AT HOME IN THE STREET
Street Children of Northeast Brazil

> If I found a box full of money? I would spend it on my
> mother. I would buy her clothing, shoes, food . . . I'd buy
> yogurt to put in the refrigerator. I'd buy a bunch of
> presents for my mother and a huge house so that when
> I die she will remember me.
>
> Eliane, aged 15

What does the future mean to children who doubt they will survive
to adulthood? What do mothers represent for children making a
home for themselves on the street? Why do international organizations make the grossly exaggerated claim that there are 7 million
children sleeping in the streets of Brazil?

Based on innovative fieldwork among street children and activist
organizations in Brazil's Northeast, this book changes the terms of
the debate, asking not why there are so many homeless children in
Brazil, but why – given the oppressive alternative of home life in
cramped *favela* shacks – there are in fact so few. At the center of
this book are children who play, steal, sleep, dance, and die in the
streets of a Brazilian city. But all around them figure activists, politicians, researchers, "home" children, and a global crisis of childhood

AT HOME IN THE STREET
Street Children of Northeast Brazil

TOBIAS HECHT

CAMBRIDGE
UNIVERSITY PRESS

CAMBRIDGE UNIVERSITY PRESS
Cambridge, New York, Melbourne, Madrid, Cape Town, Singapore, São Paulo

Cambridge University Press
32 Avenue of the Americas, New York, NY 10013-2473, USA

www.cambridge.org
Information on this title: www.cambridge.org/9780521591324

First published 1998
7th printing 2007

Printed in the United States of America

A catalog record for this publication is available from the British Library.

Library of Congress Cataloging in Publication Data

Hecht, Tobias, 1964–
At home in the street : street children of Northeast Brazil /
Tobias Hecht.
p.   cm.
Includes bibliographical references and index.
ISBN 0-521-59132-5 (hb). – ISBN 0-521-59869-9 (pb)
1. Street children – Brazil, Northeast – Social conditions.
2. Street children – Abuse of – Brazil, Northeast.   3. Children and
violoence – Brazil, Northeast.   4. Street children – Services for –
Brazil, Northeast.   I. Title.
HV887.B82N674   1998
362.76'0981'3 – dc21   97-34145
                                                                  CIP

ISBN   978-0-521-59132-4 hardback
ISBN   978-0-521-59869-9 paperback

For Isabel

CONTENTS

ACKNOWLEDGMENTS

While studying in Britain, before traveling to Northeast Brazil, I met two families from Recife. The last time I saw them in England, in March 1992, I told them that I would probably be reaching their city on the second of June. A few months later, upon my arrival at the Recife airport around three o'clock in the morning, a member of each of the families was waiting. My first Pernambucan acquaintances not only helped me to start out on the right foot, they became a source of guidance and friendship throughout the fieldwork. My thanks, therefore, begin with Zildo, Léa, Moisés, Mônica, and their families. But if I am to express my gratitude to friends in Northeast Brazil, I could never omit the names Antonio, Charles, Circe, Claudia, Dona Bernardete, Dudui, Fernando, Hozana, Índio, Jandyra, Jocimar, João, Margarete, Memê, Mêrces, Rafael, Tonho, Vera, or Zita.

Peter Adler, Sophia Avgitidou, Isabel Balseiro, Jo Boyden, Ney Dantas, Judith Ennew, Duncan Green, Keith Hart, Leo Howe, Stephen Hugh-Jones, Mary Kenny, Robert Levine, Susan Levine, Tania Regina de Luca, Virginia Morrow, my four parents (Barbara and Ted, Irene and Ron), Robin Nagle, Raquel Olegario, Catherine Panter-Brick, Zildo Barbosa Rocha, Nancy Scheper-Hughes, Fiona Ross, Lisa Sullivan, Leila Tendrih, and a consultant for Cambridge University Press who wished to remain anonymous all read and offered valuable criticism of drafts of this book. Jocimar Borges and Vera Bellato discussed the contents with me and offered many ideas. Judith Ennew and Brian Milne generously shared resources from their vast library on childhood and stimulated my thinking in various ways.

Paul Wise edited the manuscript, correcting countless mistakes. Mary Child, Brian MacDonald, Elizabeth Neal, and Marielle Poss, with Cambridge University Press, managed all stages of editing and production with finesse. Judy King prepared what I think is an excellent index. Jandyra Guerra transcribed with patience and grace tapes of interviews and conversations that rendered more than 1,500 typewritten pages. It is difficult to know how to thank Keith Hart for his criticism, support, and creative prodding during the six years I worked on this project.

I was fortunate to receive financial assistance from a variety of institutions. I thank the Simon Population Trust, the Pan American Health Organization, the Cambridge Overseas Trust, Clare Hall of Cambridge University, the Center for the Study of Nonprofit Organizations at the University of Indiana, and the Allen Fund of Cambridge University.

The last stages of writing and editing were undertaken in South Africa and I thank the Department of Social Anthropology and the Centre for African Studies at the University of Cape Town for their hospitality.

The research never would have been possible without Ruas e Praças, the activist organization for street children in Recife. The Movimento Nacional de Meninos e Meninas de Rua inspired and challenged me. I thank the many children and street educators around Recife and Olinda who shared with me their hopes and dreams, trials and frustrations.

I am deeply indebted to all of these people and organizations but take full responsibility for any shortcomings that remain.

A NOTE TO READERS

In accordance with Brazilian law, the names of children have been changed.

All translated quotations corresponding to references listed in Portuguese or Spanish are my own and thus not approved by the authors.

Although some consider the word "kids" demeaning, I do not. I use the word, one that can even celebrate a spirit of rebelliousness, interchangeably with the word "children."

INTRODUCTION

Once the place where most of Northeast Brazil's political elite was educated, the Faculdade de Direito, or Law Faculty, is situated in Recife's bustling center. The faculty is neoclassical French in design, and its cream-colored walls are surrounded by benches, tightly cropped grass, and a variety of lush trees. Around its perimeter runs a wrought-iron fence, separating the repose of the faculty from the chaos of the surrounding streets of this port city.

It's a Tuesday afternoon in 1992. Four government social workers sit nervously in the lazy shade of a broad-leafed tree. On the other side of the faculty are two "street educators" from Ruas e Praças (Streets and Squares), a street-front, activist organization. They are accompanied by a Dutch volunteer and an American anthropologist, myself. Two members of a student group concerned about street children join us, followed by a young man from the Pentecostal Christian organization Desafio Jovem (Young Challenge). Next to the eastern gate of the Law School, some 20 women officers from the Military Police survey the grounds. Behind them, across the street, stands a smaller reinforcement of male officers who, for the moment, occupy themselves boyishly surveying their female counterparts.

In all, civil and religious activists, government social workers, police, and foreign onlookers number at least 40. This unlikely assembly has come together because the Law Faculty serves as the daytime hangout for a group of street children and young, homeless adults. Yet there are no more than eight homeless children or adults on the grounds at any one time this afternoon.

I am taping the conversation between Jocimar, a street educator, and Ricardo, a man who has lived for many years in the streets of

Recife. Ricardo is lamenting the loss of his young "adoptive son" to a government vocational program, where he fears the boy will learn to steal, sniff glue, and do *tudo que não presta*, or all things bad. In the midst of this conversation, one of the government social workers comes over to inform us that the police have ordered them to leave and that they have agreed to comply. My companions from Ruas e Praças choose to ignore the warning.

About 15 minutes later, three women officers approach us. I am taping a conversation with Zé Paulo and his *menino*, or child paramour, Pedro. Zé Paulo, 32, was raised at the state reformatory known as FEBEM (the State Foundation for the Well-Being of Minors)[1] and in the streets. Pedro is 12 and has spent three of the past six years in the street, three in a shelter.

The officers belong to one of several battalions that have been deployed in recent weeks to *tirar*, that is pull or uproot, children from the streets, particularly from the city's busy thoroughfares. The officers have targeted specific stretches of some of the busiest and most crime-ridden streets in the city, attempting to remove the children block by block. The newly "cleansed" territory is then heavily patrolled to discourage the children from returning and new ones from moving in. The police are at the Law Faculty because the school's rector, convinced that the presence of the social workers is encouraging the children to loiter on the grounds, even to "satisfy their physiological necessities" there, has pulled strings so that the police will remove both the children and social workers.

There are no arrests today, but the understated recriminations tense the lips of the police and activists alike. By the time the exchange ends, the small homeless contingent has sauntered off, leaving only the social workers and police officers – the foot soldiers in this battle over where children should and should not be. In time, though, the social workers and police also depart, for their respective impoverished homes.

Points of Departure

On the one hand, this book is about street children like those who, notwithstanding periodic attempts to evict them, still lounge in the shade of the trees around Recife's Law Faculty and at many other spots in the Recife metropolitan area. But it is also about the groups that dedicate their days to working with the children, and in a more general sense it is about the attention and debate that street children elicit from state institutions, local nongovernmental organizations (NGOs), international observers and do-gooders, and casual observers in Brazil and the world over. Why did a motley group of no more than eight homeless youths bring together this diverse assembly of more than five times as many activists, concerned onlookers, and military police officers?

Over the past decade, street children, particularly those in Brazil, have become a focus of attention in the media, featured everywhere from the *New York Times* to Amnesty International reports, the BBC evening news to *Ladies' Home Journal*. Death-squad murders and underworld exploitation of street children were the subject of the American movie *Boca* (Avancini and Werneck 1994); meanwhile, street children are frequently portrayed in Brazilian soap operas watched by tens of millions. Lucrative direct mail campaigns have been launched in the United States to raise money for projects with street children. In 1985, Covenant House raised more than US$28 million in this way (Walton 1991: 25). And street children have proved a dubious curiosity for visitors to Brazil, a favorite subject for photographers. A travel article in *Ronda Iberia*, the magazine of the Spanish airline Iberia, featured shots of children "who have made their home in the street" amid photographs of *carnaval* dancers, Sugar Loaf Mountain, and the beaches of Copacabana and Ipanema (Hernández Cava 1994). Indeed, street children have been made something of a Brazilian cultural emblem. UNICEF has declared street children a top priority, and countless NGOs presenting themselves as advocates for street children have appeared. If one can imagine what sociologist Joel Best (1990) has called a social problems marketplace, street children have come to occupy a prominent place there, never more so than during the late 1980s and early 1990s.

One common trait of the talk about street children is its homogeneity. At the beginning of the 1990s it seemed that conference papers, brochures, and leisure magazine articles about street children were guided by a loosely agreed-upon recipe. The staple ingredients included a definition of the "problem," a pinch of history, a sprig of statistics about the size of the population, a dash on drugs and stealing, and a final shake in the form of suggestions for policy makers. The recipe was followed so closely by so many that even the opening paragraphs in articles about street children elicit a sense of déjà vu. Four articles began as follows:

> The phenomenon of street children has become an integral feature of the urban landscape of primarily but not exclusively developing countries. . . . In most Third World cities, they are the shadowy presence that fill the background of daily life, doing odd jobs, scavenging for food, begging. (Taylor et al. 1992: 1)

> Street children have become a fixture of the urban landscape in most developing countries – as common as the corner market stall. . . . They can be seen sleeping under bridges, begging in front of restaurants and hotels, shining shoes, selling newspapers, hawking in city markets, hauling garbage, or engaged in an array of other activities, both legal and illegal. (Barker and Knaul 1991: 1)

> Throughout Latin America there are thousands of neglected children struggling to survive in the streets of all major urban areas. These youngsters can generally be seen lingering around parks and street corners, shining shoes, begging at crowded intersections, or singing for small change on city buses. After dark, they sleep huddled together on the pavement. (Connolly 1990: 129)

> Known variously as *street urchins, street Arabs, chinches, garotos, gamines, chinos de la calle, pájaros fruteros, pelones, canillitas*, and countless other names – mostly pejorative – street children inhabit the public spaces of cities throughout the Americas and, indeed, the world. Street children are seen singing for change on public buses, begging in central squares and sleeping on doorsteps. (IAPG 1990: 5)

The last example, I must confess, is from an article I once wrote. It was prepared for an international conference on population attended by parliamentarians. I was asked to write it before meeting any street children, and by the time I finished I still had not met one. Nonetheless, the paper was warmly endorsed by a panel of "technical experts," including the heads of UNICEF and Childhope, and read enthusiastically by the parliamentarians. It was artistically laid out by professional typesetters, with graphs and emotionally charged photographs, and printed on fine high-gloss paper. The article succeeded in presenting, under a visually appealing façade, a text that coupled bureaucratic assumptions with wishful thinking.

In an informal sense, the research for this book began when I wrote the paper, more than two years before I began my fieldwork. My initial hopes of trying to do something through my article to help street children, whom I imagined as hapless victims of industrialization, were short-lived. Over cocktails in the five-star hotel in Quito, Ecuador that served as our conference headquarters, a member of Peru's Chamber of Deputies praised my work and asked if I had heard of piranhas. I replied in the affirmative to his apparent nonsequitur. He proceeded to describe how, like piranhas, street children are small and innocent in ones and twos, but when enough of them get together they attack like a school of man-eating fish. The parliamentarian had understood my publication as a call for ridding the streets of this public menace. Over time, it became clear to me that my article and the many others of which it was very nearly a replica say more about those who produce and consume the literature than about the group they purport to describe.

The impassioned attention accorded to street children during the gathering at the Law Faculty and their omnipresence in the popular imagination about Brazil raise many questions. In a city where hundreds of thousands of children suffer from hunger, disease, and deprivation in the *favelas* (shantytowns), why did the presence of a tiny number of children and young adults living in the street mobilize such a wide array of social actors? What are the aims of social activists who work with street children? How do such activists portray their beneficiaries, and how, in turn, do the children see their advocates? What are the salient features of the talk about street children, and why have street children – particularly the murdered ones – become emblematic of Brazil?

Research Perspectives and Methods

My fieldwork in Recife was preceded by a short period of research in the United States during which I interviewed representatives of inter-

national organizations that fund projects for street children. I introduced myself, when I did not already know the individuals concerned,
by saying that I was a student of social anthropology and that I was
conducting research on street children and their benefactors. I asked
about the work of the institutions, who they believed street children
to be, why they believed it important to work with street children,
and how such children could be helped. I also asked for information
about institutions in Recife and was in this way able to gain a sense
of how different organizations were regarded.

The research in Brazil was conducted during 13 months in 1992
and 1993 and three months in 1995. During the first period I lived
with my partner in Casa Caiada, a middle-class neighborhood of
Olinda, the colonial city adjacent to Recife. Coming as a couple and
living in this location had important implications for my research. My
partner had access to certain social settings from which I was barred,
such as wedding showers, and consistently lent an extra set of observing eyes. Residing among the newly rich isolated us from the *favelas*
from which street children come. On the other hand, our particular
apartment building set us across the street from the most popular
hangout for street children in Olinda. Living cheek by jowl with the
street children, albeit in absurdly contrasting circumstances, allowed
me to discover the extensive ties the children forge with the domiciled
members of the community. Housewives, shop owners, waiters, phar-
macists, and others help the children in different ways, some even
taking them into their homes. In addition, this location offered a view
of Brazilian middle-class childhood and middle-class life in general,
which also became important aspects of my research

During the second period of research I initially lived in a place
called Pau Amarelo, a sweaty 25 minutes by bus from Olinda and an
even sweatier 45 minutes from Recife. Pau Amarelo is both a summer
vacation beach area for the wealthy and a working-class dormitory
neighborhood of Recife. For the last month, I moved back to Casa
Caiada.

Participant observation is an oxymoron and in the case of my research this was especially true. Participation implies being a part of
the events one is studying; observation implies detachment, even invisibility. As a foreigner at least one head taller and several shades

Olinda with Recife in the background. Photo by Isabel Balseiro.

paler than most *nordestinos*, or northeasterners, I was especially visible. In addition, the extent of my participation was sometimes quite limited. During brief visits to the many organizations that work with poor children in Recife, it was not possible to be a true participant, certainly not in the sense of being a part of the work of the institutions. Initially, though, this had its advantages. Not being closely associated with any group, I found many doors open to me that otherwise might have been closed; rivalry among some of the groups is intense.

Over time, however, I strove to be a part of the work of one organization, O Grupo Ruas e Praças. Ruas e Praças, an activist member organization of the National Movement of Street Children, works with street youths in Recife's city center. Although not a full-time volunteer with Ruas e Praças, I participated extensively in its work, going out to the streets several times a week with the street educators, driving children and educators to the group's farm some two hours outside the city, facilitating contact with international organizations, and partaking in discussions about the group's objectives and long-range goals. I chose to work closely with this group because its members were in the street daily, because I admired its commitment to effecting larger social transformations, and because I enjoyed a close friendship with some of its members.

When I first contemplated studying street children, I was concerned about the inequalities of power. I envisaged myself in the field as the one with the upper hand. While the children would be subject to deprivation of all kinds, I would have a safe place to sleep at night, a wad of travelers checks, all the right vaccinations, and a plane ticket back to the First World. This concern proved to be warranted. I never came to terms with the material inequalities between myself and the street children. But in another sense I had it all wrong. I had the upper hand in terms of the creature comforts, but the research relationship was guided by a different dynamic. The problem of studying street children is that if you do it for long enough, you come to realize that you depend on them, not they on you.

So I searched for ways to treat the children as protagonists of my research, not as mere repositories of data. Because so many street children have been tortured by the police, I was hesitant at first to take notes in their presence, photograph them, or tape-record conversations. But after about six weeks I found, much to my surprise, how eager the children were to have their stories recorded. I discovered this by accident when 16-year-old Beto snatched from my bag the tape recorder I had resolved, precisely that afternoon, never to use. He walked off to speak to the machine on his own and to talk with his chums. Beto posed many of the questions that I had wanted to ask. He began inquiring about robberies, drug use, the families of his chums, their ages, and many other details. He also asked questions that would not have occurred to me – for instance, he asked a girl who protected her at night and how she paid her "watchman." His conversation with a boy went as follows:

> *Beto*: Hey, Carlos, where do you live?
> *Carlos*: In Ibura.
> *Beto*: What part of Ibura?
> *Carlos*: In UR-4.

Beto: You and who else live there?
Carlos: Me, my mother, my father. . . .
Beto: Are they separated?
Carlos: Yes.

I would have stopped at the question "You and who else live there?" but Beto probed further, asking whether it was really true that the father lived in the house. As it turned out, the father only visited from time to time. Although he had already asked where Carlos *lived*, Beto next asked where he *slept*. Carlos said he slept in the street. As I learned many months later, Carlos had not set foot in his "home" for years.

Having my tape recorder requisitioned and my role as interviewer usurped eventually translated into my most important research method. To my surprise, children tended to view the tape recorder not with suspicion but as a means of making themselves heard, of telling stories they rarely if ever had the chance to recount. They asked one another questions that only the most experienced interviewers might think to pose and framed the questions in ways that their companions readily understood. The questions they put to one another proved to be easily as important as the answers provided. I left the field with some 900 typed pages of transcriptions from these sessions, which the children came to call *oficinas de radio*, or radio workshops.

The term "radio workshop" evokes the sense in which many of the children used the tape recorder. They approached it at once as a toy and as a means of projecting their voices to other audiences. But whose voices were being projected and who was the audience? In the radio workshops, individual children often expressed multiple voices. In CAP (the Center for Provisional Reception), the state-run juvenile detention center, child interviewers frequently cloaked themselves in the chiding tones of the institutional social worker. Tape recorder in hand and endowed with the power to question, interviewers often suggested that their peers quit "that life" (*essa vida*) of crime and return home to work, help their mothers, and stay out of trouble. But in a moment, when they had finished asking questions and offering guidance, they would speak boastfully of their own use of drugs and participation in street crime.

In Desafio Jovem, a drug rehabilitation camp run by Pentecostal

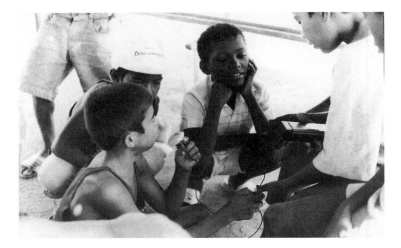

A radio workshop at a shelter for boys.

Christians, children would often assume the voices of those who pros-
elytized them. They would recite psalms and other passages from the
Bible and utter warnings about the temptations of the devil. In other
settings, children would make up stories, for instance about bank rob-
bers. One of the most popular voices was that of real television per-
sonages from *Aqui, Agora* (Here, Now), an investigative docudrama
that uncovers the grisly details of actual cases of rape, murder, or any
sufficiently gruesome crime. The television program, a sort of marriage
between the crime pages of the tabloid press and *The Twilight Zone*,
seemed to blend easily with the children's everyday experience of violence in the street. Imitating the show's hosts, the children often
used the names of their peers in describing hideous but imaginary
crimes.

The interaction in groups varied with such factors as the gender of
the participants and the physical setting of the workshop. For instance,
in CAP, boys would discuss with bravado their participation in all
sorts of crimes, even homicide. Yet in the men's prison, youths who
had recently attained their majority categorically denied any involvement in the crimes of which they were accused.[2]

Some youths were more assertive in front of the microphone than
others, and in small groups there tended to be intense competition for

control of the microphone. It was thus inevitable that in some conversations one or two individuals dominated. But as a general rule, even those most assertive initially would pass on the microphone to others once they had made their points. Sometimes it seemed that the girls were less interested in speaking when among boys or even other girls, so I tended to interview them one-on-one. This might suggest that whereas the boys were often engaged in a form of public playacting, the girls were more focused on their own private life stories and day-to-day concerns.

I never attempted to assemble a random sample of children. Yet the small size of the population, coupled with my own fascination with the method, meant that by the end of my initial 13 months in Recife at least half as many street children around the city had participated in the workshops as were counted in a municipal survey of homeless children (see Chapter 4).

In addition to the radio workshops, I taped many one-to-one conversations with children, private but recorded exchanges, which were an invaluable complement to the radio workshops. The group interviews had a group dynamic, since children, like adults, speak differently among their peers than in private conversations. For example, children who presented an almost formulaic adoration of their mothers when in a group might, in private, speak of maternal rejection.

I was wary of being seen as a social worker bent on convincing the children to quit their lives in the street. Inevitably there were times when the children saw me in that light. But there were many others when I felt confident I was hearing something not aimed at pleasing the judgmental adult. It was not infrequent for a single child to speak in two quite distinct "voices" in a single interview, that of the repentant child and that of the defiant ruffian. As I argue in Chapter 4, it is the blending of these two personae that is so characteristic of street children.

The questions the children asked in the radio workshops allowed me to define categories that were essential to my analysis. For example, my initial queries about home and the street were not readily understood by the children. But when I listened carefully in the radio workshops, I found that these themes arose spontaneously under the rubric of what children called *essa vida* ("that life" in the street) and its opposite, what I refer to as motherdom, that is, the moral logic of the matrifocal household. In other words, home is proximity – physical, affective, moral, and economic – to one's mother, whereas the street is a lifestyle, *essa vida*, that implies sleeping in the street, stealing, using drugs, and doing other things the children consider to be "no good" (*coisas que não prestam*).

In the end, the radio workshops, albeit the most important of my methods, were only one research tool, and the information gained from them was complemented by long interviews, life histories, a semistructured survey, examination of secondary sources and publicly available statistics, and participant observation over the long run. The contradictions between the spoken word and behavior took on important meanings. Where street children seemed to be most duplicitous was in describing their relationships to their mothers. For instance, an 11-year-old boy asked me to record a special mother's day message in which he apologized for being in the street, thus suggesting that his mother would really rather have him at home. But he had recently made a brief return home. According to the street educator who escorted him, the mother's first words to her son were, "But I thought you were dead. There's no room for you here."

What I inferred from the radio workshops and other sessions changed as a result of interacting with the children and others. I believe I developed a keen ability to discern when children were recounting fantasies, when they were saying what they thought their listeners wanted to hear, and when they were speaking what in everyday language might be called the truth. But like any ethnographer, I could never really be certain. There were times I was looking for something like a fact: Does a particular girl have a sibling? Has a particular boy ever been ill in the street? At other times, it was impossible to disentangle facts from the web of fantasy. For instance, one youth spoke about how he was roused in the street by a group of men, but one cannot discern from his narrative whether these men were thieves, policemen, thugs, members of a death squad, or simply elements of a story he had fabricated from beginning to end. Yet his narrative need not be pinned down as fact or fiction: the central concern of the story remains the same – the nature of violence in the street.

The survey, as Connolly and Ennew (1996: 140) note, is employed "not only as the first, but also as the only tool" in much of the research being done with street children. I twice had occasion to participate in the survey research of others while in Recife. On the first occasion, I introduced some psychologists to a group of street children living in a shelter. Their questionnaire was largely a translation of a survey designed for use with homeless adults in London and included questions such as, "On a scale of one to five, how important is it for you to decorate your room?" this notwithstanding the fact that the children had never had their own rooms and did not comprehend the abstract numerical scale. Although I had enjoyed a certain rapport with the children at the shelter before I introduced them to the psychologists, the children did not wish to speak with me the next time I went. I could only hang my head low and bemoan my poor judgment at being a helpful participant in an experiment that had treated the children a bit like rats in a laboratory. Yet the psychologists were able to collect "data" – that is, numbers capable of being analyzed by a sophisticated statistical software package and written up in a scholarly fashion.

On the second occasion, I took part in a municipal census of street children that included a brief questionnaire. The children, wakened in the middle of the night (which in many cases required forceful shaking) were offered a snack and subjected to about fifteen questions. Ticking off boxes, the researchers attempted to record such "facts" as why the children were in the street. Although there are facts involved in leaving home, I believe one can only begin to understand the torturous decisions and circumstances that lead children to find themselves in the street by knowing the children and, if possible, their families over time.

In the end, I did use a questionnaire in my own research, but it was one that grew out of the radio workshops and that was used to complement the other methods of research, not replace them. The content of the questionnaire, used with 50 street children, was not assembled until I had spent more than half a year in the field. Many of the questions used had initially been posed by street children to their peers in the radio workshops. Others were questions I devised but that the children corrected and were encouraged to reformulate in their own words. Camilla, then 17 and relatively new to the streets, gave me especially thorough coaching on how to frame the questions. The questionnaire was devised as a recorded conversation. The participants were allowed to meander, to pursue tangents that interested them, but were always steered back in due course to a common core of about 200 questions covering a wide range of topics including family life, interaction with institutions, gang participation, health, sex, education, violence, happiness, and future aspirations. I designed the survey as a guided conversation (see Rubin and Rubin 1995, especially chap. 6; Kvale 1996, especially chap. 1), beginning with questions I knew intrigued them, such as about the places where they hung out, whether they were part of a gang or had a leader, only turning to more bureaucratic issues such as their age and place of birth toward the middle of the interview. The survey suggested ways of distinguishing the merely anecdotal from something that formed part of a trend. For instance, the odd comment in conversations regarding the relationship between sniffing glue and hunger could be translated into a question that all respondents were asked in the same way: "Does glue take away your hunger or make you feel more hungry?"

Like the pool of children who participated in the radio workshops, the sample that responded to the questionnaire was not randomly assembled. The participants were chosen largely on the basis of their being in the right place at the right time. In other words, if I felt I was in a safe enough spot to use the tape recorder and the children seemed in the mood for talking, I would propose the idea. Very few refused. I conducted 33 of the interviews, and three *educadores* conducted 9. The remaining 8 were done by a young woman named Iracy who described herself as a *menina de rua*, or street girl. She lived in a house with her grandmother, but had hung out in the past with a group of kids who lived in the street, and she generally considered herself to be one of them. She added a few questions of her own at the end of the survey, such as "What do you think should be done with the police?" and "What do you think the government should do for street children?"[3]

Questions were occasionally skipped, sometimes for reasons dictated by common sense. For instance, it made little sense to ask eight-year-old boys whether they had ever used condoms. Other times questions were omitted because it seemed unfair or unrealistic to pose them to respondents in the presence of others. For example, since in Northeast

Brazil such a strong stigma is attached to being the victim of rape, it made little sense, if others were present, to ask the children whether they had ever been forced to have sex. For this reason, the sample size for a particular question varies, with 50 being the maximum.

The questions that referred to time were difficult for the respondents. For instance, the question asked of the children in shelters, "How long have you been here?" was regularly answered with such replies as *um bocado de tempo*, meaning, loosely, "a bunch of time." Various tactics were attempted to overcome this problem. For instance, those who did not know how old they were when they left home were asked if they remembered what soap opera was being shown at the time. Events that had occurred over the past year were related to important holidays such as *carnaval* or *São João*, the June festivals. Respondents might be asked "Did you last see your mother before or after *carnaval?*"

Of 50 children and young people in the sample, 36 were male, 12 were female, and 2 were biologically male transvestites who referred to themselves as women. The proportion of females included in the sample (one-third) is higher than that actually found in the general population of street children,[4] but this was intentional since I wanted to gain a comparative sense of experience by gender. The participants ranged in age from 8 to 23, the median age being 15½. Respondents who were 18 or older were included only when they had lived in the street before attaining their majority. The children lived in divergent situations: 26 were in the street at the time of the interview, 16 in shelters, and 8 at home. Many of those from the first group were interviewed in the street, in as quiet an alley or square as could be found. Others were interviewed indoors, for instance, at Ruas e Praças.

Some researchers studying illegal activities have found it necessary to partake in those very activities in order to have access to reliable data. For example, Patricia Adler (1993), who studied drug dealers and drug smugglers, writes,

> Although we never dealt drugs (we were too scared to be seriously tempted), we consumed drugs and possessed them in small quantities. Quite frankly, it would have been impossible for a

nonuser to have gained access to this group to gather the data presented here. This was the minimum involvement necessary to obtain even the courtesy membership we achieved. (24)

In my case, I did not sniff glue or steal with the children or sleep in the street. The children would have found it incongruous, even absurd, for a foreign adult to attempt to live as they do, and I drew my own limits. It was far easier to fit in among the street educators than among the street children themselves. I spent much of my time in the street hanging out, playing checkers or dominoes, talking, drawing, or commenting along with the children on the passersby. Many of the children in Recife's downtown associated me with Ruas e Praças, whose street educators I often accompanied. But when they asked about my role, or when I thought it was appropriate to tell them, I explained that I was spending some time in Brazil learning about street children and that I frequently worked as a volunteer for Ruas e Praças.

I visited the shelters where street children frequently elect to go, making quite a number of trips to two in particular. These were especially good places to conduct radio workshops because the children were not high and were especially eager for recreation. In these contexts, they tended to be gentler and their attention spans longer. The practicalities were also far simpler, since I did not have to worry about the tape recorder being stolen or the ever-present background noises of the street. For these reasons, CAP, the state detention center for children and adolescents, proved, ironically, an ideal location for these interviews. I was allowed to work there over a four-day period until a foreign free-lance photographer of street children, who happened to talk her way into the facility just after I did, drew so much attention that we were both expelled.

I spent considerable time in the *favelas*. On a few occasions I was able to visit the estranged families of street children. In a *favela* near the colonial center of Olinda I acquired some young friends and eventually even a godson, who, in a brilliant act of emotional blackmail by his adoptive mother, was named after me. I continually found reasons to visit *favelas* around the city, most frequently to visit day care centers or to accompany health promoters on their home visits.

All of the research, except when accompanying foreign visitors, was conducted in Portuguese. I had studied the language for three years before traveling to Brazil, and knowing Spanish facilitated my comprehension. Although the thick accent of Pernambuco (of which Recife is the capital) and the argot of poor children made my first weeks challenging, with time I became comfortable in the language.

Ethics

At one of the first institutions I visited, a young social worker commented that I, like so many other foreigners, had come to study their (i.e., Northeast Brazil's) misery. She spoke, I think, not so much out of knee-jerk chauvinism as from an awareness that suffering is the stuff that keeps so many foreign visitors employed. Indeed, I had the sense that much of the success of my own efforts to solicit funding for my research derived from the emotional strings the subject pulls, which, in turn, left me with the question of what was in it for the children. This has been a project fraught with ethical dilemmas.

Choosing when to intervene and when to do nothing was not easy. Sometimes such choices related to the physical safety of children, a concern discussed by Fine and Sandstrom in *Knowing Children* (1988). As the authors reflect, "Children are mischievous, sometimes aggressive, and occasionally cruel. What is the responsibility of the participant observer in that situation? . . . In some situations, an observer's presence may increase the display of aggression among minors" (26–27). One afternoon at the beach, a strong 18-year-old named Manoel picked up a huge rock and threatened to smash it over the head of Marcela, a teenage transvestite. Faced with situations like this, I took a self-consciously interventionist stance. Detailed knowledge about violent crimes, including rapes and murders, put me in an especially difficult position. I was asked for advice on wrenching dilemmas. "Should I get rid of this baby?" Camilla asked me as she contemplated her growing belly. She believed abortion was the worst sin a woman could commit, but she also knew she did not have the wherewithal to raise a child. Abortion is illegal in Brazil and for poor women it is a painful and life-threatening ordeal. Should I offer to pay for a safe, less painful, but still illegal, abortion in a clinic? What do you say to young mothers who leave their toddlers unattended and in imminent danger of being run over when they go off to steal or buy drugs? Do I listen impassively to the boy who boasts of mugging old people as impoverished as his own grandparents?

Also, should I buy food for the children? In contending with this question, I found myself treading a fine line between paternalism and stinginess, between being taken for a fool and simply sharing some of what I had been given in the name of street children. How do you deny a request for lunch when you know that otherwise the boy will go out and steal a watch to buy the food himself? But how do you oblige, knowing that this act of paternalism does nothing to resolve the need for another meal a few hours later?

The *educadores*, or street educators, at local organizations in Recife have seen countless journalists and researchers come and go. They know that many of the foreigners spend more every day in travel expenses than they take home in a month, and normally neither they nor the children with whom they work see any direct benefit from the presence of such visitors. Photographers especially are viewed as representatives of a sort of extractive industry; they make quick visits, take pictures of street children, and then sell the photographs and keep all the money. In 1993, an American free-lancer (the same one who got me expelled from CAP) came for several weeks to photograph street children in Recife. She seemed to leave a wake of resentment wherever she set foot and eventually became the subject of a multi-million-dollar lawsuit launched by a Brazilian organization against a U.S. magazine that published one of her photos of a supposed child prostitute.

So it is not surprising that street-children tourists are often greeted with less-than-open arms. My initiation to Recife was no exception. Although I encountered generous hospitality on many fronts, I was met with suspicion and cold shoulders on others. The children at the National Movement of Street Children demanded to know the objective of my research and who was financing it. Street educators from one group asked if I knew why a British researcher who had spent six months with them, eventually marrying an attractive young woman from Olinda and taking her with him, had never taken the trouble to write a letter or send a copy of his thesis.

I was fearful of becoming part of the industry of researchers that treat street children as a sort of raw material there for the taking, of translating the anguish of real children into a document that would benefit above all myself. It would be absurd to suggest that I was writing for an audience of street children. I met few that read fluently and none that knew English. Likewise, it would be pretentious to claim that this book was written strictly for the benefit of street children. But it struck me as dissonant, even violent, to translate the everyday fears and joys, murders and poems of street children into a rarefied argot.

Northeast Brazil is a world of abysmal contradictions. One middle-class friend flew her imported Scottish terrier more than halfway across the country to Curitiba for artificial insemination. Meanwhile, the caloric intake of most children in Recife is doubtless inferior to that of my friend's well-traveled pet. It struck me early on that while the latest First World technology can be found in well-stocked stores, mops do not exist. Poor, dark-skinned maids scrub the floors of the rich on their hands and knees. Street children are not incongruent with this world of contrasts that is Northeast Brazil. I hope that the dreams, spunk, and patent joie de vivre of the children are as evident in this ethnography as the violence they endure, the sadness and frustration they often feel, and the injustice of a world that leaves children to grow up at home in the street.

The Organization of the Book and the Progression of the Arguments

Readers not familiar with the setting may wish to make the Appendix, which introduces the cities of Recife and Olinda and the larger context of Northeast Brazil, the next chapter that they read.

Chapter 1 consists of extended transcriptions of two street children who introduce the reader to the feel of the street and touch on a number of the themes emphasized in this book, those themes being identity, violence, the relationship of street children to institutions, and the idea of childhood itself. Two children, one male and one female, relate vignettes that offer the beginnings of life stories. The stories contrast sharply, as do the circumstances of their authors. The boy, aged 13, is spirited and witty. He finds adventure and freedom in the street, though his relish is tempered with remorse for the things he does there, such as holding up people at gunpoint. He says that his mother searches for him in the street and very much wants him to be at home. The girl shares little of the boy's pluck or optimism. She spent her early childhood in institutions and in the care of an alcoholic mother. She was raped at the age of 13 by a demented street person and has been beaten by boyfriends and shot by members of a death squad. At the time of the interview, after several years in the street punctuated only by periodic stays at institutions, she was 17 and pregnant.

In many ways, the lives of these two children could not be more different. I selected their narratives for a number of quite subjective reasons. The first is that I was drawn to the children for the beauty of their words, the articulate nature of their sense of the world. But there are other reasons. Juxtaposed, the stories of these two illustrate the extent to which the street can be experienced differently by different children. Many of the contrasts, of course, relate to gender. I believe that, on balance, life in the street tends to be even harder for girls than for boys, not only because of their greater physical vulnerability but also because of social expectations in Brazil about girlhood and boyhood, about the street and about the home, and about the gendered nature of public and private space. Girlhood is typically more closely circumscribed, more inimical to the street, more closely allied to the home. The street is perceived as a threat to the moral values adults seek to inculcate in children, especially to those of girls, for whom contact with the street is apt to transform them from *meninas* (girls) into *mulheres* (sexually initiated women).

Despite the sharp contrasts between the two main narratives in Chapter 1, there are also similarities that I believe form part of the collectivity I call street children. For example, both children define their lives in the street with frequent reference to a mother figure; both have managed to care for themselves in the most challenging circumstances; both have lived in a variety of settings – with their mothers, with surrogate mother figures, in institutions, and among other children in the street – and both have experienced and perpetrated countless acts of violence. While I contest popular images of street children, in presenting the extended interview transcriptions I admittedly risk building my own subjectively informed iconography through a selection of first-person narratives. At issue is the ethnographic search for commonality amid a universe of individuals.

Chapter 2 aims to complement the subjectively chosen narratives that precede it by painting a broad picture of street children. It considers the daily activities, dreams, and frustrations of street children, the places where they "roam," how they meet the daily necessities of getting food and clothing, and how they organize themselves socially.

Chapter 3 begins with an examination of the divergent ways that scholars and other observers have portrayed childhood. The chapter argues that if childhood can be seen as a broad context, in urban Northeast Brazil two starkly contrasting contexts can be identified – *nurturing childhood* and *nurtured childhood*. Nurturing children, in essence, are poor children who from an early age take on serious responsibilities; they bring in resources to their mothers and nurture the household, activities they view as moral obligations. Nurtured children, on the other hand, are the coddled progeny of middle-class families. Highly differentiated from and dependent on adults, nurtured children are economic liabilities to the household. Whereas the status of nurturing children is dependent, to an extent, on what they *do*, nurtured children are valued by virtue of *being* children. Distinct as these two childhoods are, they share one thing in common: they are lived at home. And it is in relation to "home children" that street children are seen and see themselves. Notwithstanding the flurry of attention paid to street children, nearly all Brazilian children grow up in homes, and I argue that, divorced from a critical examination of domestically based childhoods, street children cannot be understood.

Chapter 4 treats the many identities, or images, assigned to homeless children and the ways those same children speak of themselves and their companions. I argue that street children ground their sense of identity in opposition to the lives of nurturing children. Although *maloqueiros* – as children living in the streets of Recife and Olinda[5] often refer to themselves in their own argot – have much in common with the poor children of the *favelas*, they speak of themselves as radically different from other poor children. The essence of their difference, I argue, revolves around their relationship to motherdom, the moral logic of the matrifocal household. Whereas poor children are expected to help their mothers, heed their advice, and stay by their sides, *maloqueiros* are physically separated from their mothers, inhabit the public spaces of the city rather than the private space of the home, and use their resources mostly for themselves. They speak of the street not as a mere physical space but as a way of life.

Intermingled in discussions of the definitions of street children, one inevitably encounters controversy over the size of this population. This chapter treats the creative speculation regarding the size of the street child population in Brazil and, through an examination of census data, gives an alternative estimate on this point. I suggest that there are probably fewer than 39,000 children sleeping in the streets of Brazil, or well under 1 percent of the figure of 7 million used in recent years by UNICEF, the World Health Organization, and other institutions.

Chapter 5 examines different dimensions of violence involving street children, considering how violence exercised both against and by street children situates these victims and perpetrators in relation to conceptualizations of childhood. Nothing seems to attract more attention to street children than the fact that their mutilated corpses can sometimes be found on city streets or garbage dumps. As child-murdering death squads threaten to displace the beaches of Rio de Janeiro as the country's most readily identifiable national icon, Brazilians have found themselves engaged in painful soul searching. What went wrong in this country where the cultural ambassadorship of Carmen Miranda's rhapsodic voice and graceful steps has been replaced by images of roving bands of thugs that hunt down sleeping children? The murders of street children are not only the subject of damning media reports and ceaseless denunciations by human rights organizations, they also hold a firm place in the world's everyday lore about Brazil. And they are a blight on the conscience of the nation. Brazilians typically discuss the violence against street children with impassioned revulsion. But just as frequently, the conversation turns to the violence in which the street children themselves engage. Violence drives the wedge ever deeper between street children and nurtured and nurturing children. The murder of children by adults, those normally expected to protect them, inverts the rules of nurtured childhood. But the violence in which such children engage also upsets the rules of nurturing childhood.

My research generally corroborates the assertions widely reported elsewhere that street children suffer myriad forms of violence at the hands of adults, especially the police. Indeed, the shock value lies not so much in the practice of these crimes as in the routinization of torture and in the imagination of the torturers. What sort of a mind decides to hang a youth upside down and slowly drip cleaning detergent into his nostrils to punish him for an act of petty thievery he may or may not have committed? But lost in the public talk about street children is a consideration of how street children interpret the violence they live. The chapter examines how children classify and explain the violence they both suffer and perpetrate and argues that the way children "read" and act out violence is varied and often at odds with the interpretations offered by their adult advocates. Furthermore, global attention to death-squad murders of street children has eclipsed concern for other, more prevalent, forms of violence experienced by poor children in general, such as systematic torture and mistreatment at the hands of the police and the hidden violence of the home.

Chapter 6 discusses many of the agencies in the metropolitan area that work with street children. Although many people are under the impression that little is being done for street children, Brazilian cities such as Recife and Olinda are home to a wide array of agencies and institutions that act in behalf of this population. In comparing the numbers of adults working with street children with the number of homeless children, I show that in Recife from mid-1992 to mid-1993 there was approximately one adult working for each child sleeping rough. The chapter examines how the different agencies struggle to remove children from the streets and situate them in the more familiar worlds of nurturing and nurtured childhood, that is, the matrifocal childhood of the *favelas* or, more fancifully, a carefree, protected, middle-class childhood in which children are highly differentiated from adults.

The belief that children are antithetical to streets harks back to ideas deeply entrenched in Brazilian social history about the opposing realms of street and home, a literature touched on in this chapter. I argue that efforts to remove children from the street are guided by the motifs of salvation, reclamation, and citizenship. By "reclamation" I refer to attempts to transform unruly street children into working children, to substitute labor for leisure, and discipline for drugs. By the motif of "salvation" I refer to a less well delineated but symbolically charged rhetoric of transforming children by "rescuing" them from the street and "restoring" their childhood to them. Finally, "citizenship" refers to efforts to endow street children with rights provided by the law, by seeking a direct relationship with society without the family as medium.

Some leaders of programs for street children – for example, Father Bruce Ritter, formerly of New York's Covenant House, the late Peter Taçon of the international NGO Childhope and UNICEF, and Ana Vasconcelos of Recife's Casa de Passagem (House of Passage) – have received extensive attention in the media and in promotional literature. But in other respects and despite all of the talk about street children, the institutions that seek to represent, aid, or even rescue these children have been all but obscured from view. What little is said about the institutions seems aimed only at raising money for them. Whereas Chapter 6 examines the motifs used by agencies to explain how they help street children, Chapter 7 turns the tables and examines how the children see the institutions. I argue that the street children in Recife tend to view the social service institutions as an integral part of street life, not as a way out. They even liken the institutions to *fregueses*, a concept I translate as, loosely, clients. The children's own visions of change, I argue, are remote from the adult concepts of salvation, reclamation, and citizenship.

For a number of reasons, I do not aim primarily to make policy recommendations. The first reason is one of deference. There is no lack of policy recommendations in Brazil coming from people who work every day with street children and do not have a plane ticket out of the country. Street children also have ideas about the way forward. The National Movement of Street Children was serving in the early 1990s as a spirited, rebellious forum in which poor children and street educators across the country could debate civil and economic rights and the need to effect change in Brazilian society. A second reason is that I believe it important to approach street children as something other than a problem to be solved. If one's goal is to legislate the eradication of a problem, one tends to lose the ability to consider what the individuals who constitute that "problem" are doing and saying and how they see their place in the world.

Many who have written on street children tend to be obsessed with two questions: What *causes* street children and what can be done to *remove* them from the streets? The first question frames street children as something akin to a disease – indeed the word "etiology" is sometimes used in this context. I have thus replaced extensive speculation about the *causes* of street children with a wider examination of the alternative – staying at home, where home is a shack and home life is steeped in hunger, deprivation, and violence. While not pretending to offer a solution, this ethnography asks as many pertinent questions as possible and in this way aims to redirect the debate about street children.

The conclusion, "The Ephemeral Lives of Street Children," offers some reflections that may be relevant to those concerned about policies. For instance, I argue that preventing poor children from working in the streets may undermine their ties with their families because the status of poor urban children in matrifocal households is enhanced by their ability to bring home resources. Forcing all children off the streets, the principal venue for urban children to earn money, endangers the welfare of poor children and families, given the present economic and social state of affairs in Brazil and many other developing countries. The conclusion also aims to situate my discussion of street children within relevant bodies of literature, such as other treatments of street children and of the cultural politics of childhood, and considers the question of the future of street children, both as envisaged in the literature and by children themselves.

This book examines street children in relation to larger expectations about childhood, for it is in this context that street children define themselves and are defined by others, and that the talk about them can best be understood. It treats the daily struggles of children on the edge, but it also offers an interpretation of how children read this reality, adapt to it, and transform it. If the most widely disseminated fact about Brazilian street children is that they are murdered, one can easily forget that they also live and that they interpret the world in which they tenuously exist.

1

SPEAKING OF THE STREET

FEBEM, as it was generally called by the children, or CAP, as the facility was officially known after 1990,[1] was Recife's "temporary" holding tank for juvenile delinquents and lost children for no less than 29 years. The compound was known to nearly all children living in the street. A few even boasted of having been in and out more than 100 times. CAP was divided into three parts, one for girls, one for young boys, and one for more "dangerous" adolescent males. Bars and gates kept the children separate in these three areas at night, though some of the time they could mix during the day. Chronically over-crowded, the facility, intended for no more than about 60 children, typically accommodated over 100. They slept on rectangular strips of foam or simply on the cement floor, ate in a large common mess hall, and spent their days watching television, chasing one another around in the courtyard, performing various chores, or engaging in "peda-gogical" activities such as gluing together popsicle sticks.

In July 1995, a group of older boys broke into the Children's and Adolescents' Court next door where, in a storeroom for court evidence, they found a vast collection of guns and drugs. In the rebellion that ensued, boys could be seen through the infrared lenses of the national television network TV-Globo sniffing glue and brandishing a variety of guns. As if imitating the heroes of American Westerns, some sported a pistol at each hip and one in each hand. For once, the police, under strict orders from Pernambuco's governor Miguel Arraes and intense scrutiny from the television cameras, exercised restraint. The three-day standoff resulted in the shooting of one policeman and the death of one youth who was allegedly organizing a gang rape of some of the girls who, mostly against their will, had remained in the compound. All shots were fired by the children. During the rebellion, virtually everything in CAP except its cement walls was destroyed, resulting in a decision to close the compound permanently.

In 1992, however, CAP was functioning much as it always had, and it was there that I met a boy I call Edivaldo, a 13-year-old who had been running away from home periodically over the previous six years. The two of us were in what sometimes served as a classroom. Although the door was shut, other children entered from time to time.

Edivaldo

Edivaldo: Do you plan to do something for these kids at FE-BEM?

Tobias: I'd like to. What do you think I should do?

Edivaldo: That's up to you. [He pauses to think.] One thing I'd suggest is to find a better place, you know, because a lot of the kids here, like me, don't like this place. We like to have a little freedom. If I were in charge of this place, the kids would have food, a place to sleep, and a bath, and I wouldn't keep them prisoners and I wouldn't let the *monitores* [the adult supervisors responsible for keeping order] hit them. I'd take them to the beach, to the movies. I think that's the right thing to do because the kids run away from home to be free. If they're prisoners at home, do you think they're going to like being prisoners somewhere else?

I'm from Caruaru [a city of about 100,000, Pernambuco's largest after the metropolitan area of Recife]. I move around a lot. I even went to Natal [a four-hour road trip to the north]. I spent two months living in the house of a woman who made fried turnovers. I met her because when I went to Natal I first stayed with a guy for a couple of days. He even gave me a surfboard. Then he had to leave and I couldn't go with him because I didn't have my birth certificate [necessary for Brazilian children to travel from one state to another] and on that day it rained a lot and I was freezing to death. I leaned against a wooden house and put the board on my head and started crying. Then the woman [who lived in the house] came and asked what I was doing there. I told her my story, she took me into her

27

house, gave me a cup of hot coffee and bread, and asked me if I wanted to live there. I told her I did. I spent two months helping her, but then she died. She lived alone and when she died, her son, who lived somewhere else, came to tell me to leave. He gave me a ticket and stuck me on a bus and made me go away.

I only ran away from home because of my stepfather. He beat me with a wire cable, left me all cut up, then he threw water and a kilo of salt on me. When I would run away I'd go all over the place. I spent two days with a truck driver, then he said, "Go away now," so I left. I stayed in the city and met a lot of kids and that's how I started learning about street life.

I think I have way too much experience now. The street doesn't have anything to offer you except experience. In the street we learn how to live because at home we get spoon-fed everything. It's not like that in the street. In the street we have to work to have something. That's what the street teaches you.

Tobias: In the street, do you roam with a gang?

Edivaldo: If you hang out with a gang, it's worse than being alone, because, look, in a gang it's the strongest one who wins. If I'm weak and, say, I steal a watch, the biggest guy in the gang is going to say, "Hey, that watch is mine, I'm going to sell it." That's why I prefer to roam alone. I only went around with a gang once, because when I'm with a group, the group wants to fight to see who's strongest. If you get caught in the middle of something you're in trouble. The one time I was with a group I got stabbed.

I've run away from home twenty-nine times. I've always come to Recife when I run away from home. I'd get a ride with the trucks. Sometimes I'd hide under the spare tire. You know how trucks have that extra tire in case one pops? I'd hide back there and come to Recife all hungry.

The first time, I was seven years old. That's when I started learning about street life. My mother came to Recife and spoke with the police. She sent the police out after me, and she even offered a reward for the person who found me.

The second time I went to the Shopping Center in Boa Viagem. I asked a guy for money. He said he didn't have any and walked away. But then he came back and bought me food and asked if I wanted to work in his house. I said yes and I went to live there. I stayed for two days and then my mother found me. She got a whole bunch of kids together and gave them money so they would tell her where I was. I liked it there. I would have stayed. I went back twice [to see the man] but he already had another boy living there and when I went the third time he had left for São Paulo.

I went back to Caruaru and stayed for two months. Then I ran away again, but my mother didn't come to look for me. I stayed in the street in the center of the city for three days. Later I went home because I hadn't really learned what street life is about.

The fourth time was when I learned how to sniff glue. I got together with a bunch of kids and started sniffing, and I got used to it. So I just started running away from home to sniff glue. It's a vice, you know. It's not that I like it, you get to be a prisoner of glue.

Tobias: What do you mean?

Edivaldo: It's a temptation that hits you: "Come on, sniff glue, sniff." And you end up sniffing.

Tobias: And what happens when you sniff glue?

Edivaldo: You get high and start seeing things that aren't in front of you. That's what hooks you.

Tobias: What happens if you sniff every day and then all of a sudden you stop? How do you feel?

Edivaldo: You get a fever, a headache, you feel like dying.

Tobias: Does sniffing glue make you hungry?[2]

Edivaldo: Yes, but only when you stop sniffing. Sometimes you sniff to kill the hunger, because when you're hungry and you sniff, the hunger goes away. But if you stop sniffing, the hunger gets you again.

Tobias: I've noticed that some kids sniff glue after eating. Why do they do that?

Edivaldo: It's so that you don't mess up your lungs, because if you eat and then sniff on a full stomach, it's not so bad for you. But if you sniff on an empty stomach, the air from the glue fills up your belly.

Tobias: Does glue cause any illnesses?

Edivaldo: Yes, diabetes.

Tobias: Have you ever lived in anyone else's house aside from with the man in Boa Viagem?

Edivaldo: Lots of times, like with the woman in Boa Viagem where I cleaned her garden.

Tobias: What was it like there?

Edivaldo: It was good. I even fell in love with the lady's daughter.

Tobias: What's her name?

Edivaldo: Paula.

Tobias: Pretty?

Edivaldo: Yes [he smiles coyly].

Tobias: How old is she?

Edivaldo: Thirteen. My age. So it's good.

Tobias: How long did you stay with them?

Edivaldo: For two years. At first I cleaned up their yard, but after a while I stopped and I became part of the family. I studied, I had food, a place to sleep, I did everything, I watched TV, I lazed around all day long. I left because they went away. I don't have my birth certificate so I can't travel. I have to stay right here. They left me in a hostel. They paid the rent for three months until I could find something else. She paid for the food, the place to sleep, the baths, television, air conditioning, video games, everything, it was great! But I cried a lot when the lady left. I missed my girlfriend. Then I went back to the street because I hadn't found anything. But I think this year, no next year, at *carnaval*, they're coming back. I'll go back there.

Tobias: Did you use drugs during that time?

Edivaldo: No. You see, the lady gave me some medicine. One day the lady gave me money to go to the movies. I took the money and bought glue, but the medicine made the glue taste terrible. So while I was with them I didn't sniff glue.

Tobias: Did you play with the street kids while you lived with the family?

Edivaldo: No, the lady said that if I kept playing with them I would pick up the vice again. The lady was doing everything for me, and it was like she was my mother.

Tobias: Do you remember the fifth time you ran away?

Edivaldo: [with a tone of boyish authority] I remember what happened every single time.

Tobias: So what happened the fifth time?

Edivaldo: The fifth time . . . I took off, caught a ride. I stayed in the bus station. I ate there and slept there. I washed the cars of the owners of the stores in the bus station. They paid me and I bought their food. It was like they were paying me to buy from them! Sometimes they didn't even pay me, they gave me a plate of food, a huge plate this size [he opens his hands around an imaginary, giant dish]. Then my mother came to look for me. She saw me the moment she got off the bus, on that bridge at the bus station. "Edivaldo, come here!" she yelled. She ran after me and caught me. I hugged her. I adore her. It's just my stepfather. If I could, I'd kill him.

Tobias: How long did you stay home that time?

Edivaldo: One day. My stepfather showed up and beat me with a piece of metal, like he was dehusking a coconut. He cut my hands all up.

Tobias: Does he drink?

Edivaldo: No, he just likes hitting. He doesn't eat or drink. He's just rotten.

Tobias: Why did he hit you?

Edivaldo: Because of his kids. They would do something then say that I did it. He wouldn't believe me if I said one thing and his kids said another.

Tobias: What happened the sixth time you ran away?

Edivaldo: The sixth time . . . I went to the bus station again. I spent a lot of time in the street. I ran away a lot. Once, the seventh time I ran away from home, I stayed at a lumberyard in Boa Viagem. While I was there I saved up all the money I earned. I didn't spend anything. I slept there and when the man went away I poured a little glue into a bottle. In the morning I'd go to the bread shop and buy some milk [and then drink it] to cover up the stench. When my mother came I had more money than she did. I paid for my bus ticket back and hers too and there was even a little money left over.

The eighth time was when I went to swim at the beach. I

jumped off a diving board and hit my head on a rock that was under water. When I woke up seven days had passed. I was in the Restauração [Hospital] and my mother was there. She had come. I didn't even have any fun that time. I just got to Recife, went to the beach, took a dip, and then I was at home.

The ninth time I hung out in the street, and my mother found me again. I was in the city sniffing glue and that's when she found out I used glue. She started crying and said, "Don't do that" and stuff.

Tobias: How did you feel?

Edivaldo: I felt like a dog because I was wrong.

Tobias: What about the tenth time you ran away?

Edivaldo: If you keep on asking one by one I'll miss lunch! [I thought he had tired of the conversation, but then, perhaps remembering fondly what had happened on the tenth occasion, he continued.] The tenth time I ran away a police woman caught me. She asked me where I lived. I told her "In the street." I lied when she asked if I had a mother and a father. I told her no. She said, "I'm gonna take you to FEBEM." I started crying. She said, "Okay, I'll take you somewhere else, you'll see." She stuck me in her car and, vroom. When I got out of the car we were at her house. So I stayed there, living in a police lady's house! It was great there. She took me all over the place. I even learned how to shoot a gun. She had this thing, a target. She had a Mauser and a Beretta. She used the Mauser and I used the Beretta. But then my mother came and found me. I was only in the lady's house for three days.

Once there was this old lady in the middle of the street who had just come out of the bank. Her bag was full. So I said, "Woohh, loot!" I grabbed her bag and took off. Then the old lady sat down and started crying. I felt sorry for her and went back and returned her money. She asked me: "Why did you rob me?"

"Because I'm hungry," I said.

She got up and said, "Let's go over there." She paid for my lunch and a Guaraná [a popular Brazilian soft drink] and I felt sorry for her. She said she had grandchildren to raise.

[suddenly, returning his attention to the noises about him] I want to get out of here. I want to sniff glue again. And here your stomach feels weird. Out in the street you eat things you can't eat here and your stomach gets used to those things and to the glue, so when you get here you feel strange, not sniffing glue and not eating those things you eat in the street.

Tobias: What do you normally eat?

Edivaldo: Anything that's food.

Tobias: On a typical day what do you eat, what do you?

Edivaldo: I wake up on Dantas Barreto [a busy thoroughfare in the center of Recife]. I go to a public bathroom. I take a bath, wash my face. Then I go over to Seu Zé's stall, grab some toothpaste, brush my teeth. He gives me a roll and some juice. I eat. Then I go out to rustle up some money. I go around and say, "Got any change?" Anyone who's eating, I ask 'em. Around noon when I've got some money I buy a huge lunch in the Bar do Gordo. Then I get up and say, "I'm gonna sniff glue now." I go up to a kid, snatch his glue, the glue's almost dead [hard, and with scarcely any smell] – you know, just so I can sniff a little. When my head is sort of feeling good I say, "Time to steal." I go around and "bam," got a watch. I run, sell the watch and buy glue. I keep on sniffing glue and stealing watches to buy food at night.

Tobias: How many watches can you steal in a day?

Edivaldo: If I spend the whole day stealing? Woohh! More than ten. Twenty. Thirty. We can make up to five hundred thousand cruzeiros [worth US$45 at the time, nearly minimum wage for a month]. But you need to know how to snatch 'em. If you don't know what you're doing, you'll never get the watches. We steal gold and silver necklaces too. Once when I had long fingernails I went to steal a lady's necklace and I scratched the hell out of her.

Tobias: What do you do with the money?

Edivaldo: I buy glue, pot, Rohypnol [a "prescription only" sleeping pill widely used as a recreational drug in Brazil], food, you name it, *loló* [a mixture of solvents that is inhaled].

Tobias: Do you share the money with the other children?

Edivaldo: [indignant] Are you kidding? If they want, they can go out and steal watches themselves. I'm the one who did the work and ran the risk. I tell them to go out and get their own watches.

Once when I earned money, I bought a Beretta. I spent ten days snatching watches, "Pah, pah" [his onomatopoeic rendition of children stealing watches]. First I bought a Mauser and then I held it against a lady's neck. I swiped her money and a bunch of videocassettes. I spent more than a month with the gun, stealing. Then I sold it and with the money I'd stolen and the money from the gun I bought a thirty-eight. Then I stole some more, sold that gun, and bought the Beretta.

I went to the street and a kid saw that my pockets were bulging, he tried to take my money. I pulled out the gun and pointed it at him. He took my money [anyway]. I said, "Give it back you asshole or I'll shoot you. You think I steal so you can come and take my money?" He gave me the money and I yelled, "Run!" He ran and I went "Bam!" but I missed. "Take another!" I missed again. When I shot again he fell. I said, "Shit, I killed a boy." I took off. The next day the kid had a Band-Aid on his toe. I only shot him in the toe.

Tobias: How would you have felt if you'd killed him?

Edivaldo: [his expression changing from one of patent excitement to that of the repentant child] I would have felt very bad. But [smiling fiendishly], I ran so fast no bullet could have ever hit me.

Tobias: What's the most interesting thing that's ever happened to you in the street?

Edivaldo: It was when a guy sold me a machine gun. I bought it, but I sold it the next day. It was one of those little ones. I kept it inside my shorts, I made it look like a bottle of glue. I went to look for someone to sell it to. I found a policeman, a friend of mine, who traded the machine gun for a revolver and gave me back two million cruzeiros [more than US$200]. In the street we get our hands on money that even rich people don't touch.

Speaking of the Street

Margarete

Amar é viver, viver é ser real.
Realidade é ser infeliz
  e felicidade é querer morrer.
A morte é fim de tudo.
Mas a vida é tão bonita e bela pra quem sabe viver.
É uma coisa que eu não sei fazer.
Por isso devo sofrer até morrer,
  acabar com tudo,
  esquecer o mundo e nunca mais chorar.

To love is to live, to live is to be real.
Reality is to be unhappy
  and happiness is to want to die.
Death is the end of everything
But life is beautiful
  for those who know how to live,
  something I know not how to do.
So I suffer and then I'll die,
  forget the world and never again cry.

Margarete[3] possessed a nearly infallible memory for the lyrics of songs and for the poems, like the one above, that she from time to time composed. Her life, as she told it to me during the many conversations we had together, was a soft-spoken collage of violence, drug-induced hallucinations, betrayals, and dreams – events and ideas that occurred to her in no particular order. Her "life story" comes in the form of vignettes, episodes of her life that she shared with me and my tape recorder.

When I met her she was 17. She had been off drugs and off the streets for several months, living on a rural farm for street children. We talked one day under the shade of a jaca tree, a sweeter, more aromatic relative of the breadfruit, in what the children on the farm called the *praça*, or central square. It consisted of several tree trunks and stumps arranged in a more or less concentric fashion. As we spoke, some of the boys would sneak up from behind to hear what Margarete was saying. She would suddenly grow quiet, speaking only to shoo them away before returning her attention to the tape recorder. Noticing that she was contemplating her growing belly, I asked her if she had wanted to become pregnant.

Margarete: It's what I always wanted, but I thought I was hysteri . . . that I couldn't catch a belly. At first I thought it might be worms, I felt nauseated, I got thin. I thought, maybe it was weak blood. [When the doctor said I was pregnant] I didn't believe him. I started to cry. It's what I always wanted, but now that it's happened . . . at seventeen, because I thought, street girls younger than me are already pregnant. I was fourteen, then fifteen, sixteen. I never got pregnant. It didn't happen until I was seventeen.

I was born in Casa Amarela, or was it Peixinhos? I don't remember, because I never really spoke with my mother, I never knew who I was. I never asked about my life, how old I was, who I was, who my family was.

At first I lived with neighbors. My mother left me there. She only took me out to go get money. Then she would start to drink. I didn't call her "Mom" because I didn't really know her. I just called her "Hey," "Hey, lady."

One day – I was little, about six or seven – I was with my mother, I think she went into a bar to beg for money. I called out to her "Hey! I'm hungry."

"Why don't you call me 'Mom'?" she asked.

I just sat there all awkward. She spent the money on alcohol and she would get food from people in their houses. She fell down in front of a lady's house. The lady yelled, "Get that woman out of here." I told the lady that my mother was too heavy for me, so she called the police. The police got my mother out of the way and they took me to FEBEM. I stayed there till I was thirteen.

When I first got to FEBEM I started crying, I was afraid of the girls in there, I thought they were going to do something to me. But they were good girls, a little like me, and the ladies there didn't let anyone pick on you.

One day my mother came to see me. She was drunk, so they

hid me behind a tree and tricked my mother by telling her that I wasn't there, that I was in some nuns' school. My mother got into a fight with another girl's mother and my mother was arrested. Then all the girls started making fun of me.

When I was thirteen and I was new in the street [a *novata*], I ran away [from a shelter] with Fátima. Marcos, they say he's nuts, he grabbed me and yelled at me to take off my clothes. I told him, "No!" He hit me in the forehead and pushed me. I fell on the ground. He ripped off my clothes and hopped on. Fátima stood there, telling him to stop, but he didn't.

At first when I was in the street I slept in a guy's house where a bunch of girls would spend the night. He let them sleep there so he could have sex with them. Whoever wouldn't let him would have to sleep in the street.

In the beginning, I liked stealing a lot. I thought, this is how I'm going to change my life. But no, things just got worse. Once I went out to do *quarador*. *Quarador* is like this. In the middle of the night you steal clothing from the clothesline, from other people's yards, in the gardens. One night me, Leila, and two boys, we were going to Ipsep, but we took the wrong bus, we were high and we got off in Jordão Baixo, in thug turf [*numa bocada quente*], but we didn't know where we'd landed. Then Leila went to knock on someone's door. I said, "Leila, don't knock there. They don't have any clothing." She said, "No, I'm just asking for water." I said, "Okay." The boys were down the street sniffing glue. I said, "Leila, come here, look who's coming." It was seven guys, all with black hoods on their heads and guns in their hands. It was what you call the death squad, the ones who kill street children, glue sniffers. They don't feel sorry for anyone. They just kill.

They started shooting at us. Leila got shot in the head, the bullet went in one side and out the other. She was hit by another one here [she points to her cheek], and it came out her mouth, and another one hit her in the ear.

She lost a lot of blood. One of the boys was scraped by a bullet that brushed across his belly and the other boy got away because he jumped over a fence. I got hit in the arm, here. I thought I was going to die, croak right there, kick the bucket.

Children playing in the street. Photo by Daniel Aamot.

Leila fell to the ground and I was afraid because I thought she was dead. They took us to the Restauração [Hospital]. I fainted. I thought I was dead, but I'd only fainted. Then they took care of me.

The thing that's most fun about being in the street is when there's a party in the streets. We party right there, in the street. Even though we're dirty, we have fun, playing in the street, with nothing to do. Some people give us these looks, they get scared, they move away from us. Sometimes I say, "Lady, I'm not going to rob you," but they see that it's a street girl who's talking, so that's it, they're scared.

In Boa Viagem there are *gringos* who like us. They prefer dark women. They get turned on and pick us up, buy us clothing, sometimes they give you a *banho de loja*.

Tobias: A boutique bath?

Margarete: That's when they dress you up, fix you all up, buy you shoes. Street girls, who never had those things, call it a *banho de loja*.

Tobias: Have you heard about AIDS?

Margarete: AIDS . . . I've heard about it. It's a disease you get through syringes and sex. A guy told me that AIDS is the rich

38

people's disease, we don't get it, only rich folks do. I'm not afraid of AIDS, but the disease I did get was the "ooze." Have you heard of it? It's this yellow stuff that oozes out from your vagina and wets your underwear. It's not just women that get it, men do too.

[freely associating, she continued] There was a boy named Bochecha who lost his penis because he had a bottle full of glue [in his shorts]. He was hanging onto the back of a bus, and when the driver put on the brakes, Bochecha fell to the ground and lost his penis [because it was cut off by the shards of glass]. Afterward, the kids would tell him, "Bochecha, you should give in to death, you can't go on living like that. How are you going to screw a girl?" He said, "No problem, with my finger or my tongue." He had been stabbed so many times and he had never given in to death. But then some nasty guys, one night they stabbed him and that time they took away his life.

Tobias: Have the police ever beaten you up?

Margarete: Lots of times. They've hit me in the back, in the belly, in my face, in the leg. Those clubs they carry around, they use them to hit us. Sometimes when they don't hit you with the clubs they hit you in the head with the butt of the revolver, or with the barrel. There's a girl who passed out because of that and because of being kicked. I got kicked in the face once, and my face hurt a lot. Sometimes the police beat up on pregnant girls. Sometimes they hit them in the stomach because they don't know the girls are pregnant, but sometimes it's to be evil or because they just feel like it

Once with two other girls I went into a store to steal a bag of underwear. I was caught [by the guard] and he took me up into a room by the toilet. He grabbed my shirt and hung me on the wall. He hit me in the stomach. Then he took out a pair of scissors. I thought he was going to stab me, but instead he cut my hair, he made a little circle in the middle like the pope has. Then he threw cold water on me and I got all wet. I went out into the street crying. The girls didn't know what to do with me. They took me to a public bathroom and I washed up.

A long time ago I went to Rio de Janeiro. I was adopted by a lady, but I didn't get along there. I fought with the lady's daughter. So the lady said, "Margarete, you can't stay here if you're just going to be causing confusion with my daughter. You'd better go back where you came from." I felt all bitter inside, I wanted to cry, but I couldn't do anything. I liked the lady's son and at night I would watch him, wanting to kiss him, but I was too shy.

Sometimes when I'm in the street I live in fear. I only get a little high because if you get really high you mess up, you fall to the ground, and then someone can come along and kill you. So many glue sniffers have already died in their sleep!

Sometimes they [big kids] are afraid [to do it themselves] so they send the little ones to steal. They used to be minors too, they already stole in the streets, and they only got sent to FE-BEM. But now they know that since they aren't minors any more they'll be sent to prison, to Aníbal Bruno. They're afraid to be sent there so they make the little ones steal for them. If they don't do it they get beaten up or they [the big ones] will snag their loot or stab them, with a knife or with broken glass, so the little kids get scared and turn over the goods.

I was always lonely, without anyone, alone, a sufferer, with no one to help me or talk with me. And when someone would come to help me, to talk with me, to give me advice, I thought the person was trying to trick me. But my stubbornness, always trying to boss others around, led me into trouble. That's why I got kicked out of the Lar Santa Luzia [a state-run facility for girls]. I would beat up the girls, yell at the director, acting like I was bigger than everyone. But I am nothing.

2

BEING IN THE STREET

In an article about research with street children in three Latin American cities, Riccardo Lucchini (1996: 168) warns against "the use of extracts from testimonies or utterances outside the contexts to which they are linked, as well as using these extracts in order to 'prove' an assertion or hypothesis." Anecdotes and carefully selected narratives – those pernicious tools of anthropologists sometimes used to conflate the individual and the collectivity – are brashly present in this book. While hoping to avoid the pitfalls of what Lucchini aptly criticizes as the opportunistic and decontextualized use of oral testimony, I have found it meaningless to portray the general without also illustrating with the specific, even though the specific is, perforce, unique. But certain problems arise.

Surrendering the tape recorder was part of an effort to allow children a voice in this study. But that voice has been altered, if not reinvented, in its metamorphosis from the original utterance, through capture on audio tape, transcription, and translation from Portuguese to English. What the children call *a língua da gente* (our tongue) – few know that what they speak is also called Portuguese – has been expressed here in standard English. Certain sayings peculiar to the private argot of Recife's street children have been translated into readily comprehensible Anglo-American expressions, with the inevitable result that aspects of the richness of the children's orality have been lost. Also missing in the transcriptions are the myriad facial expressions, gesticulations, laughs, and yawns that frame the meaning of speakers' words. One researcher of Brazilian street children has even gone so far as to relegate the orality of her subjects to the status of a " 'complementary' mechanism of communication," for, she argues, "life in the streets is defined by action, by movement, by gesticulation" more than by speech (Diógenes 1994: 24).

I risk having Chapter 1 and other portions of this book that rely on transcriptions from street children read as my own attempt to pass off the subjectively chosen text (in this case, the written rendition of what informants say) as social life itself. The stories of any number of children other than Edivaldo and Margarete could have been used for Chapter 1. It is not enough simply to say that Edivaldo and Margarete are key informants; in selecting their stories I have cast them as key figures in conveying my own view of what it is like to grow up in the streets of Recife. It must be acknowledged, as James Clifford (1988: 50) has pointed out, that "Quotations are always staged by the quoter."

Somewhat like the painting expected to speak for itself, the transcriptions in Chapter 1 have been left in quite raw form, although I shall return to them at different points, giving my own interpretation and making comparisons with the circumstances of other children. Whereas Chapter 1 revolves around highly personal accounts by two children of life in the street, this chapter takes a different approach. It combines the study of street children through participant observation over the long run with data obtained from the semistructured questionnaire. Edivaldo and Margarete are at once individual children with their own life stories and members of a larger collectivity I am calling street children. This chapter moves the focus from the individual to the collectivity.

Pontos e Galeras (Turf and Gangs)

Some of the street children in Recife, like Edivaldo, spend most of their time alone, but this is rare. Most street children are found in groups. From 1992 through 1995, there were about seven spots around the city center where street children would congregate (see Map 1). But often one would seek out the children in one or several of these places and find none. All of these locations had quite a different feel to them.

The Gramado (the lawn), indicated as position 4 on the map, was the roughest area in the sense that the kids were often aggressively involved in stealing wallets, purses, and watches. High on glue and

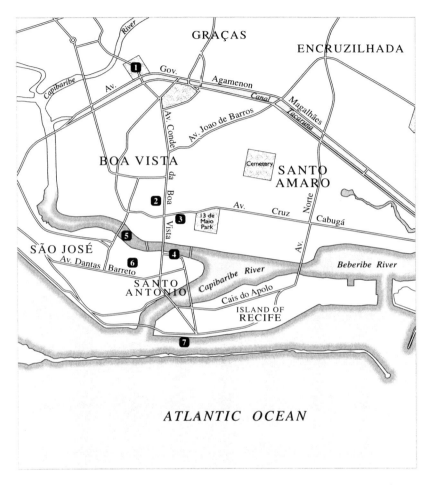

Map 1. Central Recife and the favorite spots of street children: 1. Praça do Derby; 2. Praça Maciel Pinheiro; 3. Faculdade ce Direito (Law Faculty); 4. O Gramado ("The Lawn"); 5. A Casa da Cultura; 6. Praça do Carmo; 7. Os Cais do Port (The Wharves).

other drugs much of the time, their attention spans were short. Fights broke out frequently and were often violent. Although I spent considerable time with the youths from that spot, I found it harder there than anywhere else in the city to engage them in conversation and build up a meaningful relationship. Social service groups generally avoided the area.[1]

The children around Maciel Pinheiro (position 2 on the map) tended to be far more gentle and talkative. Many of the males were gay, several of them transvestites, but females and straight males representing a range of ages also frequented the spot. Fights were less common and generally less violent. Possibly out of courtesy, the children tended not to use glue when the street educators were present. Some of the children, particularly the transvestites, would help the other children by procuring food from restaurants and sharing it. Even children who would normally hang out along the Gramado tended to be far gentler when they came over to Maciel Pinheiro.

The Law Faculty (position 3), the site of the confrontation that opens this book, was favored by a steady but shifting contingent of street children. It is across the street from a park and diagonally opposite one of the main bus stops in the city center. A large video parlor is directly across on the south side, and one block further is the frenetically busy Conde da Boa Vista, a frequent site for petty theft. There are many restaurants nearby where it is common for the children to ask for leftover food. The plentiful shops, businesses, and bus stops in the area mean there is a constant flow of people around the Law Faculty. Toward the middle of 1993, a group of prepubescent boys had moved into this area. A police booth staffed day and night was located on the back side of the grounds, and the young children in this particular group said they had made friends with the police and felt protected by their presence.

Street children tend to like to sleep in places where there is activity at night, especially near an all-night guard, say around a bank or a department store. Along Conde da Boa Vista and Dantas Barreto, two of the largest avenues in downtown Recife, there is always activity, and children can be found sleeping near those vendors who stay out through the night. Generally they sleep in groups, especially in the absence of a guard. Sometimes they sleep in *tocas*, hideouts such as abandoned vehicles or houses.

Quiet, dark places are feared. At the Capim de Cheiro farm, which is linked to the National Movement of Street Children, I observed street children positively terrified at night of the quiet, swaying cane fields. Even those 18, 19, or 20 years old who had lived in the streets fcr years would not venture away from the house alone at night to relieve themselves, no matter how urgent the need.

Despite being found in groups, the street children rarely form organized, stable gangs, though these are common in the *favelas*. Although they may refer to the group with which they roam and steal as a *galera*, the same term used to refer to a type of gang in the *favelas*, street children are just as likely to use other terms such as *turma* (any sort of group undergoing something together, such as a course) or *patota* (a group of malefactors), sometimes shortened to *pá*. And in any case, these associations are different from the neighborhood *galeras*. Raquel, aged about 16, described her experience of joining a neighborhood *galera*.

> The boss of the *galera* gets everyone together on a Sunday, he has a house for them, for us, right? Then he says, "Look, today is Sunday, this group is going to make a stop in such and such a place, that group is going to stop there. . . ." The Pró [a *galera*] has more than two hundred people. So he says, "I want everyone who's here to be here at one o'clock in the morning, not a minute before, not a minute after." And you have to be there. If you don't show up you die. . . . To get into something like that you have to be tough, have iron nerves. If you're passing by a house and he says [she looks at my cassette recorder], "Go in there and steal the tape recorder for me," you have to go in and steal the tape recorder, because if you don't, you die. Having a boss is tough, they don't want to take any shit.

In the street, there is no sense of formal group membership, as in the shantytown *galeras*. There are no rites of entry or penalties for disassociating oneself from a group. Street children will not cease to remind you "chiefs are for Indians" (*quem tem chefe é índio*) and it's "each one for himself" (*cada um por si*).

In the street, boys tend to be highly individualistic. Edivaldo's exhortations against sharing loot echo an almost Protestant work ethic in which each individual has the responsibility for securing personal resources. This also extends to what is given to them. When a group of street children is offered a snack, pushing, shoving, and grabbing typically ensue with the quickest ones making off with whatever they

I roam all over the city. Photo by Isabel Balseiro.

can before others get to it. Often if you ask street children with whom they roam they will reply, "alone, with God" (*só, com Deus*), although they are normally in the company of their peers. Street life is marked by both wrenching solitude and intense solidarity.

> *Tobias*: Within this *galera*, do you guys have a chief?
>
> *Eufrásio* [*male, about 14*]: No, no way, chiefs are for Indians. No one around here has a chief, because the day that rotten no-good Walter was with me I pulled out a huge knife right away, yeah, a two-inch knife! When he came close, I was going to give him a good slashing. . . . I was going to really kill him, stick it in with all my hatred, he was giving me shit. . . . But a chief? No, nobody has a chief. It's everyone for himself. A chief is the one who bosses you around, who says, "Go get a cigarette for me." No, what I want to do I do for myself – after all, I'm in

the street! When you're in the street, you do what you want, you know? No one bosses me around, the one who bosses me around at home is my mother, my father, my grandmother, period. Now in the street, no one tells me what to do. Just God.

Eufrásio's reference to threatening Walter with a knife related to the fact that Walter often tried to boss around the other boys. In the street, the leadership ambitions of individual children are continually stymied in this fashion, by their peers either individually or in association asserting their resistance to submitting. Despite Eufrásio's insistence that he would kill Walter "with all his hatred," the two continued to roam together in the street. Notwithstanding violent rivalries within groups of street children, tight bonds of association are also forged.

Andando e Arrumando Coisas (Roaming and Coming Up with Things)

Edivaldo had traveled a great deal around the state of Pernambuco and nearby states, and Margarete had been as far as Rio de Janeiro. Other street children have never left the metropolitan area of Recife, except perhaps on an excursion organized by a local agency. A full 84 percent in the sample of 50 children[2] were born in the metropolitan area, and most of the street children said their parents had always lived in the city. But within the city most have moved around quite a lot. Normally the first moves are made with their families and most children in my sample had lived in at least three or four neighborhoods.

On their own, street children move around the city quite a bit. "When things get hot, we go someplace else," Come-Lixo explained to me. "Getting hot" might refer to a wrathful shopkeeper whose merchandise has been stolen or to other children who have made credible threats.

Street children can often be seen moving around on the backs of buses. For most Brazilians, the phrase *pegar bigu* simply means to catch a ride. For street children it means to catch a ride on the back bumper of a bus. *Bigu* is transportation, but it is also entertainment. As I sat inside a bus one day fretting over a boy named Germano who was clutching onto the tailpipe, I offered to pay his fare. He refused, gig-

An afternoon with Preta the dog.

gling into the wind as the bus swerved from side to side, reaching ever more perilous speeds.

Possessions are difficult for street children to keep. Sometimes the children have places where they stash things, such as under a news kiosk or in an abandoned house, but these are certainly not secure storage sites. Other people have access to these places too. Money and other important items can sometimes be entrusted to an adult benefactor, for instance to an all-night guard or a street vendor, but this is by no means an everyday option. Thus when street children wake up in the morning, they typically possess nothing but a pair of shorts and a T-shirt.

Between 5 and 15 children slept in the street in the neighborhood where I lived in Olinda. They would secure food and other basic resources through a variety of means. On one side of my building was the house of a wealthy woman (position 2 on Map 2). Each morning

"Out for a ride" (*Pegando um biguzinho*). Photo by Ivaldo Bezerra.

she would allow three of the street children in for breakfast. They would push and shove to be at the front of the queue and be among the lucky ones to enter that day. Those less fortunate did not necessarily miss breakfast. Five or six other households in the neighborhood offered food in the morning, albeit not with the same regularity. The lottery ticket shop (position 3) might be convinced to allow one of the children to wash the windows in exchange for breakfast. Roberta at the pool supply shop (position 4) particularly liked one of the boys and invited him to help her at the store in exchange for clothing, food, some spending money, and even the coveted reward of assistance for his mother. Sometimes one of the more daring children might fetch a coconut from one of the tall trees along the beach. Lunch tended to be more problematic than breakfast since it proved more difficult to get food from houses, but begging in the street or at restaurants would often do the trick. Sometimes the *educadores* from Sobe e Desce would bring a snack of milk and sweet bread. In extreme circumstances one might look in the garbage for food, but this tended to result in ridicule from companions. A large dinner of leftovers could almost always be had at the restaurant. A waiter would clap his hands and one of the boys would come running to receive a bag of leftover food, which he would share with his friends.

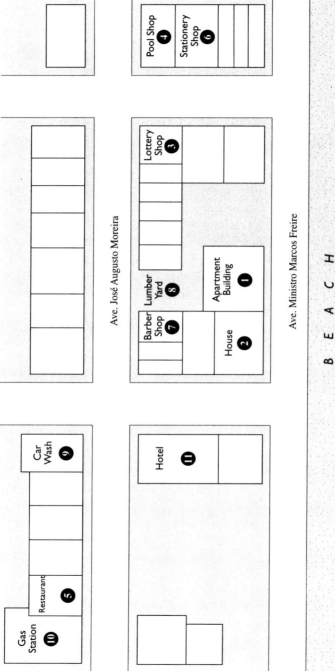

Ave. José Augusto Moreira

Ave. Ministro Marcos Freire

B E A C H

S E A

Pool Shop ❹

Stationery Shop ❻

Lottery Shop ❸

Barber Shop ❼

Lumber Yard ❽

Apartment Building ❶

House ❷

Car Wash ❾

Restaurant ❺

Gas Station ❿

Hotel ⓫

Map 2. A network of resources for street children in Olinda.

The stationery supply store (position 6) sometimes offered Aloizio, a budding artist, free paper. Otherwise he would get some chalk and draw on the walls of houses. The barbershop (position 7) would lend the children a checkerboard. The owner of the lumberyard (position 8) once took a street boy home, allowing him to sleep in his own children's bedroom, and gave the boy work at the lumberyard. In time the boy ran off, however.

The boys would watch over cars at the restaurant. The guard at the car wash (position 9) allowed some of the children to sleep in an abandoned car at the establishment. The gas station (position 10) had a toilet the children would use when no one was looking. Sometimes, in the wee hours, they would jump the fence at the hotel (position 11) and take a dip in the pool. Along the beach the children would play in the water, fly kites, and even rent canoes when they were particularly flush.

Although this particular area was the center of activity for the children, they shifted around, sleeping in different places as far as four or five kilometers away — for a time in an abandoned minivan, then in an abandoned house, under the awnings of a bank, outside the Bom Preço supermarket, even next to a beachside bar so they could watch television. Their main source of liquid income came from selling stolen goods. The loot had usually been procured in other neighborhoods — "never on my turf," as Come-Lixo explained. In forays called *madrugas* (a mispronunciation of *madrugada*, meaning dawn, and a reference to what they would do in the early hours), they would break into houses in the middle of the night to steal a variety of goods.

> *Come-Lixo*: At night we wake up, have some coffee . . . and wait to pull a *madruga*. When it's *madruga* we wake up and climb around the houses to enter through the window and take everything — [with great excitement] televisions, record players, video games, and everything! And that's how it goes: bicycles, clothing, basketball shoes, whatever turns up goes with us.

These goods would quickly be sold to fences in an Olinda slum. The proceeds from such forays were sufficient to buy a nearly constant supply of drugs, with cash left over for candy, fizzy drinks, and video games.

Street children engage in a multiplicity of income-generating activities. The activities most frequently cited in the survey were begging, stealing, and taking care of parked cars, or washing windshields. Yet many of those who said that they had begged also made such remarks as, "But no one gives me any money so I have to steal." And most of the older children who said they had taken care of cars claimed to have done so only when younger. Although many resources can be obtained in kind, the principal method of earning money in the street is stealing. Prostitution is an important element of the income of some of the youths (both male and female), and the very young children, those under about 10 years of age, can earn a small amount of income through begging.

Age and success at begging are, not surprisingly, inversely related. As children become physically larger, less "cute" and more "threatening," sympathy for them diminishes. On the other hand, as the kids get older they become physically stronger and more daring, which facilitates self-defense and enhances their skills at snatching wallets, watches, and purses.

It was extremely difficult to obtain information on how much money the children earned. The survey contained the questions, "How much do you earn in a day?" and "And on a good day?" But, inflation of 30 percent per month made it senseless to ask the question of those at shelters who had left the street at some difficult-to-determine point in the past. Even among the children on the street it proved difficult to get precise figures. Like Edivaldo, who boasted of being able to steal more than 10 watches a day, a few of the children can come up with what, by the standards of poor people in Brazil, are large quantities of money, say the minimum monthly salary after just a couple of particularly fruitful days. Other street children, especially the ones who do not steal or who steal only infrequently, collect only small amounts of money, perhaps a couple of dollars per week.

Clothing is easy to come by on clotheslines, but this is by no means the only way to get it. A neighbor named Hozana, a retired school-teacher, invited two street children and me for breakfast one day. Our hostess asked one of the boys about some nice clothing she had seen him wearing once.

Hozana: Germano, do you remember one Sunday when you were here, you were taking a bath? You had on some beautiful new shorts and a striped shirt. Were those [taken] from a clothes-line?

"Chiefs are for Indians" (*Quem tem chefe é índio*). Photo by Daniel Aamot.

Germano: No, a man bought that clothing for me, a man who was going to take me to Natal.

Hozana: And where's that clothing now?

Gilson [*the other boy*]: He throws it away when it gets dirty.

Tobias: Then you have to get more clothing later?

Germano: Yes, but there are other people around to give you clothing. We have a bunch of *freguesas* who take care of us.

Hozana: [incredulous] *Freguesas*?

Germano: Yes. Just yesterday I "won" a bag of clothing and today I'm going to "win" another.

For most Brazilians, *freguêses* (*freguesas*, in the feminine, as referred to above) are regular clients. For instance, a butcher will refer to his steady customers as *freguêses*.[3] But among street children the term is used to refer to people who help them out regularly, particularly by providing a free meal. The resources to be had from *freguêses* are always available, although one must be *esperto*, or cunning, as well as persistent, to extract them.

Aside from individual *freguêses*, the children have two other sources of free food: institutions and restaurants. A number of organizations in Recife provide meals, though most of them only erratically. The girls might look for meals during weekdays at one of two institutions: the Casa de Passagem and the FUNDAC (government) project called first Projeto Renascer then later CAE (Center for Reception and Referral). Some of the boys go to another FUNDAC project in Abreu e Lima, just outside Recife, where they are given vocational training as well as meals. Ruas e Praças used to offer snacks, but eventually desisted, complaining that the street children came to expect food as just another paternalistic handout. Different religious groups, particularly the Spiritists, would from time to time give out free food and clothing. Restaurants and bars are a vital source of food for most of the children. Many establishments give the children leftovers. But street children by no means live outside the cash economy. As Edivaldo and Come-Lixo point out, they obtain money and buy food. When I visited the shelter with the two researchers I was helping to conduct interviews with street children, they were amazed at the enormous plates of food the kids were gobbling up. When one of the researchers commented on this, a boy interjected, "This is nothing compared with what we ate in the street."

Such comments obscure the fact that street children do experience hunger at times. But most street children are probably better nourished than their siblings at home. Although proving such an assertion was beyond the scope of my research, a careful examination of this issue in relation to children in Nepal was carried out by a team of biological and social anthropologists from the University of Durham. One hundred eleven homeless children in Kathmandu evidenced slightly less stunting and a slightly lower incidence of weight deficiency than 62 squatter children and 52 village children (Panter-Brick, Todd, and Baker 1996). Similarly, a study of street and working children in Tegucigalpa, Honduras, found that while impoverished children working in city markets were more likely to eat regular meals than truly abandoned street children, "second- and third-degree malnutrition has so far been found only among the market children; no such cases have yet been seen among the children 'of' the street" (Wright, Wittig, and Kaminsky 1993: 88). In any case, in informal conversations, street children tended to affirm that they ate better in the street. An exchange with one boy about the comparative benefits of eating at home or in the street went as follows:

Being in the Street

Tobias: How are you finding it being in the street?

João: On the one hand it's better because I eat. I eat, I fill my belly, and there's still some left over, but not at home. At home I even gobble up the plate.

Gender, Age, and Race

As illustrated by the narratives of Edivaldo and Margarete, the experience of living in the street differs in important ways for boys and for girls. Although neither narrative can summarize the diversity of experiences for either gender, the very starkness of the differences between their lives serves to highlight certain gendered ideas about street life. When they explain their genesis as street children, girls and boys often tell markedly different stories. When asked why they have left home, the girls frequently cite sexual abuse. Camilla was one of the few street children who disliked the tape recorder, but I spent many afternoons hanging out with her. She told of how her stepfather had tried to rape her. Her mother, whose protection she sought, sided with the stepfather. The sexual aggression of Camilla's stepfather, coupled with her mother's devastating refusal to help, compelled Camilla to leave home at the age of 17.

Edivaldo highlights how leaving home was, on the one hand, a response to abuse from his stepfather and, on the other, a reflection of his patent fascination with life in the street. Upon meeting street children, adults often ask them why they are in the street; boys will typically respond to the blunt question with an equally blunt answer: they say they left because they felt like it (*porque eu quis*).

> *Airton [male, aged about 17]*: A lot of people who live in the street blame their mothers and fathers, but that's not it. I'm in the street because I want to be. I left home because I felt like it. No one made me leave.

Over time boys typically reveal other factors such as beatings, fear of the *favelas*, or a sense of rejection or simply boredom at home. What they are least likely to cite, at least initially, is maternal rejection. In certain instances, I knew of boys whose mothers refused to have them at home. Yet when I would ask the boys why they were in the street,

55

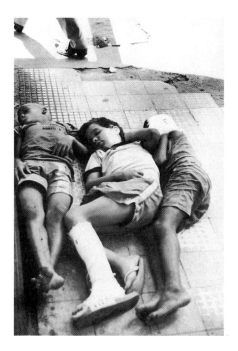

An afternoon nap on a busy sidewalk.

they would insist they were there because they "felt like it." In explaining their status, boys like Edivaldo often highlight their own defiant initiative, whereas girls (perhaps more honestly) are more likely to refer to their ill-treatment at home.

Some of the groups of street children around the city are age- and gender-based. For example, one group behind the Law Faculty consisted exclusively of boys ranging in age from about 9 to 15. An afternoon conversation with the boys at this spot in the company of a street educator named Jocimar revealed much about their feelings on gender and authority in the street.

>*Tobias*: In your group, are there girls?
>*Edi*: The people we roam with?
>*Tobias*: Yes.
>*Edi*: Only boys.

Tobias: And if a girl wanted to join you, would you guys accept?

Another boy: I'd accept.

Edi: I wouldn't.

Tobias: Why not?

Yet another boy: Because he's a faggot [*frango*].

Edi: I am not! You're the faggot!

Tobias: Why wouldn't you accept?

Edi: I don't know.

Jocimar [to a boy called Carioca]: And would you accept?

Carioca: Of course I would. To do it.

Jocimar: Do what?

Carioca: It!

Jocimar: What's "it"?

Carioca: It!

Jocimar: What kind of "it"?

Carioca: Business!

Jocimar: What kind of business?

Carioca: Man, grab her and fuck her.

Jocimar: Oh yeah?

Carioca [laughing]: Yeah, stick it in her twat.

Jocimar: Is that what girls are for?

Carioca: Yeah, stick it in and ciao!

Jocimar: How crazy!

Edi: Ask me questions!

Tobias: Does one of you tell the others what to do?

Edi: No, it's each one for himself.

Some of the smaller boys were apparently prepared to consider roaming with girls, although others believed it was not appropriate, citing possible threats to their sexuality. In other words, being with girls would jeopardize their sense of boyhood by being in some way a homosexual and (to their understanding) less male thing to do. On the other hand, Carioca, who was just reaching puberty, saw roaming with girls as desirable because of the possibility of confirming his male identity by being able to "stick it in."

The affirmation at the end of the dialogue, that no one tells anyone else what to do, was followed by a discussion of abuse at the hands of older and larger *cheira-colas*, or glue sniffers. Although there was argument over how a gender-integrated group would in different ways be both undesirable and advantageous, there was broad consensus against roaming with the bigger youths, who would steal from them and boss them around. But whereas these boys, like many other young children in the street, were deeply afraid of the older and stronger youths, the latter (particularly those who could be arrested as adults) tended to be interested in befriending younger children who could steal for them. Sometimes the older children, as Margarete explains in Chapter 1, coerce the little ones into such relationships, threatening them physically if they do not cooperate. At other times, a small child will seek the protection of a big one.

Gender divisions, from the perspectives of girls, are sometimes marked by two stances, both based on physical and sexual vulnerabilities. Some girls will avoid being with boys, in this way eluding the boys' likely attempts at subordinating them (sexually and otherwise), while forming close bonds with one another. At other times, girls explain that they seek to be with boys for protection. Camilla explained to me, "I'm ashamed to beg and I don't know how to steal. That's why I'm with Tadeu." She put up with extensive beatings from her boyfriend while he was her only source of income. As another girl told me in no uncertain terms, "If you don't have a boyfriend, all the other boys want to hop on." But boyfriends are seen as far more than a source of protection. When street girls draw pictures, they tend to include their boyfriends in them. Those who do not know how to write will ask someone to decorate their drawings with a message about their latest flame, such as "Katia and Chefe love each other." The girls often talk about their partners with great passion and make considerable sacrifices for them. For example, a 15-year-old named Renata explained that she preferred to prostitute herself than have her boyfriend steal. We were speaking at a drop-in center.

> *Tobias*: Patrício is your *namorado* [boyfriend], right?
> *Renata*: He's my *macho* [my man]. *Namorado*! Has anyone ever seen a woman in the street with a *namorado*?
> *Paula* [*a street educator*]: Do you have sex only with him?
> *Renata*: With him, and with the Chinese, with johns who've got the money, real money! I won't do it for cheap.

Erica [*another street educator*]: Does he know about this?
Renata: He knows.
Paula: He doesn't get on your case? He doesn't do anything?
Renata: I split the money with him.
Paula: And the money he comes up with, does he share it with you?
[Renata nods her head.]
Erica: And how does he come up with money?
Renata: Ah, well, only when he. . . . He doesn't steal now. I prefer to give him money than have him steal in the street.

For boys there are two contradictory stances on having girlfriends. On the one hand having a girlfriend can be a matter of prestige for the adolescent boys; on the other, there are those who claim the girls just want to live off them. Immediately after we talked with Renata, Patrício spoke with us.

Erica: When Renata is in the street, how does she live?
Patrício: She goes home every day. She goes home at three or four o'clock, she eats there, sleeps there. Her friends at the brothel give her money. They like her.
Erica: And the girls don't receive anything in return? Does she give something in return?
Patrício: The girls there, from the *zona* [red light district], at the brothel, they know her, they like her. Sometimes they just give her money.
Erica: After she started going out with you, did she stop going to the brothel?
[Patrício does not answer.]
Erica: What if she wanted to go?
Patrício: I wouldn't let her, of course.
Erica: And if she were to have sex with another person?
Patrício: Then, she'd have to stay with him and I'd take care of myself [*vô me virá só*], like I used to do.
Erica: What if she were to have a child?
Patrício: Only if it were for a baby. If she were supporting her baby, it would be alright.

Thus, whereas Renata says she is supporting Patrício through prostitution, he presents himself as a sort of street patriarch, reassuring the female street educators that Renata goes home every day and that he would forbid his girlfriend to prostitute herself. He suggests the unlikely scenario that the girls at a brothel give her money because they like her, and he proudly affirms that he would refuse to allow her to have sex with other men, unless she were doing it to support her baby.

Young homeless males who dress like women, only a handful in the city, tend to congregate among themselves and with girls. The ultimate outcasts, not only growing up outside the home but from a young age defiantly referring to themselves as females, transvestites speak of being at once rejected and sexually exploited by adolescent males.

> *Marcela [aged about 17]*: [What we want is] a Foundation Queer Queer [Fundação Veado-Veado], also known as Defense for Street Queers, you understand? To have a house for transvestites, homosexuals who live in the street, that at the same time would be a defense, because, I say, what good is it for you [referring to some boys in the group who consider themselves heterosexual] to call me over to have sex today when tomorrow you hit me, reject me? No, it doesn't get us anywhere, my friend.

Like the street girls, with whom they closely identify, transvestites sometimes cite sexual abuse from a man at home as the reason for their being in the street.

> *Tobias*: What was it that prompted you to go and live in the street?
> *Marcela*: It was because of my stepfather, who wanted to have sex with me. I never wanted to, he hit me. When I came to the street I learned how to fight, to cut – I got cut in the face – I cut other people too, then I started to fight. When I went home, [my stepfather tried it again] and I grabbed my mother's knife and stuck it in his ribs.
> *Tobias*: This happened when you were seven?

Marcela: Seven years old.
Tobias: Is your mother with him still?
Marcela: Yes, she's still with him. She says he's the only person who can feed her.

Like most people in Recife, the street children are typically of mixed race, though some have very black features and some rather white. Race is often incorporated into nicknames. For instance a small, dark-skinned boy may be called *Neguinho*, a big one *Negão*, and one with light-colored hair is likely to be known as *Galego* (literally, Galician). They are apt to view lighter skin and hair as favorable characteristics; one particularly dark-skinned youth told of using a "special" lotion to lighten his hair.

Beto: How many years ago did you start to rob?
Zé Pretinho: Since I was nine.[4] The first time when I started to steal was in Bom Preço [a supermarket]. My first arrest was at Bom Preço. I "won" something when I was going out of Bom Preço, the police caught me and stuck me inside the "little cockroach" [a police vehicle] and took me to the courthouse.
Beto: What kind of thing was it [you stole]?
Zé Pretinho: It was Johnson's Oil, that stuff you rub in your hair to make it lighter. We use it at the beach.

Another boy asked me with apparent frustration why his hair was so kinky. Others simply told me they thought that white people were "prettier." The street children, however, by no means associate or disassociate with their peers for reasons of race; a gamut of skin colors can typically be found in any group of street children, although children who are very light-skinned, and hence likely to be middle-class, are rarely found on the street.

Ficando Doido (Getting High)

Most of the children who have spent more than a few months on the street have used drugs. Glue and marijuana, the drugs used most frequently, are both readily available at accessible prices, glue being the cheaper. Although children are frequently refused glue in hardware stores, traffickers purchase large quantities and resell it to the children for a profit. Sufficient glue to fill a small bottle costs the equivalent of a dollar or two and lasts several days. Of 26 children in the survey living in the street at the time of the interview, 14 (54%) said they currently used glue.

Many kids who have spent a long time on the street experiment with different kinds of "prescription only" medicines. The most frequently used ones are Rohypnol and Artane. Of 49 children questioned, 77 percent (33) had used Rohypnol; of 47 children, 64 percent (30) had used Artane.[5] Rohypnol (flunitrazepam) is a sedative. Artane (Trihexyphenidyl), a synthetic antispasmodic meant for people with Parkinson's disease, has a euphoric effect.

In the literature about street children, the use of glue is explained as an attempt to ward off hunger and cold. For example, the caption to a photograph in an article published in *World Health* reads, "Glue sniffing in Colombia: A negative and destructive way of forgetting the pangs of hunger" (Rialp 1991: 9). Even in Recife, adults frequently say hunger and cold are the reasons street children sniff glue. Yet in my survey only 1 of 26 current users cited hunger and only 1 cited the cold when asked about their motivations for using glue. The answer given most frequently was something to the effect of *eu gosto*, or "I like it."

In my first radio workshop one boy asked another not whether glue diminished his hunger, but whether it increased it. The reply was yes. Many other children told me the same thing. Edivaldo explained that sniffing glue on an empty stomach was unhealthy, and I often observed children sniffing glue after eating. I therefore decided to include in the survey the question, "Does glue diminish or increase your hunger?"

Only a minority (38%) said sniffing glue diminished their hunger but most of these were adamant about it. On the other hand, one-third said it actually increased their appetite; another 21 percent said it both decreased and increased their appetite – that is, while they were sniffing glue they felt less hungry, but once the high was over (*quando passou a lombra*) they felt a strong urge to eat. Others (8%) said that glue did not affect their appetite in any way, though it might do other things such as make them thirsty. The replies to this question seem to suggest that the relationship of glue to hunger varies dra-

Table 1. *Anthropological Interviews: Drug Use among Street Children*

Questions and responses	Number
Why do you/did you sniff glue? (*Porque você cheira/cheirava cola?*)[a]	
To diminish hunger	1
To diminish cold	1
I like it (*eu gosto*)	11
I got hooked (*fique viciado*)	7
Gives me courage to steal (*me dá coragem pra roubar*)	3
Other reasons	9
Does glue take away your hunger or make you feel more hungry? (*A cola tira a fome ou dá fome?*)[b]	
Diminishes hunger (*tira a fome*)	15
Increases hunger (*dá fome*)	13
Diminishes and increases hunger	8
Other	3
Do you/did you spend more money on drugs or food? (*Você gasta/gastava mais dinheiro nas drogas ou na comida?*)[c]	
On drugs	24
On food	19
Other	3

[a]$N = 27$ street children currently using glue. Responses add up to more than 27 because some children cited more than one reason. Question posed in an open-ended fashion.
[b]$N = 39$ children who currently use or have used glue and who responded to the question. Question posed in an open-ended fashion.
[c]$N = 46$ street children who currently use drugs or have used them in the past.

matically from one user to another. Although I did not include a question about the relationship between marijuana and hunger, those children who touched on the subject were unanimous in saying that smoking marijuana made them voraciously hungry (*dá uma fome canina!*). It is also interesting to note that when asked whether they spent more money on drugs or on food, 52 percent said they spent more on drugs.

To suggest that street children sniff glue principally to ward off hunger and cold makes little sense in light of the way the kids themselves speak about drugs and the lengths they go to get them. Moreover, this approach ignores the possibility of initiative on the part of street children, who are portrayed as hapless victims rather than as people making a choice, albeit a choice with life-threatening consequences.

The kids in this sample, like Edivaldo, are aware that inhaling glue has detrimental effects on one's health. A full 95 percent replied in the affirmative to the question, "Does sniffing glue cause any illnesses?" When asked to name the illnesses, the children mentioned nearly everything from swelling of the head to diabetes, from wasting to kidney damage.[6] Sixty-eight percent of the children named at least one condition they believed was provoked by the substance.

Twenty-one kids who had formerly used glue were asked what had motivated them to quit. The answers varied to the extent that it was not always easy to classify them, but most fell into the categories of "sniffing glue doesn't get you anywhere" (7), health problems (5), and "I don't like it any more" (5). Of those who had quit, about half (52%) said it was difficult to quit; the other half said it was not.

Families, Institutions, Literacy, and the Perils of Being a Street Child

Like Margarete and Edivaldo, the children in my sample had lived in different settings: not just with their biological mother and in the street, but with an aunt, a grandmother, a neighbor, a godmother, or a stranger they met in the street, or in one or several institutions. Of the 46 children asked whether they had lived with someone not related to them, 37 (80%) answered in the affirmative. Of the 50 respondents, 39 (78%) had been to at least one live-in institution. Considering only those 34 children who were somewhere other than at an institution at the time of the interview, 23 (67%) had been to at least one institution.

Typically, those children who lived in the street at the time of the interview but had been to an institution in the past said they had liked the place. In all, 19 of the 23 (83%) said they had liked at least one shelter. When asked why they had left, the children provided diverse answers. Sometimes they had turned 18 and were forced to leave, sometimes their mother had fetched them. But of those who left of their own accord, most stated that they did so because "I felt like it" (*porque eu quis*) while a number cited poor food, fights with other children, or restrictions, such as not being able to smoke or having to take a bath (see Chapter 7 for an elaboration on this subject).

A few street children read and write quite well, but this is rare. Only 16 percent of those in the sample had gone beyond the fourth year in school. Most of Recife's street children are illiterate or know only how to write their names or read a few basic words.

All of the 48 children in the sample who were asked whether they had siblings replied yes to the question. A total of 29 (60%) had four or more. Yet 67 percent said that none of their siblings had ever lived in the street. In other words, typically the child in the street is the sole child from the family living in that situation. Only a single child said that more than one of his siblings had ever lived in the street.

Others have pointed out (e.g., Kendall 1975; Felsman 1982; Swart 1988) that children who sleep in the street in different cities around the world are not necessarily cut off from their families. Many street children in Recife bring home money to their mothers. But, as will also be discussed in Chapter 4, many street children use the resources they secure mainly for themselves and many have only tenuous links with their families or no links at all. Of those in the sample, only 32 percent said that they had been home over the past week, while 23 percent said they had gone home only between a month and a year ago; a further 17 percent said it was more than a year since they had returned. The amount of time elapsed since the last visit home increases with age, with some of those 13, 14, or older not having been home in years.

The relationships of the children to their mothers varied dramatically. There are mothers like Edivaldo's who comb the streets looking for their children whom they cannot persuade to stay at home. The mother of one youth explained to me how there was almost nothing she could do to convince her son to come home, try as she did.

> *Dona Beatrice*: [Alejado] left home when he was eleven. He used to shine shoes in Boa Viagem. Sometimes he came back at night, sometimes he didn't, and I would go out to look for him. Sometimes I found him, sometimes I didn't. He got together

Table 2. *Anthropological Interviews: Last Time at Home*

Questions and responses	Number
When was the last time you were at home? (*Quando foi a última vez que você esteve em casa?*)[a]	
In the past week	15
Between 1 week and 1 month ago	6
Between 1 month and 1 year ago	11
More than 1 year ago	8
Impossible to determine	6

[a] $N = 46$ children who responded to the question.

with some of his friends and started sleeping in the street. Now he stays in the center of the city. In December it'll be a year since he set foot in the house. I always look for him whenever I come into the city, but it's been a month since I last saw him. I talk with him to see if he wants to come home, but he says, "We'll talk about that later, I'll take care of it later." Time goes by, he gets older, and that's how it is. . . . He just wants to be with his *colegas* [peers] in the street.

Alejado's mother was clearly distressed about his not coming home, and when the youth was eventually imprisoned not long after turning 18, she faithfully visited him in jail, bringing him food and other necessities. On the other hand, some children have no family whatsoever to return to. One such child was Bia. When she was seven, her mother, a prostitute, died. Bia had an older sister, also a prostitute, but the sister lived precariously herself, in brothels, and introduced Bia to prostitution at a very young age. One young boy told me with great embarrassment how his mother had sold him to a couple who subsequently abandoned him.

Lucas: I was in São Paulo in the street, sleeping on the sidewalks on a bunch of paper. One day my mother sold me to a couple for a thousand cruzeiros – which [because of inflation] isn't worth anything any more. They brought me here [to Recife]. Then the woman, the one who adopted me, brought me here [to Desafio Jovem, for street children].

Street girls tend to get pregnant. Recall Margarete's surprise at not getting pregnant until the age of 17. Of the 12 females in my sample, 9 had been pregnant in the past or were pregnant at the time of the interview. The remaining 3 were among the youngest in the sample: 2 were only 14 years old, 1 was 15. By the time I returned to the field in 1995, the 15-year-old, by then only 17, was pregnant for the third time. I was unable to locate the girls who had been 14 during the survey. Street girls typically forgo any prenatal care and are apt to continue sniffing glue and using other drugs while pregnant. Beatings from the police and other children make them susceptible to miscarriages. They are likely to be suffering from a sexually transmitted disease. Some girls terminate their pregnancies by taking large doses of Citrotex, a prescription drug intended for ulcers that has strong side effects. Another method involves getting very high and standing against a wall as a friend gives a forceful kick in the belly.

When babies are born to street children, sometimes a relative will take in the infant. But more frequently the mothers keep their babies with them in the streets until caught by the police, who take the infants to the state institution, the Casa de Carolina. A few girls manage to hold onto their babies. For example, Afra, who had lost most of her front teeth in fights with her boyfriend, had managed to keep her baby for two and a half years when I met the twosome. Somehow, the toddler had not only stayed alive but appeared quite healthy.

The ability of children to survive in the streets and to find moments of joy, despite the odds stacked so heavily against them, is testament to their resilient spirit. But it is difficult to be sanguine about the futures of individual street children in Northeast Brazil. Violence in the street ends the lives of many children. Falling off the backs of buses and other sorts of traffic accidents have killed and maimed countless children. Those who do manage, somehow, to grow older often find themselves taken to adult jails rather than to FEBEM. As adults, they can find themselves spending months or years in the dreaded Aníbal Bruno prison for an act of petty theft. Others end up in Tamarineira, Recife's mental hospital. A few become adult street people, and a few settle into cardboard shacks in the *favelas*, trying

"The person I love most in the world is the baby in my belly."

their best to blend in with the domiciled, wretched poor. Although I
know of only one street child in Recife who was tested and found
positive for HIV, it is difficult to imagine that a large proportion are
not seropositive or will not become so. Nearly all the street children
are sexually active from an early age, some intensively so through
prostitution. Few even experiment with condoms. A small minority
use injectable drugs, sharing needles in the process. Sexually transmitted diseases such as syphilis, for which the risk factors are similar
to those for HIV, are common. Indeed the mortality rate and the
bleakness into which children who spend several years on the street
tend to sink give one the sense of seeing the children at the end of
their lives, not the beginning.

I met a minute, barely pubescent 15-year-old at FEBEM named
Eliane who still sucked her thumb. I later ran into her in the street
and over time I got to know her. She told me how she had been
picking up johns for a couple of years and had recently held up someone at gunpoint. I asked her what she would do if she found a box
full of money.

Eliane: I would spend it on my mother. I would buy her clothing, shoes, food, I'd do the shopping, lots of shopping. I'd buy yogurt to put in the refrigerator. I'd buy a bunch of presents for my mother and a huge house so that when I die she will remember me.

3

"HOME CHILDREN": NURTURED CHILDHOOD AND NURTURING CHILDHOOD

The culture of childhood shares many of the attributes of primitive cultures. It is handed down by word of mouth, it includes many rituals and magical formulas whose original meanings have been lost, it is hidebound and resistant to alien influence and to change.

(Stone and Church 1973: 354)

There is nothing natural or inevitable about childhood. Childhood is culturally defined and created; it, too, is a matter of human choice.

(Nandy 1992: 56)

We are faced with two competing ways of viewing childhood. On the one hand, childhood is seen as a sort of unchanging, universal social order experienced in a similar fashion by children around the world and over time. On the other hand, social anthropologists, historians, and others have increasingly come to accept that childhood is socially constructed and hence variable according to the context in which it is lived. This chapter considers, first, competing ways of viewing childhood and children. It then presents an ethnographic account of what I argue are the two dominant ways of experiencing childhood in Northeast Brazil: nurtured childhood and nurturing childhood, as I call them.

The British journalist Anthony Swift wrote a booklet for UNICEF entitled *Brazil: The Fight for Childhood in the City* (1991a). In it one reads not about the struggles of millions of children in the *favelas* and rural settlements across Brazil, but about the plight of the comparatively tiny number living in the street. Thus the booklet's title juxtaposed with its contents might lead one to draw two conclusions.

First, childhood is a thing that one can have or, if terribly unlucky, not have. Second, street children lack this thing called childhood. The reader is left wondering whether those stunted children in the countryside with worm-infested bellies have attained childhood while those in the streets remain excluded.

As the title of Swift's publication might suggest, childhood is frequently seen to possess readily defined, self-evident characteristics. If children live particular experiences, they are said to have a childhood. But rarely are these characteristics or experiences defined. Because childhood is seen as universal, though intangible and evanescent, it defies description and becomes readily apparent only in its absence. In her masterful study of British media images of children, Patricia Holland (1992: 148) observed that "Without the image of the unhappy child, our contemporary concept of childhood would be incomplete." She suggests that images of abused children, famine-stricken children, and children in other situations of great suffering solidify adult notions of childhood as an inherently weak, helpless, and dependent status. Although not disagreeing with Holland's point that victimized children highlight many First World assumptions about the nature of childhood, I would argue that such children are also presented as the obverse of childhood itself. And through persistent suggestions that children in seemingly unnatural circumstances – living or simply working in the street, for example – have been robbed of their childhood, light is shed on just what is meant by "childhood." The dust cover of a book about working children in Colombia, written with support from UNICEF, reads:

> At the age when life should be dedicated exclusively to tenderness, study and play, countless little people, like those in this book who tell their sad tales, are forced into arduous conditions of exploitation. They, who for the simple fact of being children deserve the best life has to offer, must compensate for the irresponsibility of adults and help their parents to survive. (Muñoz and Palacios 1980)

The contrast between the role of children as depicted by the reviewer and the way the children in the book describe their own lives is striking. For instance, one child states: "I believe all children should work and help their mother . . . if they need rice, then the kids have to help her to get it" (46). Another says, "children should not be given [money] because they are given food. Everyone has to learn in order to get by in life later" (49–50). Rather than focusing on the "irresponsibility of adults," the children speak of their own need to take responsibility, principally by helping their mothers and acting from an early stage to "learn to get by in life." By alleging that they lack childhood itself, the reviewer reduces the children to that lifeless state of victimhood in which attention is turned inevitably back to the behavior of adults. It is adults who victimize the children and it is adults who must also redeem them.

In "Childhood and the Policy Makers: A Comparative Perspective on the Globalization of Childhood," Jo Boyden (1990: 186) argues that international organizations are guided by a vision of a "safe, happy and protected childhood," one in which children neither work nor suffer, where they are free of hardship and pain. She suggests that the monolithic character of the model is expressed in UNICEF's discourse on the "world's children"; and this model, though globalized in the minds of social planners, is "culturally and historically bound to the social preoccupations and priorities of the capitalist countries of Europe and the United States" (186). Although not disagreeing with Boyden's assessment of the origins of this image, I believe the image is also widespread among the economically powerful upper strata of Latin American society, as I shall argue further on in this chapter with reference to the case of Northeast Brazil.

The idea that the world of childhood can be lost is common in Brazilian media reports about exploited children. For instance, an article on child prostitution in the weekly *Veja* was entitled "Em busca da infância perdida" (In search of lost childhood) (Pereira 1992). Clearly what has been "stolen" or "lost" is not the biological development from infancy to adulthood, but rather the conditions germane to a particular type of childhood, in this case one that takes place at home – not in a brothel – and one free of sexual exploitation.

The sociologist José de Souza Martins (1993 [1991]) assembled a collection of articles by fellow Brazilian academics entitled *O massacre dos inocentes* (The massacre of the innocents). The book offers a view into the life of poor youths in a variety of settings: in rural land struggles, interned in urban institutions, working both in cities and in the context of agro-industry, and struggling to survive as members of a culturally ravaged indigenous group. One can discern through the essays in this collection the challenges of growing up poor in Brazil. But while the book makes evident that there are many ways of being a child in Brazil, there is a countervailing tendency to speak of what Martins calls in the introduction the "suppression" of childhood, the idea being that when children are exposed to the brutality of social relations in the Third World, they are excluded from childhood itself (9). Indeed, the subtitle of this collection, *A criança sem infância no Brasil* (Children without a childhood in Brazil), encapsulates the notion that childhood is both distinct from physical immaturity and something one can be deprived of. In one of the volume's essays, Campos (1993 [1991]) examines children who work and children who grow up away from their mothers and concludes that for many poor children in Brazil there is no separation between "work and childhood." As a result, these children are "unable to live fully their childhood" (151). Although the volume does not define what childhood positively is, the implicit suggestion is that childhood can be seen as what is left over when children do not work, when they are not exploited or institutionalized. When all those things that can go wrong are excluded, one is left with the notion that childhood is a time of innocence, joy, and dependence mediated by the institutions of family and school. In discussing child abuse campaigns in Britain, Jenny Kitzinger (1990: 158) has made the point that childhood is frequently defined not "by age but by some set of qualities or experiences which are incompatible with being assaulted. The images of unhappy and frightened children (usually white) represent, not individuals, but a concept."

Another vision of childhood, encapsulated in the quotation by Ashis Nandy heading this chapter, suggests that this concept is not merely the absence of suffering, exploitation, war, and famine in early life. In its purest expression, the argument is that childhood is not only elastic and variable around the world, but a recent European creation. In *Centuries of Childhood*, Philippe Ariès (1973 [1960]) posits that the idea of childhood did not exist in medieval Europe. Through the study of medieval icons he argues that children beyond the stage of infancy were depicted only as small adults. He portrays childhood as a more

73

recent invention that took shape between the fifteenth and eighteenth centuries.[1] Although others have refuted Ariès's methods and conclusions (e.g., deMause 1974; La Fontaine 1986), the growing consensus among sociologists, historians, and others is that childhood, as distinct from biological immaturity, is socially constructed (James and Prout 1990; Thorne 1993). In a recent reassessment of Ariès's thesis, the sociologist Chris Jenks (1996: 66) writes, "critiques of Ariès have rarely succeeded in achieving more than a modification of his central ideas."

Just as there are competing ways of viewing childhood, there are competing ways of seeing children. Although children have been considered in social anthropology since its beginning, they have also been relegated to the margins of the field. As Jean La Fontaine (1986: 10) points out, children have for the most part remained the central specimens of other fields, particularly psychology. Jean Piaget, who founded developmental psychology in its current mold, attempted to relate the actions and behavior of children to distinct, genetically governed stages in human development. These stages of development, because of their basis in biology, transcended culture. While Piaget (1982: 213) admitted the possibility that "factors other than those of maturation are playing a part" in child development, he also wanted his theories to extend beyond the reach of his own field and into sociology.

> Child psychology constitutes an irreplaceable instrument of psychological inquiry, as many people these days are increasingly coming to suspect, but there is less often an awareness that it could play an almost equally important role in the field of sociology. Comte rightly holds that one of the most important phenomena of human societies is the formative action of each generation on the following one, and Durkheim reached a conclusion which favored a collective origin of moral opinions, legal norms and even logic itself. (207)

For Piaget, a child's socialization is "his development in terms of the specific or general social influences which he undergoes while his character is being formed" (207).

Piaget's idea that children develop psychologically in accordance

with more or less preordained biological rules seemed to find a place
in "commonsense" ideas of education and psychology (Prout and James
1990). It likewise meshed with social anthropology's functionalist and
subsequent structural functionalist approaches to children. Functionalism was concerned with studying "primitive societies," which were
seen as self-contained and self-sufficient microcosms. It sought to explain social practices in relation to their contribution to the workings
of society as a whole. Denying the usefulness of history in studying
"primitive societies," functionalists portrayed their objects of study as
existing in a sort of perpetual, unchanging present. For Malinowski
(1944: 108), the prime mover of this school of thought, children were
"drilled towards conformity, obedience to custom and etiquette." Subsequent structural functionalists were concerned, among other things,
with how social control is maintained. Not unlike Malinowski, structural functionalists tended to believe that children reproduced the social forms of adults. Radcliffe-Brown wrote in the preface to *African
Political Systems* (1970 [1940]: xv–xvi), "Good behavior may be to a
great extent the result of habit, of the conditioning of the individual
by his early upbringing." In his treatment of the education (or "socialization," to use a more contemporary term) of the Tallensi, Meyer
Fortes (1970 [1938]: 201–202) wrote, "It is agreed that education in
the widest sense is the process by which cultural heritage is transmitted from generation to generation. . . . It is agreed, correlatively, that
the moulding of individuals to the social norm is the function of
education such as we find it among these simple peoples." Further,
"Between birth and social maturity the individual is transformed from
a relatively peripheral into a relatively central link in the social structure; from an economically passive unit into a social personality irre-
trievably cast in the habits, dispositions and notions characteristic of
his culture" (202–203).

In short, there is, on the one hand, a tradition in social anthropology, linked to tendencies in behavioral psychology and even "commonsense" notions, of seeing children as the *tabula rasa* on which adult
culture is written (James and Prout 1990). Children have been reduced
to "human becomings," to borrow a phrase from Qvortrup (1987: 5),
in which the end product of their development is known (Benthall
1992: 23); what is of interest, according to these schools of thought,
is the process children undergo in order to reproduce adult social struc-

tures. On the other hand, there is in anthropology a long, if somewhat muted, tradition of seeing children as social actors with a degree of autonomy. The American anthropologists Margaret Mead and Ruth Benedict, for instance, treated children as informants on the same footing as adults. In *Coming of Age in Samoa*, Mead (1977 [1928]) sought to refute the assertion that adolescence was universally a time of distress and conflict. She asked, "Are the disturbances which vex our adolescents due to the nature of adolescence itself or to the civilization?" (17). Her answer was emphatically "the civilization"; in other words, the biological stage of puberty is not universally characterized by the social conflict prevalent in North American and European adolescence.

In Britain, the Opies saw children as social actors, but in a world of their own making. In *The Lore and Language of School Children* (Opie and Opie 1959), children were said to inhabit an autonomous social reality.

> [The] folklorist and anthropologist can, without travelling a mile from his door, examine a thriving unselfconscious culture (the word "culture" is used here deliberately) which is unnoticed by the sophisticated world, and quite as little affected by it as the culture of some dwindling aboriginal tribe living out its helpless existence in the hinterland of a native reserve. (1–2)

The culture to which they referred was the culture of childhood. The Opies argued that children in England preserve lore, games, and cosmology dating back to the times of Shakespeare and before. Literally behind the doorsteps of adults, children were seen to have their own secretive, tribal world. These "others" at home were made out to be as different as possible from adults.

By the 1970s, some social anthropologists came to consider that children, like women, were a muted group – muted, that is, in the sense that they remained overlooked in social research. Inspired by the Opies, Hardman (1973: 87) sought "to discover whether there is in childhood a self-regulating, autonomous world which does not necessarily reflect early development of adult culture." Although it has been argued that this perspective led to a vision of children that artificially cut them off from adult society (James 1993), I believe it also quickly opened up the way for a more fruitful examination of adult–child relations and of children as social actors worthy of study in their own right than that offered by functionalism and structural functionalism.

In her study of children in urban Kano in Nigeria, Schildkrout (1978: 112) approaches children as "independent and mutually interacting variables" upon whom adults can even come to depend for their social roles. She argues that " 'sex roles' in Hausa society could not be defined as they are without children performing certain roles which are distinct from and complementary to adult roles" (114).

I take as a point of departure in this ethnography the propositions that childhood is socially constructed, and hence variable from one context to another, and that children are worthy of study in their own right precisely because they can and should be seen as social beings. I also believe, as Schildkrout suggests, that children are influential components of the social worlds inhabited by adults, shaping the values and roles of their elders. In an analogous but expanded articulation of Schildkrout's thesis, Sharon Stephens (1995) argues that,

> As representatives of the contested future and subjects of cultural policies, children stand at the crossroads of divergent cultural projects. Their minds and bodies are at stake in debates about the transmission of fundamental cultural values in the schools. The very nature of their senses, language, social networks, world-views, and material futures are at stake in debates about ethnic purity, national identity, minority self-expression, and self-rule. (23)

Street children have been placed at the center of adult debates about the use of public space, about the family, about crime and "social decay," and even about citizenship and the meaning of democracy.

Allison James (1993: 94) has argued that childhood should be seen "not as an object, a 'thing,' but as a context within which children socialise one another as well as socialise with each other." While James is concerned largely with the child-centered constructions of childhood, her vision of childhood as a context also lends itself to understanding the varied adult-defined notions of childhood.

This chapter posits that if childhood can be seen as a context, competing contexts can be forged. Despite alarmist media reports, nearly all children in Brazil grow up in homes and never spend a night on the pavement. It is against this backdrop of "home children" that street children are defined, define themselves, and become social agents. I argue that in Northeast Brazil there are two competing contexts for childhood: nurtured childhood and nurturing childhood.

Rich Children and Poor Children

In Northeast Brazil there are many ways to distinguish a rich child from a poor one. For one thing, rich children tend to be far larger because of superior nutrition. The standard fare of poor infants is a mixture of manioc flour or corn starch and water, the latter often straight from the tap and rife with parasites and bacteria. Rich infants, on the other hand, are more likely to be breast-fed, and if they are raised on the bottle, their mothers typically use standard milk formulas mixed in appropriate proportions with purified water. A study published in the *American Journal of Clinical Nutrition* (Linhares, Rourd, and Jones 1986) compared the height and weight of 226 children aged 7 to 17 hailing from the *favelas* of Recife with a control group of 674 wealthy children in the city. The mean height of wealthy children was almost identical to the mean height of the American and British children. The poor boys fell below the fifth percentile when compared with the control group. In terms of bone growth maturation, 84 percent of poor boys and girls had a delay of over two years.

One wealthy white mother in Recife attributed to race the difference in size between poor children and her own children – the youngest of whom, at only 15, was tall, broad shouldered, and muscular. She said that her white children were so much larger because the poor had more black blood and the black race was made up of small people. She made the comment at the time of the 1992 Summer Olympics and did find it puzzling that Magic Johnson and his black teammates on the American basketball team had managed to grow to such dizzying heights.

Different styles of dress also distinguish poor kids from rich ones. The same wealthy mother told me, "I don't let my son go out without a shirt and wearing rubber thongs; he might be taken for a criminal." Poor children usually go barefoot or wear only open rubber slippers.

A child at home in a Recife shantytown. Photo by Daniel Aamot.

Rich children may wear fashionable rubber slippers of bright colors at the beach, but not in the street, and normally their feet are not visible at all since they wear enclosed, laced shoes. While poor children often go shirtless (the girls at a very young age and the boys at any age), rich girls never do and rich boys do so only at the beach. Poor children are almost never seen wearing long trousers, while this is common for rich children. Sometimes poor kids wear the clothing that once belonged to rich kids. This happens, for example, when the rich children wear out a piece of clothing and have their mother pass the item on to the maid who, in turn, gives it to her children. But by the time of donation, the item is usually faded and old. Poor children often don campaign T-shirts donated by vote-buying political candidates, wearing the shirts until they are quite tattered and stained. Rich children, on the other hand, tend to sport colorful, clean designer T-shirts. A knapsack is a dead giveaway since this item, used to tote binders, pens, and pencils, is almost certainly the property of a child attending a private school.

In addition to physical stunting, there is another telltale mark that identifies a poor child. Known locally as *pano branco*, or in English as tinea versicolor, it is a stain, a white blemish on the skin caused by a fungus. *Pano branco* can crop up anywhere − on the face, arms, legs, or torso − and extend over large portions of the body. It is slightly contagious, but truly thrives only where hygiene is poor and nutrition inadequate, and when left untreated for prolonged periods. When rich kids contract it, as they do from time to time, they can eliminate it with an ointment available at pharmacies, sometimes complemented by a course of pills. But for poor people, the cost of the medicine generally proves prohibitive, and, in any case, one tube of ointment is inadequate over the long term since continuing to live in the same cramped, unhygienic conditions of *favela* homes means reinfection is likely. As the condition becomes advanced, the blemish turns indelible, even if the original infection has disappeared. I never saw a wealthy child with visible signs of *pano branco*, but most poor kids seem to have at least a few spots.

Poor children tend to have other scars that physically distinguish them from their rich counterparts. As infants and small children, they are exposed to mosquitoes and other biting insects in the slums. As they scratch, some of the wounds become infected and leave permanent scars. Small cuts and abrasions likewise can become scars because of frequent infection. Rich children, on the other hand, have fewer encounters with biting insects since their houses are located away from the swamps and oriented in such a way that the strong breezes of Northeast Brazil discourage the insects. When rich children do suffer bites or abrasions, basic hygiene prevents the development of scars.

Children Who Are Nurtured and Children Who Nurture

The physical signs that distinguish rich children from poor children are merely one aspect of the children's radically different social and economic worlds. In urban Northeast Brazil, rich childhood is a nurtured status; poor childhood is a time for nurturing the household. Whereas nurtured children are loved by virtue of *being* children, the love received by nurturing children is to a great extent a function of what they *do*, and they struggle to win the affection of their mothers.

Viviana Zelizer (1985: 11) has observed that in the United States children came to be viewed in the twentieth century as an "exclusively emotional and affective asset [which] precluded instrumental or fiscal considerations. In an increasingly commercialized world, children were reserved a separate noncommercial place." From the perspective of rich adults in Northeast Brazil, parenting is a largely selfless task in which they painstakingly nurture their progeny and expect little in return save the satisfaction of seeing their children thrive through play and learning and that of imagining their future assumption of adult roles. The wealthy couples I knew in Recife tended to have few children, normally from one to three, even if they came from large families themselves. They described having children as a sacrifice, albeit a satisfying one. Having just one child entails considerable expense. Wealthy couples in Recife do not subject their children to public schools or the public health system, and private schools and health insurance do not come cheap − nor do stylish clothing or leisure activities such as judo classes and scuba diving. Nurtured children are the ultimate consumers, unfit to offset with productive activity their own need to be fed, clothed, and pampered. No one has understood better the extent to which wealthy parents are willing to pay for their children than the kidnappers who abduct rich children and demand a ransom from the parents.

Rather than being a bottomless pit of expenditure for their parents, poor children in Northeast Brazil are expected from an early age to contribute to the production and income of the household. And the children see supporting their mothers and nurturing the household as a virtue. Eufrásio, a 14-year-old boy so stunted from malnutrition that he had no trouble convincing the officials at FEBEM he should be sent to the little kids' pavilion, explained that bringing home money was expected behavior on the part of a child.

> I bring home money [to my mother] whether she's out of a job or working, *because she's my mother*. I bring it home to her, to my whole family. Even if there's nothing left over for me, I share. I've pushed a cart around [to collect bottles, cans, cardboard, and other items to sell], I've gone out into the street to beg. I've begged lots of times.

Eufrásio lived in the street in my neighborhood and I came to know him well. I believe that his explanation − recorded during a radio workshop in the company of peers − was a description of what he

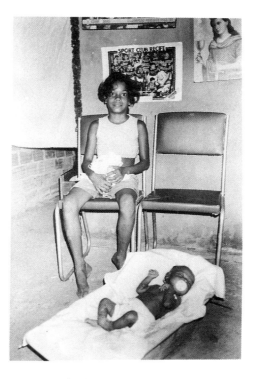

A girl watches over her little brother.

thought he ought to be doing rather than of what he in fact would habitually do, for, to the best of my knowledge, he never returned home at all while I was doing fieldwork in Brazil.

One day in a slum on the outskirts of Olinda I spoke with a mother of a dozen children, one of whose names, to her exasperation, she suddenly forgot when reciting the long list of her progeny. She complained that the doctors would not give her a tubal ligation; I took her for a 50-something-year-old fretfully awaiting menopause. She was 38. She told me, "My luck in life is my children, who bring me money and food. I can't work with so many little ones around. Where would I be without them?"

The idea of children bringing in resources to the household may today look anomalous in the eyes of middle-class families in many parts of the world, but this was of course more the rule than the exception until the latter part of the nineteenth century, if not well into the beginning of this century. In *Children of the City*, David Nasaw (1985: vii) writes that during the first decades of the twentieth century, urban working-class children in the United States "were expected to work in their spare time after school, on weekends, and during holidays" and that although the children inevitably pocketed some of their money, "they were expected to turn over all their earnings to their mothers" (viii).

But whereas poor mothers in Recife expect their children to work, they see them as far more than an economic lifeline. In a meeting of mothers of working children, a mother with tears in her eyes said,

> My husbands were all no good. Every one of them left me with a kid to lug around. I depend on the garbage dump [where I rummage for food], the traffic signal [where I beg]. Some days my kids eat, sometimes they don't. I get home, I put one hand on my head and say, "Lord, my kids ain't got a droppa milk today." Sometimes I feel like stealing, killing . . . killing everyone in sight. Then I think, "Who would take care of my kids? No, I'll hold on. No one is mightier than God. . . ." I ask God to help me, to look my way so I'll have a normal life. What I want is for my children to have their food. [with tears streaming down her face] They suffer so much! I only ask God that they have bread, then I will sleep in peace. I would like to wake up every morning and find that my children have bread instead of them waking up hungry, crying "Mommy, I want bread!" "Mommy, I want milk!"

Painted in broad strokes, the nurtured childhood of the rich in Brazil has much in common with the ideal of contemporary middle-class childhood in Europe and North America. But it exaggerates the forms. Not only are nurtured children not expected to contribute to the family income, they are not expected to clear their dishes from the table, make their beds, or clean their rooms. These are the tasks of maids and, on occasion, mothers. It is not enough to sleep late during summer vacation; many very rich, nurtured children (particularly from cities thousands of kilometers to the south of Recife such as São Paulo,

Curitiba, and Porto Alegre) are shipped off in groups for several weeks at a time to Florida for a sort of luxury summer camp experience where they stay at five-star hotels, shop for exotic electronic gadgets, and make the obligatory stop at Disney World. In 1992, word that a group of children from Recife had been "abandoned" in Florida by an unscrupulous tour operator who had falsified the return tickets made the front page in the *Diário de Pernambuco* for several days.

One upper-middle-class father who lived comfortably in a beachside apartment building and himself had been one of nine children told me, "We decided to have only one child and give him everything we can." The father worked for a company that manufactured car radios and his wife worked as a consultant to various public schools. Their seven-year-old boy, Rogério, had a bedroom of his own and a separate game room where he had the latest video toys as well as a miniature soccer table. His mother drove him to and from school, where he had already become a good reader. A picture of him in cap and gown on the occasion of his kindergarten graduation adorned the wall in the living room. He played in the apartment, often alone with a large supply of video games but sometimes with a young cousin or friend, or downstairs within the entrance terrace to the building. The terrace was surrounded by a high wall, topped with razor-sharp coiled wire and guarded 24 hours a day. Like other young children of his social class, he was never permitted to play alone in the street and could only go to the beach accompanied by one of his parents or another adult deemed responsible. In an assignment for school he was once asked to draw a picture of an activity he did at home to help his mother. He drew a picture of himself washing the dishes, but his mother made him tear it up, out of fear, as she later explained, that the seven-year-old would be labeled a homosexual.

The physical setting in which nurtured and nurturing children grow up relates to the cultural construction of their childhoods. Apartment buildings, like Rogério's by the sea, are surrounded by a wall beyond which the kids normally venture only when accompanied by adults. Nurtured children seldom ride public buses so they must be driven by their parents. Most of their socializing outside of school is with members of the extended family, especially first cousins. Most areas of the city are considered dangerous for rich kids to walk in on their own, so they are shuttled by car from home to school, and to the

houses of relatives and friends. In a book on the development of gender
roles among children in the United States, Barrie Thorne (1993: 29)
writes that "The landscape of contemporary childhood includes three
major sites – families, neighborhoods, and schools." In Recife, the
category of neighborhood could almost be eliminated when speaking
of nurtured children because their physical movements are so tightly
controlled. Nurtured children have limited opportunity to socialize
with other children merely on the basis of residence, since they are
rarely allowed to play freely in their neighborhoods. Alternatively,
visits to the houses of nonkin friends are facilitated by parents. The
street is known to nurtured children as a place through which they
pass in automobiles traveling at high speeds. Only at a beach house
far outside the city is the nurtured child allowed to roam free and
barefoot.

The houses in which nurturing children live are so cramped one
might expect to find an entire family of six or seven living in a space
no larger than a rich child's bedroom. In the *favelas*, as one youth
summed it up for me, "There's no space." *Favela* houses – small,
closely packed together, and poorly situated – rarely catch the inces-
sant winds of Northeast Brazil that keep the homes of the rich both
cool and free of mosquitoes. Unlike the fortresses in which the rich
live, the *favela* shacks are nearly impossible to secure, often lacking
even a lock for the front door, and never difficult to penetrate even if
locked. Lacking proper sewerage, they are permeated by what residents
themselves call a *catinga*, or rank smell.

"Where is it more dangerous, in the *favelas* or in the street?" I
asked a youth.

"I think [it's more dangerous] in the *favelas*," he replied. "The
favelas bring together all sorts of bad elements." When I posed this
question in the survey, of 43 children only slightly over half (54%)
said it was more dangerous in the street. Thirty-five percent said it
was more dangerous in the *favelas*, and 12 percent said it was just as
bad in both places. Unlike the secure homes of nurtured children, the
homes of poor children – far from being a refuge from the mayhem
of urban life – are sites of violence and danger, and many children
deem them more perilous than the street.

In *Death without Weeping: The Violence of Everyday Life in Brazil*, based
on research in a *favela* of a small Pernambucan city the author calls

Hoping the tide won't rise, a Recife *favela*. Photo by Daniel Aamot.

"Bom Jesus," Nancy Scheper-Hughes (1992: 362) writes that "malicious child abuse is extremely rare on the Alto do Cruzeiro." Although Scheper-Hughes may have been referring to the physical beating of infants, children in the *favelas* of Recife old enough to speak for themselves generally possess a wholly different opinion on the subject. They speak of beatings as not only common, but normal and even deserved, if also hated and apt to make them *revoltar*, or rebel.

"Does your mother hit you?" one youth asked another, speaking into my tape recorder.

"She hits me because she's a mother [*bate porque é mãe*]."

The children complained especially of beatings by their fathers or stepfathers. Recall Edivaldo who explained, "I only ran away from home because of my stepfather. He beat me with a wire cable, left me all cut up, then he threw water and a kilo of salt on me." Sometimes mothers defend the beatings of their children. One mother, whose son had grown bigger than her and whom she could no longer physically punish without running the risk of being hurt by him, told me, "I hope the police give him a good beating. He's got to stop sniffing glue and stealing." The foster mother of a young infant told me that she decided to take in the baby because the biological mother had been beating her son, even extinguishing cigarettes in his tender skin.

Rich children at a private school celebrate the June festivals as dads videotape them.

But the most consistent testimony of violence against children comes from the children themselves: "The only reason I would go home at night," a young man told me, recalling his childhood, "is because I knew that if I didn't, my mother would find me in the street, drag me home, and beat me." Of the 40 children asked in my semistructured questionnaire about violence at home, 32 said they had been beaten by their mothers.

It is not merely the frequency with which poor, nurturing children speak of being beaten that draws one's attention, but the moral content with which they often imbue tales of their own castigation. Frequently, children will discuss the beatings they suffer and then lament how difficult they are for their mothers. Although it would be a mistake to overlook the ways in which nurturing children protest this violence and the fact that many children swear their mothers never "laid a finger on me," it would also be a mistake to forget the assessment "she hits me because she's a mother."

Among rich families in Northeast Brazil, physical violence against children is rarely discussed. This is not to say it does not exist, but physically hurting children is generally considered aberrant and reprehensible. Whatever its frequency among wealthy families, as in North America and Europe, it is something of a guarded secret. In the wealthy urban families of Northeast Brazil, both biological parents generally reside in the home. The men, while not infrequently having *casos*, or affairs, are normally expected to have children by only one woman and the women by only one man. Nurtured children stay at home until they marry. "If they're living on their own," a mother warns me, "there's a problem. Either they're drug addicts or homosexuals or something like that." The nurturing of rich children can easily go on for more than two decades.

A visit to the home of Beto, who spent his days and nights in the streets of Recife, speaks volumes about the strong ethic among poor children who seek to nurture the household and of how their success at bringing in resources relates to their status within the household. The bus ride to his mother's home lasted more than 45 minutes and took us far away from the sluggish traffic at the center of Recife into the winding, dusty roads of an area called Camaragibe. To arrive at the house from the bus stop we climbed a dirt road and then descended along a steep, muddy trail. From a distance, set against the verdant hills, the *favela* was picturesque.

The house had two bedrooms, a small sitting room, eating room (perhaps a misnomer for there was nothing edible in sight), and kitchen. Two large families lived in the house. It belonged to another woman. Beto's mother was only there temporarily, hoping to find somewhere else to live. She told the story of how she had lost her shack in another *favela*. Her favorite son, Alexandre, used to work in Boa Viagem, a rich beach-front section of Recife. Alexandre shined shoes and showed tourists around. He would sleep in the street for a couple of nights and then come home with the money he had earned. A younger brother, Daniel, would accompany him. About a year earlier, Alexandre had contracted a respiratory infection and died. As Beto's mother told the story, she sifted through some papers trying to find her son's death certificate. A few minutes into the unsuccessful search she gave up with an exasperated, "What good is it anyway?"

Without the income from Alexandre, the family lost its shack. Dona Marinefe, Beto's mother, had nine children from several men. The children ranged in age from 6 to 22. I knew Zezinho, the oldest, from the streets of Recife where he lived. Then came Carmen, who had one child and was expecting another. Carmen and five siblings along with their mother and Carmen's baby occupied one room in the house. Beto visited sometimes, but the mother said that "there's no space for him." He normally slept in the street. But the lack of space in the house, while hardly an exaggeration, was surely not the only reason Zezinho and Beto were not especially welcome there. Unlike Alexandre who had earned money through lawful work, Zezinho and Beto survived through theft and spent much of their money on drugs. As I was leaving, the mother, pointing at her youngest daughter, asked me, "Do you want to take her?" (*Quer levar ela?*). The six-year-old clung to her mother and cried in a long, shrill voice, "*Não!*" while her mother stared me in the eye, awaiting an answer.

The virtues of rich, nurtured childhood are innate – playfulness, imagination, innocence, the ability to learn and enjoy life. Among the poor, certain admired characteristics are inherent, such as light skin or other culturally favored physical characteristics. But, to borrow a concept from Allsebrook and Swift (1989), virtuousness in this type of childhood is achieved, not ascribed. Beto's late brother, Alexandre, had attained a special status in the household through working, bringing home resources, and staying out of trouble. His siblings showed no surprise that he was talked of as the elect child and had achieved a place in their mother's heart that they clearly had not.

Another vital aspect of how nurturing children experience childhood is a phenomenon that could be called child shifting, or in Portuguese *crianças em circulação* (Fonseca 1989). Unlike the rich nurtured children who typically grow up in a household presided over by the biological father and mother, poor nurturing children not infrequently are shifted among distinct matrifocal households and often grow up under a maternal figure other than the biological mother.

Frequently, the *mãe de criação*, or foster mother, is simply referred to as *mãe*, or mother, even if in other kinship terms she might be called the grandmother, stepmother, aunt, or guardian. For instance, in the fragment of the interview included in the Introduction, a youth identified as Carlos speaks of living with his mother in a slum called UR-4. Many months later, when he was in prison, I went to deliver a note he had dictated to his "mother." When I met her, she described herself as Carlos's stepmother, the biological mother having abandoned him many years ago when she left for Bahia. But, in a tone of self-

A girl with her mother in the street. Photo by Daniel Aamot.

flattery, she remarked, "He always called me *mãe*." The foster mother of an infant who had been abused by his biological mother referred to the baby as her son, and others in the community referred to the boy's new guardian as his mother. As Ruth Cardoso (1984: 202) has pointed out, informal adoption among the poor in Brazil serves as a "culturally acceptable means of creating *real* kinship ties."

Far from being a recent symptom of the breakdown of a previously predominant nuclear family system, the practice of informal adoption is deeply rooted in the history of poor families in Brazil. Fonseca (1989) examines court records of custody cases in the southern Brazilian city of Porto Alegre. The disputes involve mothers, fathers, grandparents, aunts, third parties, wet-nurses, and legal guardians. She argues that in the early twentieth century "the working-class family . . . had not assumed the form of a well delimited, self-contained domestic unit" (104). The consolidation of the nuclear family was impeded because of the fluidity of the domestic unit, conjugal instability, and child labor. Foster parents were considered, even by the courts, to have similar rights over the children as biological parents, and often the latter lost the custody disputes. "The files suggested that the central question was who would have the right to direct the upbringing of the child and to enjoy the services of the child, not who had the moral right to claim the identity of mother" (122).

For nurturing children in Recife, it is crucial whom they designate as their "mother," but like poor children in southern Brazil in the early twentieth century, they often find themselves shifted from one household to another. It is quite common for poor children to speak of having lived with an aunt and a grandmother or their godmother, in addition to with their biological mother.

Nurturing children frequently regard the father as something of a transient figure in the household. As nurturing kids would sometimes tell me, "Your father can be anyone, but your mother is like no other" (*Pai é qualquer um, mãe é uma só*). Two girls and I had a discussion about mothers and fathers:

Tobias: What is the difference between a mother and a father?

Raquel [*aged about 16*]: It's like they say, "Your father can be anyone, but your mother is like no other." If it was our mother's first man who had us, then we should respect him until the end of our death [*sic*]. He can be horrible, he can be anything, but he's our father, just like our mother [is our mother].

Syneide [*aged about 12*]: Are you sure yours is really your father?

Raquel: Yes, because I look like him.

Syneide: You look like him! Just because something *looks* like something else doesn't mean that's what it is!

Raquel: Well if he weren't, that would be lucky [the two girls laugh].

Syneide: I like my mother more [than my father], because my mother is everything for me – mother, father, aunt, grand-mother. Everything that I have is my mother.

Tobias: And what is your father like?

Syneide: Like anyone.

Raquel: My father might be terrible, but I still like him. What he did with me [he tried to rape her], I will never forgive, but if someday I get somewhere in life and he needs me, if he knocked on my door, I'd serve him with all the pleasure in the world. I wouldn't deprive him of anything. Just like I'd do for my mother.

Syneide: If it were my father and I got somewhere in life and he came knocking at my door, I'd throw water in his face. My mother suffered so much at his hands. I'd throw a bucket of cold water in his face so that he'd stop coming. And if my father did what yours did with you, asking to do bad things, he'd be dead before he could count to three.

This chapter has considered nurtured children and nurturing children as opposites: whereas nurtured children are an endless expense, nurturing children bring money into the household; whereas nurtured children are highly differentiated from older members of society, nurturing children take on the responsibility of adults progressively from a young age; whereas nurtured children are highly dependent, nurturing children are highly independent. But this dualism breaks down at a certain point. In spite of the stark differences between these two types of children, they share one vital experience: they live childhood within the home.

While the social life of nurtured and nurturing children may be vastly different, childhood as a socially understood context is congruent with and dependent on domesticity. This is true both for the protected, nurtured childhood of the rich and the matrifocal, highly independent, nurturing childhood of the poor. As different as the early lives of nurtured and nurturing children may be, the locus of their childhood is the home. But how are young people who are not "home children" viewed in relation to these competing ideals of childhood? How do they view themselves in relation to dominant cultural constructions of childhood? The following chapter begins to take up these questions.

4

BETRAYING MOTHERDOM: *MALOQUEIROS* AND "THAT LIFE" IN THE STREET

Given the ubiquity of the image of street children in popular conceptions of Brazilian social life, one might expect to see homeless children everywhere in Brazilian cities. Living in the street, homeless children are indeed in the public eye. As one would expect, they can be seen begging and stealing along the thoroughfares and sleeping on the sidewalks. But sometimes they are harder to find than one might think. On many occasions, I would go out to the street and have to search long and hard to find any. And some days there were simply none on hand.

But for whom was I searching? Thus far, this book has referred to street children as if the meaning of the term were self-evident. How is it possible to distinguish street children, or *meninos de rua*, as they are called in Brazil, from other children? The preceding chapter discussed nurtured and nurturing childhood, two contexts in which children in Northeast Brazil grow up. This chapter considers street children in relation to these two ideal types, particularly to childhood within the world of Brazilian matrifocality in which poor children are expected and themselves expect to nurture the household. If children can be imagined as social actors rather than as merely the passive recipients of adult culture, they can also be seen to have a claim on defining their own identity. Perhaps because all street children in Recife and Olinda have also been poor "home children," the rules of nurturing childhood function as a backdrop against which street children evaluate their own lives. This chapter considers conceptualizations of street children offered by adults – researchers, activists, and bureaucrats, among others – and by homeless children themselves in Northeast Brazil. I argue that *maloqueiros*, as children living in the streets of the Recife area tend to refer to themselves, forge their own sense of identity based on their interpretation of how they differ from other poor children who nurture the home. They are street children not merely because they inhabit the physical space called the street but because they have betrayed motherdom, the moral and economic logic of the matrifocal home.

The use of the term "street children" in English is not new. Sporadic examples of its use date back to the nineteenth century. For instance, in his 1884 book *Street Arabs and Gutter Snipes: The Pathetic and Humorous Side of Young Vagabond Life in the Great Cities with Records of Work for Their Reclamation*, George C. Needham (1884: iii) uses the term in passing to describe the children who, in his words, "through the stress of circumstances, are forced into a course of life which tends to the multiplication of criminals and the increase of the dangerous classes." But until about a decade ago, terms such as "street urchin," "waif," or "street Arab," used in the early part of this century, or "runaway" or "abandoned child," employed subsequently, were far more common terms than was "street child." Williams (1993: 832) notes that Unesco began to use the term to refer to vagrant children after World War II and that the term became common following the United Nations Year of the Child in 1979.

In *Death without Weeping*, Scheper-Hughes (1992: 240) observes that in the 1960s the children who regularly slept in the streets of "Bom Jesus" "were referred to affectionately as *'moleques,'* that is, 'ragamuffins,' 'scamps,' or 'rascals,' or any small black child." But as a descriptive term, *meninos de rua* has existed for some time. One instance of its use can be found in Jorge Amado's 1937 novel *Capitães da areia* (translated as *Captains of the Sand*) where a group of children sleeping in Salvador's abandoned wharves are referred to, at least in passing, by the term. But it was not until the 1980s that the phrase became common, and *meninos carentes* (needy children), *crianças abandonadas* (abandoned children), or the more derogatory and still common terms *pivetes* (knaves) or *trombadinhas* (scoundrels) began to make way for *meninos de rua*, a term considered free of derogatory connotations.

It was the international bureaucracies and their consultants that brought the English term "street child" into the mainstream, and I suspect that *menino de rua* was the literal Portuguese translation, made widespread through the cooperative project of UNICEF and various Brazilian organizations that became the National Movement of Street Children. Use of this term in Brazil preceded slightly the country's legal renaming of children in general. Until the end of the 1980s, those under the age of 18 were referred to in official documents as *menores*, "minors" or, literally, "lessers." In everyday parlance the term was used (and continues to be used) almost exclusively in condescending reference to poor children (Schwartzchild 1987). In 1990 the Minors' Code was replaced by the Children and Adolescents Act, which divided young people into two groups, those aged under 12, now referred to as children (*crianças*), and those 12 to 17, called adolescents (*adolescentes*). Both terms were advocated as being free of the stigmatizing connotations of the word *menor*. Thus the advent of the term *meninos de rua* came in tandem with a larger legal and social redefinition of young people.

But it was also clear that there are different types of children and adolescents. One kind came to be referred to as *meninos de rua*. Over the past decade, debate has not ceased over just what is meant by the term "street children" in either Portuguese or English, or by the Spanish equivalent, *niño de la calle*. In 1981, UNICEF issued a series of documents (Taçon 1981a; Taçon 1981b; Taçon 1981c) that coincided with the beginning of the widespread use of the term among institutions. The author of these reports spoke interchangeably of children without families, abandoned children, and street children. He described them as follows:

Who really is this ragged, foul-mouthed little "enemy of the people"? He is the child most rejected and, at the same time, most in need of acceptance; the most difficult for adults to love and the most in need of adult affection; the least trusted and the most in need of trust; the most abandoned and the most in need of family; the most repressed and the most deserving of freedom; the most forgotten and the most worthy of our remembrance; the least helped and the most in need; the least fed and the most hungry; the dirtiest and the least able to find a good bath. (Taçon 1981a: 20)

Not surprisingly, different nongovernmental organizations began (and have continued) to use the term "street children" in different ways. In 1986, representatives from the Inter-NGO Programme for Street Children and Street Youth met to discuss the problem and to devise a standard definition. They settled on the following, "Street children are those for whom the street . . . more than their family has become their real home, a situation in which there is no protection, supervision or direction from responsible adults" (cited in Glauser 1990: 143).

But this definition seemed to spawn only new confusion. Just what is meant by "family," the "real" home, or "protection"? To make matters worse, the definition was translated, with liberal reinterpretations, into Spanish, Portuguese and other languages. But the greatest difficulty was that it combined the apparently subjective view of the child regarding the conversion of the "street" into the "home" with the malleable concepts, presumably to be judged by adults, of "protection," "supervision," and "direction." And in any case, just who is a "responsible adult"?

In the literature on street children there is a tendency countervailing to the contemporary anthropological approach to childhood. While social anthropologists have accepted the elasticity of childhood, the promotional, journalistic, and even academic literature on street children almost always homogenizes street children. Indeed, the "recipe" for writing about street children, referred to in the introduction to this book, not only dictates how one is to write about street kids, it informs their very iconography. Practices such as sniffing glue, snatching wallets, and watching karate movies have been sufficient for many to group together street children from around the world. As one observer writes, "Names people use to refer to them may differ from country to country . . . but it appears that Latin American street children have much in common" (Ortiz de Carrizosa 1992: 406). Comparisons are made not only between street children in Guatemala City and Bogotá (Connolly 1990), but even between those in the Sudan and Ireland (Veale 1992) and the United States and Honduras (Wright, Wittig, and Kaminsky 1993). Despite making almost no explicit references to research on street children in the United States, the last of these articles concludes that, "Despite the many glaring differences between Honduras and the United States, the material, social, and medical circumstances of the very poorest and neediest children prove remarkably, even disturbingly, similar in both nations" (90).

Rarely are the words "street children" far away from the word "problem." Indeed, not only are street children in diverse contexts made members of a single "phenomenon," their very lives are reduced to a condition to be cured. Thus, when one reads about the "etiology" of street children, it is worth considering whether one could contemplate an etiology of other groups such as taxi drivers, dentists, or stockbrokers.

With the burgeoning interest in street children in the mid-1980s, homeless children have been displaced even from history and recast as a wholly new phenomenon. As the authors of a review of the literature on childhood in Brazil note,

> The conspicuous presence of children and youths as a contemporary feature of large Brazilian cities has been accompanied by the proliferation of publications on the question of children, leading one to suspect that we might be witnessing a recent phenomenon followed closely by the inquisitive eye of the social scientist. (Alvim and Valladares 1988: 3)

But children are not new to the streets in Brazil. In *Sobrados e Mocambos*, Gilberto Freyre (1968 [1936]b) refers to *moleques*, which in the English version translated as *The Mansions and the Shanties* (1968 [1936]a) accurately appear as "street urchins." The context is interesting. The English translation reads,

> The street urchin – that vivid expression of the Brazilian street – was showing a growing lack of respect for the great house [in the late nineteenth century] as he defaced walls and fences with scrawls that were often obscene. Not to mention relieving himself on the doorstep of illustrious portals. (xxvii)

Not only were there children in the street but, as the passage suggests, their mischievous presence was alarming to the urban elite. In a history of legislation on and assistance to children in Brazil, Irene Rizzini (1995: 116) notes that by the end of the nineteenth century, there were "innumerable references condemning the presence of children in the streets, the most notable of which was 'How to Proceed with Regard to Young Vagabonds (notices of 1885 and 1892).' " Indeed just as children are not new to the open spaces of the cities, neither is the idea that street children are a scourge in need of elimination Rizzini (119) also cites a 1902 police reform bill in Rio de Janeiro that calls for physically capable beggars, vagabonds, and "vicious children," among others, to be placed in correctional facilities. Written six decades ago, Amado's novel *Capitães da areia* (1989 [1937]) opens with a newspaper article describing the activities of a band of "child muggers" (*meninos assaltantes*) in Salvador:

> Living from theft, they are said to number more than 100 and range in age from 8 to 16. Urgent steps must be taken by the police and the Minors' Court to extinguish this band, gather up these precocious criminals who prevent the city from sleeping in peace, and lodge them in reformatories or prisons. (10)

In his reports for UNICEF, Taçon drew attention to the plight of street children not only by describing the hardships they encounter in daily life, but by suggesting that Latin America, particularly Brazil, was home to millions of such children. Hyperbolic speculation about the numbers of street children informs notions of who street children are. A 1978 article in *Time* referred to 2 million Brazilian children "abandoned by their destitute parents." In her review of the movie *Pixote* (Babenco 1980), *New Yorker* movie critic Pauline Kael (1981: 170) credited the country with "three million abandoned children – swarms of scavenging, thieving street kids." Connolly (1990: 129) claimed Brazil had 20 million street children, while an article in UNICEF's *Ideas Forum* suggested that "more than 30 million children live in the streets of Brazil" (Morch 1984: 1). If true, this latter figure would leave Brazil with few urban children living in homes.

When one sifts through all the numerical estimates of street children in Brazil, there is one figure that arises with great frequency: 7 million. The number is said to refer to what some of the institutions call "hard-core" street children, or children who live and habitually sleep in the street, and it is cited by institutions, journalists, and academics alike (Bitar de Fernandez 1989: 187 [for the Organization of American States]; Amnesty International 1990a: 4; Lamb 1991: 22; Burns 1993: 490; Childhope n.d.: 1). Invariably, the figure is referred to as someone else's estimate. Amnesty International cites a study by the Brazilian Institute of Geography and Statistics (IBGE), Childhope cites the *Los Angeles Times*, and a group of Brazilian and American academics (Campos et al. 1994: 320) cite a Childhope publication. If one chases down the citations, one is invariably referred again to someone else's estimate, or the reference is simply omitted. It is a curious example of shared hearsay given the allure of truth through an endless and circular process of one source citing as fact the reference or estimate of another.

Claims about the size of the street children population are similar to what Joel Best (1990) has dubbed the "numbers game" in analyzing reports about missing children in the United States. Best observes that "Numbers tend to be treated as facts, regardless of how they came into being. . . . Once the press begins repeating a figure, the number takes on a life of its own" (45–46). The relative lack of attention accorded a problem in the past tends to be accompanied, logically, by a dearth of official statistics. Faced with such an absence, advocates – what Best calls claims-makers – can both point a reproachful finger at negligent officials and offer figures of their own. In time, these figures have the potential to become the "official ones," as seems to have happened in the case of both missing children in the United States and Brazil's street children. In the United States, the figure of 1.8 million missing children per year was common currency in news reports and in the literature of a wide range of advocacy organizations during the early 1980s. Best argues that the highly unusual instances of stranger abductions resulting in rape or murder were used in the United States to typify far more widespread situations; in fact, even by the admission of advocates, the vast majority of "missing children" (whatever their numbers) were in fact runaways, and another large subgroup were children taken by parents who lacked legal custody. The varied circumstances of children labeled as street children – comprising those who work, those involved in prostitution, and those who are impoverished, among others – has added elasticity to the concept in a way that makes counting impossible. But the figure of 7 million

Brazilian street children is typically used in more specific reference to homeless children. In other words, this figure – the origin of which is unrelated to any real census – has definitional specificity.

If Brazil had 7 million street children out of a 1993 urban population of about 114 million,[1] then homeless children would have constituted over 6 percent of all people in cities. If the ratio held true for Recife, there would be some 80,000 street children there, out of a 1991 population of about 1.3 million. Yet a carefully executed 1993 survey commissioned by the city of Recife (CIELA 1993) rendered a very different tally. The study was conducted under the direction of professional researchers, and the census takers were experienced street educators, familiar with the children of the city and the places where they sleep. Five teams of at least four street educators surveyed distinct areas of the city, including sites rarely visited by any of the NGOs, such as the city's bus station and the wealthy neighborhood of Boa Viagem. The teams worked during three nights in June 1993, from approximately 10:00 P.M. until 3:00 A.M. Any children found in the street were given a snack and asked to answer a short questionnaire. Over the three nights, a total of 212 children under the age of 18 were found in the street.[2] Approximately 150 children were found on all three nights (the remaining 62 were found on only one or two of the nights).

During my fieldwork I believe I became familiar with all of the children who slept regularly in the street in Olinda. I conducted two censuses in Olinda, one in August 1992 and one in March 1993. My method was simple. Across the street from my apartment was a vacant house. The patio area in front of the house was the single most popular spot in the city for the street children to congregate. On both days I waited for a time when at least a dozen kids were at the site. I counted each of the children, children I knew slept in the streets, and asked them to name all of the other street children that they had seen on that day and the day before. I clarified that I only wanted to know about the children who slept in the street. On the first occasion my count reached a total of 22, on the second just 19.

A survey cited in *Veja* magazine in which 23 institutions participated found 895 children in São Paulo who spent the night in the streets (Pereira 1994: 68).

Research by the government institution IBASE counted, in 1993,

797 children in the streets of Rio de Janeiro (cited in Impelizieri 1995: 11).

In Fortaleza, the Italian organization Terra Nova and the Brazilian government institution CBIA counted approximately 200 children sleeping in the streets (Save the Children 1993).

Taken together, the children sleeping in the streets of these five cities number 2,126. The combined population of the five cities, by the UN's rather conservative and slightly outdated 1991 counts, is 18.5 million people, or about 16 percent of Brazil's total urban population. The census data would suggest that there are about 115 children living in the street for each 1 million urban residents in these cities. If this ratio holds true for all of Brazil's urban population, Brazil would have about 13,000 street children. It is, of course, possible that these censuses undercounted the true number of children sleeping in the street. I observed, for instance, that the crew I worked with one night in Recife drove along some streets where we probably should have walked since the children are often hidden and difficult to spot from a moving vehicle. If only one-third of the children were counted in each census, the total population of children sleeping in the street in Brazil would be about 39,000, an enormous and frightening number in itself: 39,000 children sleeping, stealing, falling in love, crying, dancing, and dying in the street. The only consolation about this number is that it would suggest that more than 99 percent of UNICEF's 7 million street children were a figment of this distant institution's imagination.

Among some of the street educators who participated in the Recife survey, there was mild surprise that the census did not find a larger number of children in the street. But none appeared unduly shocked. One street educator had remarked to me before the census that he found offensive the "exaggerated" figures he had heard of hundreds of thousands of children in the street in Recife. Rather than encouraging people to help the children, he felt it made them fatalistic, leading them to believe that there was nothing that could be done for such an enormous number of children. Others even went as far as to say that such scare tactics encouraged the death squads to fight back against this "invasion." Yet for institutions, particularly the international ones portraying themselves as advocates of street children, the high numbers are an essential component of their own persuasive pow-

Table 3. *Population of Street Children in Brazilian Cities*

City	Population (1991)	Year of street children census	Population of street children
Recife	1.3 million	1993	212
Olinda	0.3 million	1993	22
São Paulo	9.6 million	1993	895
Fortaleza	1.8 million	1993	200
Rio de Janeiro	5.5 million	1993	797
Total	18.5 million		2,126

Sources of urban population data: UN 1996: 271. Source of street children census data explained in text.

ers. Thus when Taçon wrote that his UNICEF report "seeks above all to be the voice of some 25 million street children in Brazil," the use of numbers served both to awaken outrage about the plight of children and to add weight to the voice of the advocate.

In "Street Children: Deconstructing a Construct," Benno Glauser (1990) points out that the use of the word "street" in conjunction with the word "child" denotes an aberration. Children who play in gardens are not called garden children, nor are children who play in the attic referred to as attic children. Both are merely children, and the location of their play simply says something about where they co things, not who they are. Yet the combination "street" and "child" suggests that the child's location is so peculiar that it becomes a mark of identity. The incarnation of an oxymoron, street children upset broad expectations about the street and about childhood. As Roberto DaMatta (1991 [1985]) has observed, in Brazil, the street is the place of commerce, of men, and of prostitutes. It is decidedly not a place for children.

The question of where children are versus who, in a more elemental sense, they are has been pivotal to the debate about what constitutes a street child. The prepositions "in" and "of" have been used by institutions to describe two types of relationships that children have with

Playing the rock game.

streets. The children "in" the street, like Glauser's children who happen to be in the garden or attic, simply do certain things there. They
work in the street, they dance in the street, they beg in the street,
but the street is the venue for their actions, not the essence of their
character. The preposition "of" is generally added to modify those
children who do all of these things in the street and something else:
they sleep in the street. But how often does a child have to sleep *in*
the street to be *of* the street? Is a girl who sleeps in the street one or
two nights a week a child *of* the street? Is she a *menina de rua?*

Children of one family I met in Recife would sleep in the street
occasionally. They went to school in the morning and would beg along
a busy avenue in the afternoon and evening. Returning home, a place
they were not particularly welcome when arriving empty-handed, involved a long bus ride and a treacherous two-kilometer walk through
one of Olinda's more violent *favelas*. Eleven children and their mother
lived in a mud and wattle hut no larger than 10 meters square. The
barraco, as such makeshift constructions, especially those fashioned
from odd-sized planks, are called, was precariously lodged on the steep

edge of a ravine. It lacked running water, sewerage, a stove, a refrigerator, and practically any other amenity one could imagine, save a television – that ever-present Brazilian symbol of modernity. It otherwise contained a table, a couple of chairs, a bed, and a naked bulb dangling from a wire. Most of the children slept on the dirt floor since the home's only bed could not accommodate everyone. The mother stayed at home taking care of her small babies, so aside from the wages of the oldest son, David, who was employed as a silk-screener, the household income derived solely from the activities of the young children who washed windshields and begged in the street.

Not surprisingly, the children would weigh the perceived benefits of returning home against the relative convenience of sleeping in the street, closer to their school and closer to their place of economic activity. Sleeping on a dirt floor at home was not so different, in terms of comfort, from sleeping on a cement doorstep. Unless they were bringing food with them, it was generally easier to get a meal in the street than at home. So on days when they had little to bring to their mother or finished their activities in the street late at night, they would often simply curl up in a hidden spot in the street. In a radio workshop held at a weekend retreat for children of the National Movement of Street Children, David and his siblings talked about how they first began sleeping in the street.

> *David*: I was hanging out in the middle of the street, working, begging for money to bring home. . . . One day I hadn't come up with any money, nothing, so I was afraid to go home. . . . The first day I slept [in the street] I liked it. I went home the next day and then I went back to the street and slept there again.
>
> *Syneide* [*David's younger sister*]: I slept with him [pointing to David], my sister, and my cousin. We'd spend the whole day trying to get food, then at midnight we'd eat, we got together, then we'd go to sleep with full bellies.
>
> *Boquinha* [*Syneide and David's 10-year-old cousin who possessed mesmerizing skills in the Brazilian martial art and dance known as* capoeira]: We'd find some paper to sleep with. Then we got wood, we stuck it in a place where no one would see us.
>
> *Syneide*: We'd fill up the tunnel with paper and make a little cavern to sleep in.

Boquinha: It's just like sleeping with a sheet. It [the paper] keeps you warm.

David did consider himself to have been a street child, whereas his younger siblings and his cousin did not place themselves in that category. In part, the difference had to do with the amount of time they spent in the street. Whereas David had once spent a period of about two years without returning home, the younger ones returned regularly and considered their house their normal place for sleeping, not the street. But the larger issue had to do with moral judgments about their relationship with their mother and, concomitantly, about their economic life. When David spent a long uninterrupted period in the street, the money he earned through begging and stealing was his. His siblings spent some of their own money, but they also brought money to their mother. Even when children live in the street and try on occasion to help their mothers, their assistance is at risk of being rejected. Many told me that their mothers called their money *dinheiro errado*, or bad money. The children complained that the money they earned through theft would run out right away while another sort of money, *dinheiro suado* (money earned by the sweat of one's brow), would last a long time. Rather than nurturing the home, David spent his money in the street. In the street, he received no discipline or advice from his mother, whereas his siblings were always subject to her guidance. In short, David made use of the street in a way that defied motherdom, whereas his siblings made use of the street in a way that was consistent with the moral and economic logic of their matrifocal home.

In a study carried out in Colombia, Lewis Aptekar (1988) was rightly concerned to place street children in relation to larger kinship arrangements. Aptekar describes two competing kinship patterns in Colombia, what he calls the Spanish patrifocal family and the African matrifocal family. The former demands obedience on the part of sons, the latter values self-reliance and responsibility. In many ways, the children of the Colombian patrifocal families are similar to what I call nurtured children in Northeast Brazil, and the children of the Colombian matrifocal families are comparable to what I call nurturing children. Aptekar portrays the Colombian patrifocal family as follows:

> Both boys and girls were encouraged to stay at home far longer [than children in matrifocal families], and neither left without the blessings of both parents. Boys learned from their fathers . . . how to be "men." The streets were out of bounds. Girls were socialized to be women by the mother. . . . The father was considered to be the principal source of family wisdom, although the mother, in spite of her "inferior position," was on many occasions consulted in private about relationships between the sexes. (162)

In contrast, based on his interpretation of secondary sources, Aptekar argues that the boy in matrifocal families was "socialized to leave home before puberty and to be independent of his mother. This ensured that by the time he reached puberty he would have had many experiences on his own away from home, and often with other children, on the streets" (162). Aptekar continues,

> A woman's relationship with her son had some similarities to her relationships with her serial companions. Her son, after his immediate dependency needs were met, was encouraged to leave home and be independent. When the son reached puberty the emotional ties of mother to son were lessened, and he was valued and held responsible in the home as an adult. Thus, only later in life, as an adult, after a son had made secure his own economic situation and was able to contribute to his mother's home, would the affective care he received before puberty be resumed. (163)

Aptekar asserts that street boys were natural expressions of matrifocality. They were, he writes, "often merely accepting the independence that their type of family expected of them" (195). However, if boys in typical matrifocal families were encouraged to live in the street, then we might truly see millions of homeless children in Colombia and elsewhere. Yet Aptekar himself explains that the numbers of street children are exaggerated.

Although the poverty of the suburbios and barrios [working-class and poor neighborhoods] was no doubt a partial cause of children being abandoned or abandoning their families, it cannot explain the phenomenon in full. Only a small number of children from families living in these conditions were not living at home. (181)

In the context of his study, the claim that matrifocal families encourage boys to live in the street becomes increasingly problematic because Aptekar also emphasizes that street children in Colombia have "made one important life decision – to leave home at a time when most children are fully dependent on the decisions of their families" (77). Thus, one line of argument places emphasis on the defiant initiative of street children who shun control and make a truly unusual decision, while another line of argument holds that street children are merely conforming to the expectations of socialization in the matrifocal family.

In a similarly contradictory vein, Aptekar points out that street children are rare on the north coast of Colombia, where matrifocal families are the norm, as opposed to in the central highland cities such as Bogotá, where, he argues, patrifocal families are typical and street children common. Thus, in the end, one is left wondering how street children fit into matrifocality, whether they are normal expressions of it or rare deviants. The thrust of Aptekar's argument seems to be that "Street children were developing normally in matrifocal homes in a tradition of urban poverty" (164). Although it makes little sense here to dwell on Aptekar's findings in Colombia – the context differs in important ways from Recife – I highlight his argument that street boys are natural expressions of matrifocality because I believe precisely the opposite can be said about Recife. In Recife and urban Northeast Brazil more generally, the street is not an acceptable *alternative* to the home, it is a *resource* for nurturing the home. And, in any case, the street is a resource used with considerable trepidation. Looked at from the perspective of children in Northeast Brazil, living in the street is not an affirmation of matrifocality but a betrayal of it.

In an effort to know what street children in Recife believed differentiated them from their peers in matrifocal households who lived at home, I would ask them, early on during my field research, what they perceived to be the differences between home and the street. My question was usually met with blank stares. The problem, in retrospect, was that whereas I was naming physical spaces that for the children held only limited meanings, houses and roads, they associated what I was really probing for with complex notions about ways of living – ways of living that, as in the case of David and his siblings, revolved largely around the relationship to a mother figure.

As poor Brazilians will tell you, one can grow up *na rua*, in the street, without ever spending a night on the pavement.

"I grew up in the street," Lena told me as she sold bottles of mineral water during *carnaval* in Olinda. "I know what it's like. That's why I wouldn't sell my son to that *gringo*," she said of an offer she had purportedly received from a visiting foreigner. But Lena, like many Brazilians who consider themselves to be or to have been street children, had always slept in houses. The difference is that Lena, unlike her siblings, was not raised by her mother. Instead, from an early age she was left with neighbors and acquaintances of her mother, shifted from one house to another and forced into arduous domestic work in exchange for food and shelter. Selling her infant son would be tantamount to putting him in the street. In an unusually candid conversation about her mother, Iracy, the street girl who administered some of the questionnaires, explained simply, "I am a street girl because I don't have a mother, or even though I do, she never helped me. When I needed her most she kicked me out of the house and made me live with my grandmother."

For the children who sleep in the street in Recife, an essential element that distinguishes them from poor, home-bound children is their relationship to a mother figure, be it their biological mother, be it another woman who raises them – grandmother, stepmother, godmother, aunt, or unrelated foster mother. Home and the street are not concepts attached primarily to physical spaces; they are notions revolving largely around the children's relationship to their mothers and the concomitant implications of this relationship. Being at home is being with one's mother, even if the physical space called "home" is nothing more than a few makeshift walls under a bridge, the same type of physical space where children might sleep on their own without their mothers.

Shooting the breeze (*batendo um papo*).

But "home" is far more than physical proximity to one's mother: it implies first and foremost "helping" one's mother, doing things in the home that she wants done, accepting her advice and discipline, and augmenting the family income, or sometimes supplying it entirely. One friend told me,

> By the time I was seven I was footing the bills. In the morning when we woke up there'd be nothing to eat, so I would go out and carry around vegetables at the market, watch over cars, beg, anything, and by noon I'd have some money to take home to my mother so we could eat.

Home also frequently implies attending school. In a general sense, home means sticking to what the children refer to as the *vida boa*, the righteous life, or the right track. And always, the right track revolves around an adoration of their mothers.

In a radio workshop, 17-year-old Índio described a confrontation with his mother, who had accused him of stealing her butane tank and selling it. He explained in a deadpan voice that he had told her, "Ah, Mom, your son wouldn't do that. He might do other things, like be a murderer and stuff, but, no, I don't have the nerve to steal from you." Índio then proceeded to recount how, when he found that

The tattoo reads "God said, 'True love is mother love' " (*Deus disse amor só de mãe*).

the mother of his child had cheated on him, he shot and killed her
Afterward, he had to face his mother:

"Mom, now that I don't have your love, I'll go away."

"Where, my son?"

"To the street."

Índio may have left for the street to avoid arrest or a revenge attack
on his life from the relatives or friends of his girlfriend, but he presented the punishment of losing his mother's love and living in the
street as if in his mind they were one and the same.

Children define the street in terms of its contrast to the concept of
"home." One boy at FEBEM asks another, "Is it fair, André, to leave,
to run away from home, to hang out with no-gooders [*quem não presta*],
to let your mother be very sad, to worry about you?" The street is as
much what it is not – proximity to one's mother, working, studying,
and generally being "good" – as what it concretely is. When the
children refer to life in the street they refer to it generally as *essa vida*,

literally "that life," or more explicitly as *essa vida de malandragem*. Although there is no adequate English translation of *malandragem*, the concept brings to mind vagabondage, debauchery, living by one's wits (invariably through crime), or simply engaging in what Latin American technocrats label "antisocial behavior." In the street one steals, sniffs glue, fights, and generally does things that *não prestam*, or simply are no good. A radio workshop I held at FEBEM went as follows:

Valber: Why did you end up here?

Aloizio: I was sniffing glue.

Valber: Do you take Rohypnol?

Aloizio: I've been taking the stuff for seven years.

Valber: You just steal, pickpocket, right?

Aloizio: I steal clothing from clotheslines, sometimes I steal gas cans, water cans. . . .

Valber: Why do you steal that stuff from clotheslines? What kind of a no-good, small-time thief [*ladrão peba*] are you?

Aloizio: You think I go for the tacky stuff? I go for the cool clothing, Sea Way shorts. Anyway, I have to steal. If I don't steal, I don't eat.

Aloizio: Isn't there food at your house?

Valber: Yes, but I don't want to be at home, because at home I just stick to the righteous life [*fico na vida boa*], going to school, working with my mother. . . .

The children speak of sleeping in the street as a vice. For instance, a working child explained his theory about why young popcorn vendors sometimes begin to sleep rough:

Perhaps because there is so much popcorn being sold in the street, a kid won't be able to bring money to his mother. So his mother gets worried, frustrated because there's nothing to eat, and hits the kid. The kid, afraid to go back home without money and get hit, just sleeps in the street. He picks up the vice [*pega o vício*] of sleeping in the street. He gets hooked [*fica viciado*], afraid to go home. Then he picks up other vices like sniffing glue, smoking pot.

Like any vice, the street – despite its hardships and dangers – exerts an addictive power. Home is a good habit and, like any good habit, requires continuity and a certain moral resolve.

"Why are your brothers and sisters all at home and not you?" I asked a 16-year-old who had 12 siblings, none of whom had ever lived in the street. He replied, "I am *da rua* [of the street], when I'm at home I can't stop thinking about the street. I can't stop! Then this urge hits me to get the hell out and steal." As another, younger boy explained it, "Last month I ran away from home [again]. I don't want to be at home. I'm just not used to it [*não sou muito acostumado em casa não*]."

While children speak of the street as a vice, they are constantly reminded of their status as pariahs. At home they are chastised. David recalls that when he began to sleep rough "[my sisters] called me 'glue sniffer,' 'thief,' 'pot-head.' "

And children who regularly sleep in the street often speak of themselves as a danger. Children can sometimes be heard speaking about themselves in terms akin to those used by supporters of the death-squad murders of street children. For instance, a boy named Elvis was incredulous that the street educator I was with one day wanted to take a van-load of street children on a trip.

> If I were a street educator I would round up all the street kids. I'd tell them I was taking them on an excursion. Then I'd drive them halfway between here and Bahia and leave them on the side of the road so they could never get back.

Another boy who lived in the street once told me in more graphic terms, "I'd round them all up, tie cement blocks to their feet, and throw them in the river."

A common derogatory appellation for street children is *cheira-cola*, or glue sniffer. One can sometimes hear it muttered at the adolescent who begs for change – "get a job, *cheira-cola*." Children who live in *favelas* will taunt those who live in the street with the slight. As one would guess, *cheira-cola* finds its origin in the fact that children who live in the street often sniff glue, which they tote around in small bottles or cans. Children who live in the street will also often refer to other youths in the street as *cheira-colas*.

Activists in Recife and elsewhere object to the use of the term *cheira-cola*. One street educator explained that it dehumanizes the children, replacing what they are with a description of what they often do. This emerges as an interesting parallel to the problem of speaking of children as being *in* or *of* the street. When, if ever, can one consider a practice tantamount to a state of being?

The National Movement of Street Children defines *meninos de rua* as

> the children of the workers whose insertion in the productive market is characterized by underemployment, intermittent employment, and unemployment, children deprived of the fruits of development whose rights are abused, especially their right to be children. (MNMMR 1992: 7)

In other words, children of the street, in the view of the movement, are the millions of poor children in Brazil. But children who live in the street have been a pivotal aspect of the identity of the National Movement of Street Children, especially as that identity has been projected to the public. They are, however, a symbol of the movement, not its essence. The most visible young spokesperson for the movement in Recife in the early 1990s had lived in the street for a number of years. Yet he was virtually the only child activist in the movement in Recife who had lived in the street. Videos about the movement's second and third national congresses of street children were centered around children who have lived in the street. I found, however, that most children I met in Recife who lived in the street had not heard of the movement.[3] When adult activists from the movement invited children to speak at the Second International Conference on Street Youth and AIDS in Rio, a handful of children who lived in the street were chosen. But in Rio, as is true nationwide, the overwhelming majority of children activists in the movement are very poor children who live at home. An adult leader of the movement in Rio put it to me bluntly: "It is called the National Movement of Street Children for reasons of marketing. If it were called the National Movement of Children, no one would listen."

In a general sense, *street* is clearly included in the title of the movement as a way to draw attention to the excruciating difficulties experienced by poor children in Brazil, particularly to the violations of

Boy being interviewed by a news team as the Pernambuco delegation prepares to depart for Brasilia for the Third Congress of the National Movement of Street Children.

their human rights. It is an adjective, or, in Portuguese, a prepositional phrase, that conjures up images of hardship, oppression, and struggle. Thus the National Movement of Street Children, which in the early 1990s was one of the most visible social movements in Brazil, has been instrumental in widening the definition of street children to include all poor children whose rights – civil and economic alike – are violated.

Although it is to be expected that the first word of the compound noun "street children" can present analytical difficulties, the second can also be surprisingly problematic. Williams (1993) has pointed out that street life has been seen for over a century to endow children prematurely with an adultlike status. He cites a mid-nineteenth-century observer who wrote of "street Arabs": "they are older when young than any other class." Because it exposes children to experiences believed to be the province of adults, the street is often said to convert children prematurely into "little adults." On a number of occasions foreigners in Brazil pointed out to me how it seemed to them that boys working in the streets had the facial expressions and body language of men. But in the contemporary literature about street children, there is a countervailing tendency to highlight the youthfulness and innocence of this population. When accompanied by photographs, articles about street children typically feature very young, prepubescent boys and girls, often amid comparatively large adult street educators (e.g., Filgueiras 1992). Yet as a Brazilian ethnography (Milito and Silva 1995) aptly points out. most Brazilian "street children" are in fact street adolescents. And perhaps because Brazilian legislation makes such stark distinctions between the legal penalties imposed upon adults and on those who have not reached the age of majority, many adolescents want to remain just that for as long as possible. I even knew youths who were "17" over a three-year period. A Recife NGO was working with people it referred to as *meninos* and *meninas*, many of whom were in fact in their early 20s. They argued that because these youths had never had a "childhood," they were still children. The street, seen as inimical to childhood, is thus also represented as a force that retards normal maturation, excluding children from adulthood.

My own understanding of the term "street children" when I set out for the field revolved around those people under the age of 18 who regularly sleep in the street. Indeed my research was ultimately centered around that group, although I used some flexibility with the age limit. But how do children (or young people) who sleep in the street speak of themselves? They talk about their lives as a sort of chiaroscuro where home means helping one's mother, working, studying, and generally doing "good" things, whereas the street is its opposite: not obeying one's mother, stealing, using drugs, and generally doing "bad" things. The children who regularly sleep in the street will often refer to themselves as *meninos de rua* (street children) or even *meninos abandonados* (abandoned children), but generally only when speaking with adults, especially street educators. Among themselves, they tend to employ the term *maloqueiros*, usually pronounced without the long Portuguese *ei* as *maloqueros* and sometimes shortened (interestingly, to its etymological root) to *malocas*.[4] For most northeasterners, the term conjures up images of naughty children stealing fruit, taunting old people, or generally making a nuisance of themselves. Or it may be used simply to refer to slum dwellers. When children living in the street use the term, however, they are almost invariably speaking of themselves. "I've been a *maloca* all my life," Mônica, an 18-year-old known throughout the city center for her brazen acts of theft, told me. "I'm not going to leave this life [*sair dessa vida*]." *Maloqueiro* is more than a description of activities, it is a lifestyle, and it is that life, *essa vida*, that I try to evoke when speaking of *maloqueiros*, or, interchangeably for the purposes of this book, street children.

Like street children in Bombay who are said to refer to themselves as *Sadak Chap*, literally "those who carry the stamp of the street" (Patel 1990: 10), *maloqueiros* are both talked about and see themselves as different from other poor children, as if they carried an invisible stamp. "Once a kid spends a week in the street, you can forget about him," a struggling middle-class friend who had once tried to adopt a street girl told me. "There is nothing you can do to help the kid." The *maloqueiros* are frequently spoken about as being beyond *recuperação*, or recovery, and are in this way radically set apart from other children. And the *maloqueiros* tend to separate themselves from other poor children in ways that often mystify adults. For instance, an organization called CAMM, Center for Support of Women and Children, runs two programs for youths. One is a live-in farm for those who previously slept in the street. The other is for poor children who reside at home. The director of CAMM once confided his inability to understand why, when they had parties to mix the two groups, the former street dwellers refused to interact with the other children. "They are all from the *favelas*, in some cases even from the same *favelas*, and have grown up with similar hardships. But the street kids just stick together, get all quiet, and can't wait to leave."

Feelings tend to be mutual. Glue-sniffing street children (*cheira-colas*) are the frequent target of ridicule by poor "home children," even if the poor "home children" do many of the same things, such as stealing and using drugs, even glue.

"We've fought," explained Neide, who had a pronounced scar across one cheek from when she was stabbed by Tânia. "Tânia, Neguinha, Luisa . . . we've all fought, but friends are like that." Although shouting matches and internecine brawls are perpetual among *maloqueiros*, street children also stick together – stealing together, using drugs together, roaming together – often without apparent interest in doing these things with other children.

Together, *maloqueiros* share the ostracism for their "vices." In the *favelas* they are taunted as glue sniffers and thieves; in the city center and in FEBEM they are spoken of as "unrecoverable." And they are unmistakably separated from their mothers – although they generally go to great pains to try to convince others that their separation was their own choice, not their mother's. Their "vice" is at once public and indicative of danger, as they are constantly reminded by the nervous strides of passersby. *Maloqueiros* are the ones apt to ask themselves, "Will I ever quit this life?" (*Será que eu vô saí dessa vida?*)

5

WHEN LIFE IS NASTY, BRUTISH, AND SHORT: VIOLENCE AND STREET CHILDREN

In 1980, Hector Babenco, Argentinian born though also an important exponent of Brazil's *Cinema Novo*, made a film entitled *Pixote: a lei do mais fraco*, released outside Brazil in 1981 as *Pixote*. The film, based loosely on José Louzeiro's novel *Infância dos mortos* (1977) and employing children from the *favelas* of São Paulo as actors, wove together the violent and violated lives of children in a tale that raised questions about human nature as disturbing as those it raised about Brazilian politics. The film's protagonist, Pixote, a young boy of about 10, is detained in a police sweep in the wake of a bungled pickpocketing-cum-murder of a judge. Interned in a reformatory, he is witness to the rape of a young boy, finds that some of his peers are murdered by the police when singled out arbitrarily in revenge for the death of the judge, and practices, along with older boys, mock bank robberies. Pixote eventually flees the reformatory and in the company of friends embarks on a spree of street crime in São Paulo and Rio de Janeiro. Snatching purses and wallets, selling drugs, and (in collusion with a prostitute) robbing half-dressed johns, the protagonist is at once a young, prepubescent boy eager for affection, companionship, and care and an incensed, gun-toting would-be tough capable of murder.

Pixote became the third most commercially successful Brazilian film (Levine 1997). In the United States, it was named the Best Foreign Film by the New York Film Critics in 1981 and elsewhere it was generally well received. But as a foreign-language film (for most of the world) and an intellectually challenging and unsentimental one at that, it was not widely distributed. It was nearly a decade later that the violent lives of Brazilian street children came to be well known internationally.

Violence and Street Children

In 1989, the National Movement of Street Children held its high-profile Second National Congress in which poor children and street educators from throughout the country convened in Brasilia to protest violence, poverty, and other human rights abuses and to debate a draft version of the Children and Adolescents Act. The event was covered extensively by Brazilian and foreign news media. A year later, Amnesty International (1990b) issued a report on the executions of Brazilian children. On the first page of the report was the photograph of a young child lying dead in the street, surrounded by many onlookers. The caption below the photograph read,

> Patricio Hilario da Silva, aged 9, whose corpse was dumped in the fashionable Rio de Janeiro suburb of Ipanema on 22 May 1989. A note tied around his neck read, "I killed you because you didn't study and had no future. . . . The government must not allow the streets of the city to be invaded by kids." The boy is believed to have been the victim of a death squad.

It was also in 1990 that the well-regarded Brazilian journalist Gilberto Dimenstein published a book called *A guerra dos meninos* or, in its English-language version, *Brazil: War on Children* (1991). Dimenstein argued,

> In the back streets of the country's big cities, a silent war of extermination is being waged against young petty criminals. The war involves the use of beatings and torture. Although the exclusively police death squads of the 1970s have practically ceased to exist, this latest war is promoted and organised by members of the police force. The groups involved are often given names such as "death squads" and *justiceiros* ("avengers"), and the police encourage their activities on the grounds that the children are dangerous and will never mend their ways. . . . Children are increasingly to be found among their victims because growing numbers are forced on to the street to make a living, to contribute to the family income or because there is no school for them. (20)

The murders of street children came to be debated by the European parliament and were for a time a veritable thorn in the side of Brazilian diplomats and politicians. During a trip to Italy in 1991, President Fernando Collor de Mello was forced to account for violence against street children (Gama 1991). Prior to the Global Summit on the Environment held in Rio de Janeiro in June 1992, British Prime Minister John Major was widely encouraged by parliamentarians to broach the subject of youth murders with the Brazilian president (Rocha 1992), and on a visit to Brazil, Major, under the watchful gaze of an entourage of photographers and bodyguards, made a point of eating breakfast with street children at a local shelter.

In his book, Dimenstein asserted that "The war on children is one of the least known aspects of Brazil's social crisis" (20). Yet, the death-squad murders of street children came to be one of the most widely known facts of any sort about Brazil. The popular press was important in disseminating reports about Brazilian death squads. For example, the widely circulated women's magazine *Marie Claire* ran a feature article entitled "Why Rio Is Murdering Its Children" (Lamb 1991). The U.K. version of the article was preceded by a story entitled "Sexual Fantasies: Five Women Reveal Their Secret Desires" and was flanked by advertisements for Neutrogena Face Bar and Soft and Gentle Anti-Perspirant. By the early 1990s, though homeless in Brazil, street children and their disfigured bodies had become a household concept the world over.

Just as attention to the war on children seemed to be ebbing, a number of sleeping children in Rio de Janeiro were murdered in cold blood. The incident, known as the Candelária Massacre (*a chacina da Candelária*), was reported around the world. On July 25, 1993, men arriving in two cars opened fire on a group of youths sleeping outside the Candelária Church in the center of Rio de Janeiro. Four were killed instantly, one managed to stumble a few streets away, and a sixth died of his wounds a few days later. The killers then attacked another nearby group of children, killing two more and wounding one. According to Human Rights Watch (1994: vii), "A twenty-two-year-old garbage collector named Wagner dos Santos, who survived the shootings with a bullet lodged in his neck, identified three policemen from the Fifth Battalion of the Rio state military police and a civilian as being among those responsible for the slaughter." In an unprecedented victory for human rights advocates, one of the perpetrators, a member of the Military Police, was convicted in 1996 for his participation in the massacre.

Although the frequency of media treatment of violence against street children has now subsided, the general impression that death squads routinely hunt down street children probably has not. "Violence against [street children] escalated to a level of deliberate 'extermination' of undesirable children," writes the author of a 1995 book entitled *Street Children and NGOs in Rio* (Impelizieri 1995: 15). A 1996 article that treats the killings of poor youths in Brazil seeks to dispel the idea that these murders happen merely in the context of a violent society. "Latin America has no cultural monopoly on violence. And in any case, some other explanation is needed for the increased violence than a simplistic unvarying construct called 'culture of violence'" (Huggins and de Castro 1996: 89). The authors argue, convincingly, that a particular kind of youth – poor, male, and dark-skinned – is identified as a "social problem" and made out to be a "symbolic assailant." But Huggins and de Castro cite data from São Paulo indicating that 64 percent of homicides of males aged 15 to 17 during 1990 were carried out by "unknown" assailants. The "known" types of murderers listed in the article are: public police (17%), extermination group (9%), family (5%), private police (2%), lone assailant (2%), and friend (1%). Unfortunately, the alleged perpetrators in these killings were evidently divided into different categories based on questionable data culled from newspapers, morgue statistics, and police reports. Because the vast majority of murders in Brazil are, to all intents and purposes, not investigated – let alone brought to trial or solved – scant reliable data are available on murders in Brazil.[1] What is more, as the authors themselves note, many murders are not even reported. Thus, in actuality, the "unknown" category is almost certainly far larger than that identified by the authors. Be that as it may, Huggins and de Castro inexplicably conflate "unknown" (i.e., unsolved murders or murders in which responsibility remains unattributed) and assassins who are "unknown" to the victims. These "unknown" assassins, they assume, are members of death squads. In this way, the category of death-squad murders becomes vast.

Just as Huggins and de Castro have renamed unsolved murders death-squad murders, elsewhere the killings of all youths are spoken of as if the victims were street youths. For example, the NGO Child-hope (1992) published an advertisement in the British daily the *Guardian*, that began, "*Q*: What is the going rate for killing a street child? *A*: Seven pounds. 167 street children have been murdered in Rio de Janeiro so far this year." Yet an article published in the same newspaper the previous week explained, "Brazilian government statistics show that in the first four months of this year 167 people under 18 were killed in Metropolitan Rio" (Rocha 1992). In other words, Childhope was describing 100 percent of Rio's murdered children as street children. In other cases, simply speaking of street children and murders of all children in the same breath is enough to give the misleading impression that most murders of children are tantamount to murders of street children. For example, a mass electronic mailing from the International Child Resource Institute (1995) called for

> assistance in a worldwide effort to stop the killings of street children in Brazil. The lack of political will to effectively tackle the violence against the children of the poor in Brazil and to prosecute their assailants is one of the key reasons for the four daily murders of children and adolescents in that country.

The widespread, unquestioning acceptance as fact that Brazilian adults are systematically hunting down and murdering young children like so many rabid dogs is not only based on dubious statistics but has a number of unintended consequences that are not necessarily in the interests of children. One such consequence is to reduce street children to the status of animal-like prey (indeed, the use of the compound verb "hunted down" in reference to the way they are targeted is telling). Stripped of human agency and placed in a pantheon of faceless victimhood, street children become objects in a largely adult debate that does more to enhance the status of those who crusade in their behalf than to shed light on the myriad ways children in fact live violence. In her article "Youth and the Politics of Culture in South Africa," Pamela Reynolds (1995) suggests that in studying children under apartheid,

> One can easily be seduced by the brute force of oppression in South Africa into offering an analysis of structure while ignoring

agents' interpretations – another version of symbolic domination.
. . . To dub youth, as is often done [in the context of contemporary South Africa], as the "lost generation" is to demean their contribution and to deny the inventiveness inherent in processes of inheritance and change. (223–224)

Likewise, in a context of global attention to the annihilation of Brazilian street children, it is sometimes difficult to remember that street children can be living, breathing people. Denunciations of violence against street children, however well intentioned, have left little space for a consideration of the ways violence is experienced and interpreted by children.

What follows in this chapter is an attempt to look at violence from the perspective of street children in Recife and to comment on the social constructions of violence against and by those children. I argue that street children have complex systems for classifying violence and that their interpretations are often at odds with those of their adult advocates. The chapter is also an attempt at making sense of my own uncomfortable conclusion that street children in Recife are far more likely to die at the hands of their peers than as victims of death squads. Finally, I argue that while a constellation of advocates and media figures has centered attention on the relatively rare if heinous death-squad murders of street children, the everyday mistreatment of children at the hands of the police is all but ignored, as is the violence they suffer at home. And the public discourse on violence and children has drawn a rigid – and ultimately harmful – distinction between violent murder in public places and quiet, private violence in the home.

Schooled in Violence

Mistreatment at the hands of the authorities begins at a very young age for many Brazilian children and takes myriad forms. Some *malo-aueiros* described to me the terror of finding themselves as small children locked up in the midst of much larger, violent youths. One young man named Edson, who was tenuously seeking to remake a life for himself off the street by working at a shelter, recalled how his first contacts with the authorities shaped his initiation into street life.

What [the juvenile detention center FEBEM] has to offer is nothing but a bad upbringing for children, because the child gets in there even without being a street child to start with. When he gets in there he might be shy, but no, they don't want to hear anything about it; to them all the kids are thieves, glue sniffers, and they live in the street. They put the kids together, big ones with little ones, thieves with the children who just wander around in the street. . . . When I lived in the street, I didn't steal or anything like that, I just sold candy for a lady in the city. One day when I was leaving work at noon – I was coming back here to São Lourenço, I lived with my mother at the time – the police, the Minors' Court, they caught me and a chum who was also from São Lourenço. I started crying and everything, asking them to let us go, saying we worked, and they went, "You don't work, all those kids we catch say they work." That's what they told us.

They stuck us in the car and took us away. We spent four months there [in FEBEM] without anyone from our families knowing. Then one day my mother showed up. So I'm there, I'd spent a year and four months there,[2] I had to learn something about debauchery [*tinha que aprender alguma coisa da malandragem*]. So it went on and on, and when I thought it couldn't happen, before I knew it I was into that life of *malandragem*, learning slang. I was too timid to steal, though. But in there, some chums, they said, "Edson, let's *botá mola!*" I said, "What's *botá mola?*" They said, "Steal, brother, don't you know what stealing is?" I said, "I know what stealing is, I just never stole anything." So they taught me. I went, I stole a watch. And I thought it was pretty good [*aí nisso, eu achei bom*].

During a hearing I attended at the Children's and Adolescents' Court, even a judge described the facility as "a school for criminals." FEBEM is a place where young children are exposed to the violence both of their older and larger peers and of the authorities. Their internment at the facility is often the first step in launching them into *essa vida*, not only because they learn about crime but because they come out stigmatized. Edson continued his story about FEBEM by describing what happened when he went home.

So I got out, I spent eight days in the street, and the whole time during those eight days I was stealing and everything. Then I went home. When I got home I found all my brothers and sisters, but they started calling me "glue sniffer," just because I'd been taken prisoner. They discriminated against me, you know. So I got more angry than ever and I fell back into street life.

One of the most frightening aspects of the FEBEM facility in Pernambuco was known as the *cafua*. In the midst of a radio workshop in which the kids were discussing sexual relationships at FEBEM, a description of the *cafua* arose.

Verinha: Sometimes it was because one girl wants to [have sex with another girl], sometimes it was the two of them. When it was just one, she would do it by force.

Nego Nic: That's right. Some of them [now referring to boys and girls] know how to read, so they send a little note to a guy to meet in such and such a place. He reads it and then he goes to that place and they do whatever they want. But if the *monitor* catches you, it's *cafua*. That's the law: if they catch you, *cafua*! The *cafua* is the same thing as a hole in the ground. You go down steps. Down below there's a tunnel, that's where the *cafua* is. . . . We went into a room, like a room without light, to sleep with the cockroaches, with the mosquitoes, with the lizards.

Tobias: And how long would you be left there?

Nego Nic: Man, it depends on the *monitor*. If he wants to leave you there for ten days, he leaves you there. Now, if he feels like it, he'll take you out after two days, three days. But it makes you really scared. Because it's very dark – flocks of rats, flocks of cockroaches, flocks of mosquitoes. The mosquitoes don't let you sleep, you sleep on the ground, without a sheet, without anything.

Violent Authorities

When I handed the tape recorder to the children in my radio workshops, any participant's mention of an arrest would provoke the in-

"Off to FEBEM." Photo by Daniel Aarnot.

evitable questions: "Did they beat you that time?" "How many blows did you take?" "Did they stick your head in the toilet and give you a whirly?" Recalling his last arrest, one youth said, "They hung me upside down, poured water in my nostrils, made me drink Pine Sol and bleach. Then they beat me with a strip of rubber." When I indexed my notes I found what seemed an endless number of entries under such headings as "police violence."

The children employ an elaborate terminology to speak of the police and the things the police do to them. The police are known by the words *cobaia* (guinea-pig); *cabeça de pinoco* (chamberpot head); *cagüeta*, a variation of *alcagüete* (snitch); *caboclo* (usually used to refer to someone of mixed Indian and white ancestry); or, collectively, *os homens* (the men). In addition to all of these things, the police are referred to as *malandros* (rogues) and are known to employ their own blend of cunning and brutality to steal, even from street children. Not long before being murdered himself, one adolescent male explained,

> When we're sleeping we're woken up to kicks, clubs, buckets of water they throw on us – they mess you around in a thousand and one ways. Say you got money, two thousand, three thousand cruzeiros [a dollar or a little more] in your pocket, they take you to the police booth, snatch what you've got, smack your hands a bunch of times with a club, and send you out of the area.

While street children fear having their possessions or money taken by their peers, they also must contend with the police stealing from them. The street children in the city center complained of this routinely, and they also spoke of having to make payoffs by sharing their loot. It is perhaps this unpredictable nature of the police that makes them so dangerous. Children need to determine whether the police aim to use them as proxies in their own illegal pursuits, remaining content with a payoff, or rather to punish them arbitrarily (and, perhaps as an afterthought, to rob them).

Street children typically experience violence at the hands of the authorities over a long period of time and they distinguish between different sorts of mistreatment. In one enactment, the police are punishing them for a crime, real or imagined:

> *Sócrates* [*aged 17 or 18*]: It's my turn to talk [he grabs the microphone from another youth, almost breaking it]. Last Sunday something happened to me. Two policemen out there on Guararapes [Avenue]. A boy snatched a necklace from a lady and another one took her watch. So there I was, walking. The cop started looking at me and just because I looked back – I wasn't even looking at him – they grabbed me by the hair, gave me a kick in the foot and in the stomach. Then they punched me in the face three times, then a kick in the head, a bunch of kicks in my ribs, a bunch of punches here next to my heart, in my stomach. I even vomited a little. Then they kicked me, afterwards they shoved me. When I fell to the ground, they kicked me. They grabbed my hair, they hit me in the eye, me screaming and all. A transit policeman came running 'cause he thought

they were killing me, but they weren't killing me – well, really, they were killing me 'cause if a person gets kicked a lot in the belly he might what? Die! Yeah, he might die.

In this passage, Sócrates asserts that he is being punished for a crime, albeit a crime he did not commit. When the police believe, rightly or wrongly, that a poor youth has committed an infraction, the youth's expectation is typically of immediate physical punishment. Younger children are not always hit by the police. They tend to be taken to FEBEM rather than to the regular police stations for adults (where by law no one under 18 should be taken). But in general, street children take it for granted that if caught for (or suspected of) stealing, vandalizing property, possessing drugs, or in any way angering the police, they are likely to be beaten. When detained, they say, it's "a clubbing every time" (*pau, sempre pau*).

Another form of police violence directed at street children could be called retribution. An extreme case was described by a 17-year-old at FEBEM.

> *Cheira*³ [*meaning "he sniffs," or short for* cheira-cola, *glue sniffer*]: The late Come-Rato [Rat-Eater], he killed a Major, you know, but he wasn't the one who killed him, it was his *colega* [peer]. Come-Rato was here [in FEBEM]. There was a rebellion, a rebellion to get out of here. So they caught him, they took him to Cabo [the jail for adolescents]. He spent two years there. He played [soccer] every Sunday in the field by the distillery. One Sunday, when I was there . . . he went to play ball. On the way back two guys on a motorcycle made the FUNDAC⁴ van stop. They said, "Look, stop, if you don't stop I'll shoot you in the head." So the driver, he was about forty, he was nervous, he stopped. The guy looked inside. There was a bunch of people inside the van. A lady said, "Don't do that!" He goes, "Don't worry, I won't do anything to you. I just want that nigger who killed the Major." He started shooting. He shot him more than fifteen times. So he died right there.

Although similar to physical punishment, retribution differs in its severity and in the fact that you never know when it will strike. The manifestations of physical punishment described above are immediate and spontaneous. Retribution, on the other hand, can come back to haunt you long after the alleged crime was committed. The act of retribution tends to be carefully planned and devastating in its consequences. Retribution is usually "payment" for an act that directly offends the police, such as assaulting or killing an officer or a relative of an officer.

Sometimes the violence of the police is attributed to *malícia* (malice) or *safadeza* (being low and dirty). One girl, about 15, described how the police had made her and her friends undress and parade naked.

> The "men" come along without us having done anything, we're not even sniffing glue or smoking cigarettes, and there they come to hit you. There's this skinny one in the city, he grabs us when we haven't done anything. He grabs us to see our bodies, to have us take off our clothing.

This type of violence is attributed to the nature of the police, who are widely viewed as evil thugs. Not seen as a direct or retaliatory punishment of any sort, this type of violence is particularly frightening because of its unpredictability; it is viewed as one of the risks of living in the street, rather than as a risk implicit, say, in stealing, an act that when successfully carried out renders a tangible benefit.

Michael Taussig (1987) employs the term "culture of terror" to describe how society can be dominated through the pervasive use and threat of violence. The police may not really dominate street children – indeed, the children are haughtily defiant – but the presence of the police in the lives of street children is pervasive and terrifying. The reach of police violence is extended by the fact that it can be exercised both directly and by proxy. And it is terrifying both in the savage extremes to which it is taken and in its unpredictability. It is what Taussig (4) has called "power on the rampage – that great steaming morass of chaos that lies on the underside of order and without which order could not exist." When enforced by the police themselves, violence against street children can take countless forms, from *bolos na mão* (smacks to the hand) to pistol whippings, from kicks and punches to electric shock. As a general rule, the older the detainees, the more severely they are beaten. Although children as young as nine told me of being hit with cudgels, the most severe beatings tend to be reserved for adolescents. It is not uncommon for physically mature 16- and 17-year-olds, and on occasion kids far younger, to be taken to regular, adult police stations. In my questionnaire I asked the children whether they had been to any of the adult police stations. Of the 50, 29 (58%) said they had. They were then asked what happened there. Of those 29, 17 (59%) spontaneously mentioned they had experienced incidents of violence, such as severe beatings and forced confessions.

The most feared of the police stations is a special one called the Delegacia de Roubos e Furtos, which is located in an outlying area of the city on a street ironically named Avenida Liberdade. The station's mandate is to pursue and arrest thieves of different sorts. Sometimes Roubos e Furtos is but a stop on the way to the men's prison, Anibal Bruno, located just across the street. But whether the prisoner is released or transferred to prison, the officers at the station often inflict punishments of their own. When in the questionnaire I asked the respondents if they had been to Roubos e Furtos, 14 replied in the affirmative. Of those, 10 mentioned spontaneously that they had been tortured.

One of the most common forms of torture at Roubos e Furtos and at other police stations is *pau de arara*, literally "the parrot's perch." This involves having your hands tied together around your bent legs (bringing the knees close to the chest). A stick (the "perch") is inserted above your cuffed arms and below the bent knees. As the stick is raised and hung, the weight of your upper body spins you upside down. You are left like this, hanging upside down. Water or, in severe cases cleaning detergents such as Pine Sol may be dripped into your nostrils

Bia was beaten so severely at Roubos e Furtos that she spontaneously aborted. Other youths were transported to Roubos e Furtos in the trunk of a sedan by police officers who neither identified themselves as such nor wore uniforms.

At Roubos e Furtos, torture is frequently made the responsibility of other prisoners. After four or five *entradas* (detentions), one can expect to become a *preso de ordem*. In answer to my question "What's a *preso de ordem?*" one youth explained as follows:

> *Negão*: That's when you boss around the other prisoners at the station. You keep the key in your hand, you feed the prisoners,

Table 4. *Anthropological Interviews: Physical Abuse at Police Stations*

Questions and responses	Number
Children who cite beatings and other forms of physical abuse when asked "What happened there? (*o que foi que aconteceu lá?*)" in reference to a detention at a police station[a]	
Spontaneously mention physical abuse	17
Do not spontaneously mention physical abuse	12
Respondents who cite beatings and other forms of physical abuse when asked "What happened there? [when taken to the special Roubos e Furtos police station]."[b]	
Spontaneously mention physical abuse	10
Do not spontaneously mention physical abuse	4

[a]$N = 29$ children who had been to a police station other than Roubos e Furtos.
[b]$N = 14$ informants who had been to Recife's Roubos e Furtos police station.

right. You wash the cars in front of the station, run errands, go and buy bread for the prisoners, hit the prisoners too, right. All those things.

Tobias: If you were free to run away, for instance when you went to buy bread, why didn't you do it?

Negão: I didn't run away because I knew that if I did, they would catch me again. And if I did, the club would come down twice as hard [*o pau era dobrado*]. And then I'd go to the *cela batida*.

Tobias: What's that?

Negão: It's a cell where it's dark day and night, day and night, no one can see anything. It's just dark. I'd spend seventy [many] days in there without seeing the sun.

Using prisoners to torture other prisoners aids the work of the police not merely because it saves them the trouble of soiling their hands but because the *preso de ordem* is said to be left *marcado*, literally "marked," or on the hit list of his victims. In other words, the system takes advantage of the children's own sense of retaliatory justice. Margarete explained the death of one youth as follows.

> *Margarete*: There was this kid named Jameson. He died in a *boca* [a drug den] in Santo Amaro. They say he died for snitching or else he killed the grub of another prisoner [*matou o rango de um prisioneiro*].
> *Tobias*: What do you mean, he killed someone's grub?
> *Margarete*: He didn't put enough lunch on the guy's plate. . . . So the prisoner put him on his list [*marcou a cara dele*]. The prisoner was from a *boca* in Santo Amaro. He got out and so did the other one [Jameson]. Jameson went into Santo Amaro to buy some glue and then that prisoner who was there he asked, "Remember me?"
> "Yeah."
> "Remember what you did to me?"
> "Come on, I would have been beaten by the police."
> The other one didn't want to listen and shot Jameson three times. So he lost his life right there.

The *preso de ordem* system has the effect of achieving the results the police want, the beating or murder of certain repeat offenders, without directly implicating the authorities; it also extends the reach of the police into the world of street culture. With attention focused on police murders, it has become a system of pitting those seen as socially dangerous against one another in a sort of war by proxy. During a visit to the men's prison Aníbal Bruno, I listened to inmates speak eagerly of the imminent arrival of a certain "snitch" who was then across the road at Roubos e Furtos, allegedly beating detainees.

Violence and Social Transformations

Early on in my fieldwork, I placed a youth in danger by failing to understand the stigma of murder. Germano, then about 16, though he was far from certain, tried to find me one day. He wanted me to accompany him to the Institute of Forensic Medicine to identify his father's body. His father had been hit over the head with a board and shot. He was found some time later with stones forced down his throat.

I only learned of the murder two days after the fact, by which time Germano's father had been buried, and the boy was out and about on the street like normal, although with obvious sadness on his face. I went to speak with him and as we talked other street kids came to listen. To my surprise, they did not know that Germano's father had been killed. As I told them, I noticed Germano growing nervous. I encouraged him to go home to spend some time with his mother, a washerwoman in a northern *favela* of Recife. One young boy agreed with me, "When my brother was murdered, I went home to be with my mother." But the other, larger kids were silent. One smirked. Germano asked me for some money to go home and I decided to oblige. He jumped onto the back bumper of a bus, thrust a hand through an open window to steady the ride, and disappeared down the avenue.

But Germano did not go home. Instead, he hopped off the bus a few blocks away. When I saw him the next day he had a black eye and a bruised cheek. Marconi, one of the street kids who had overheard our conversation, had reportedly taunted the boy: "Your father was killed because he was no good." Germano threw a rock at him, but was easily overpowered by Marconi's superior strength. Murder tends to be seen as a stigma for those close to the victim, not a call for compassion.

An 18-year-old male street educator who used to live in the street described how he was almost murdered.

> Many of our *colegas* are dying, it's the police killing, dragging them off, taking them to the forests and killing them, finishing them off one by one. This is what they say, "Since they can't be caught, since they run away no matter what you do, let's just kill them." They caught me, took me to the forest, tore off my clothing, left me in my underwear. They pointed a revolver at my forehead, in my mouth, in every hole they could find, and threatened to shoot. But I'm still here, alive, thank God, because I don't have anything to pay for.

I believe the last sentence is crucial, for while street children speak of the violence they suffer as cruel, horrifying, and unjust, they also frequently imbue it with moral overtones whereby the victim is paying for his "sins." The violence is often seen as retribution. As Camilla (aged 17) interpreted it, "No one just dies for no reason [*ninguém morre de graça*]."

In my questionnaire I asked various questions about rape. The first, posed as a way of initiating a conversation about sexual violence, was "What is *suruba?*" Edson described *suruba* as follows:

> *Suruba* is when five or six boys grab a girl and force her to have sex. They do everything. Here in São Lourenço [just outside Recife] there's a girl, she wasn't of the street, but she hung out with us, at night she'd always come. One day she snitched on the boys and the boys caught her and dragged her to the cane fields. Fifteen boys got to her. She spent two weeks at home before she could walk straight. Her uncle took care of her, but I think she liked it so much that she went back to the street.

The rationale for the rape offered in this case is that the girl blew the whistle. Like the retribution enforced by the police, sexual violence is sometimes used by street children to strike back at someone who has broken a sacrosanct rule. It is carried out by a group, not by a single individual. Rape is seen to have a transformative effect on the victim. Females are believed to become promiscuous as a result of rape, like the girl just mentioned who is said to have wanted to return to the street because she allegedly "liked it [being raped] so much." Rape is discussed as a peculiar domain where the term "victim" hardly seems to apply, for the onus of responsibility is placed on the one who is raped, not on the one who rapes.

I held a radio workshop in a *favela* where a young girl had recently been gang raped. While the boys, some of them no more than 13 years of age, laughed and joked about ripping off the girl's clothes, they ridiculed their victim for having made the mistake of sniffing *loló*, a mixture of hallucinogenic solvents. The young girl became the laughingstock of the *favela* for having, as the boys saw it, let down her guard.

In the case of boys who are raped, the act is said to turn them into homosexuals. A youth told me about FEBEM, where homosexual rape

.s common, "When you go in there you have to go in being a man,
otherwise you'll come out a faggot [*bicha*]." In discussing Brazilian
notions of the perceived feminization of men who practice receptive
anal sex, Richard Parker (1991) has observed,

> The *viado* [queer] or *bicha* [faggot], the "passive" partner in
> such exchanges . . . is unavoidably transformed, not merely in his
> own eyes, but in the eyes of his partner or partners and in the
> eyes of any other individuals around him who might happen to
> have knowledge of his sexual practices. He is emasculated. He
> becomes, through his sexual role, a symbolic female. (46)

Like voluntary receptive anal sex, homosexual rape is likewise seen to
transform the "passive" individual into a symbolic female. In the case
of street boys, forced anal penetration is a pervasive fear, because of
both the terrifying violence of the act and the humiliation that ensues.

> *Ismael*: A group of boys got me out there in Caxangá. They
> grabbed pieces of broken glass, bottle necks, sticks, and right
> there they forced me to have sex with every one of them.
> *Tobias*: How many of them were there?
> *Ismael*: There were fourteen. I was alone, right, in an old house
> in Caxangá, which they knocked down just a little while ago. I
> was alone, I couldn't do anything, you know. I wasn't about to
> resist, if I'd resisted . . . that would have been it for me – all of
> them armed and me with nothing in my hands. They got me
> when I was all alone. I suffered it with every one of them.
> Then, little by little, I met up with each of them [in the
> street]. They gave me shit [*tiravam onda*]. I stabbed one of them
> in the ribs, and this part here [he touches his chest] opened up,
> because he was the one who told the group to rape me.

Children talk of two effects of the violence that is part and parcel
of their daily existence. Violence, they say, makes them *revoltar*. *Revoltar* means to rebel, revolt, or strike back. It is frequently used to
explain why they do things that they describe as no good. Cheira, a
17-year-old male, explained, "The worst thing in the world is for a
person, a person who's a thief, to be beaten by someone he never saw

Before the police apprehended the boy, he was beaten by the crowd.

before. That creates an enormous *revolta* in us. We start to rob . . . to do so many things to people . . . the police hitting us, we get even more *revoltados*."

Cheira's words cogently suggest that *revolta* is part of a spiral of violence. One is a thief, then one is beaten, which incites *revolta*, which in turn induces one to rob and "do so many things to people." Fueling the *revolta* is something called *raiva*.

> *Cheira*: When my mother comes to visit me, the police yell at her and I feel like exploding. This business, man, of sticking us in here [FEBEM] and keeping us prisoner doesn't do any good because it fills us with even more *revolta*. When you get out of here, you leave with even more *raiva* and start stealing again.

Raiva means fury, anger, or hatred, but it also means rabies and, like the dog with distemper, a person brimming with *raiva* lashes out.

> *José* [*aged 17*]: It looks like he [the judge presiding over FE-BEM] is punishing us. We're all full of *raiva*, I think we're going

to start a rebellion. . . . When your mother comes, they say "Turn up on such and such a day." This shit is filling us with *raiva, raiva* for the social worker, *raiva* for the director, for the *monitores*. It's true that the *monitores* don't have anything to do with it, but they're the ones who have to pay.

Rather than turning it outward against the *monitores* in FEBEM, their *colegas* in the street, or the stray cats and dogs in their path, the children may turn *raiva* inward against their own bodies. Girls in the street often carry razor blades in the roofs of their mouths or rolled up in a piece of paper in their underwear, a practice that induces veritable panic in many Recife residents, rich and poor alike. Sometimes the girls use the razor blades when they fight among themselves, sometimes when they hold up a victim, but frequently their own bodies are the target. Most girls who have spent a couple of years or more on the street have slits up and down their forearms. The same is true for the male transvestites. Sometimes self-mutilation is a means of defense; girls will cut themselves before being arrested in the belief that in this way they will not be beaten. Margarete explained it as a more general release of frustration, however.

> Sometimes it's because of a boyfriend that one girl takes from another and she doesn't know what to do. She can't cut her, she can't get back at her, so she cuts herself in the arm. Sometimes it's because she gets hit by the police, she gets taken in, drugged and all. She can't cut them [the police], so she cuts her own arm.

There is a dimension of violence involving street children that the advocates eschew. When it comes to violence, street children are never portrayed as possessing agency. But anyone who has spent a day with street children cannot help but notice how often they fight. Normally the fights are limited to pushes, shoves, and unlikely threats, but at other times they suddenly spiral into bloody brawls. Nearly ubiquitous on the bodies of children who have spent a year or more on the streets are knife and bullet wounds. The bullet wounds are often inflicted by the police or private security guards, but the knife wounds tend to be the work of other *maloqueiros*.

Tobias: Ever been stabbed?

Milton: Yes.

Tobias: [pointing to a scar on Milton's leg] And what is this?

Milton: I was slashed with broken glass.

Tobias: Who did that to you?

Milton: A kid, he came to take my glue, and jabbed me with a broken bottle.

Tobias: Ever been shot?

Milton: No [pause], but I was hit over the head with a club.

Tobias: Who did that to you?

Milton: A glue sniffer.

Death Squads and the Violent Status of Victimhood

During a conversation in a bar one night with an off-duty police officer I'd just met in the small city of Caruaru, the subject of death squads arose. He made it clear that he had intimate knowledge about the activities of such groups in his city. He was able to quote the going rate for murder (between US$30 and $90) and even to describe where the bodies were dumped. According to him, most of the members of local death squads were policemen, but hired *pistoleiros* figured among their ranks as well. "Sometimes they kill for free, for the pleasure of seeing a certain person fall." Coming just minutes after he had had an argument with an aggressive, trouble-making patron that nearly erupted into violence, the police officer's explanations were couched in a certain tone of empathy for the perpetrators of such acts. On another occasion, a lower-middle-class man described to me with pride his participation in the extrajudicial group slaying of four youths who had allegedly raped an 11-year-old girl.

My own accidental encounters with people who may have been members of death squads are probably not inconsistent with Brazil's larger panorama of an informal economy of crime and punishment. Street children have not been immune to this climate of vigilante justice. At various times, they have been targeted for murder by paid or unpaid networks of killers.

The death squads are a terrifying threat to street children. Many street children even claim to be able to identify the vehicles used by these professional murderers. "It's a black four-door with tinted windows," one boy told me. But when I asked the kids to describe the murders of all of the *colegas* they had lost, the list of those killed by other children was generally longer than the list of those killed by the police and death squads.

Tobias: During the time you've been in the street, do you know of any kids who have been killed?

Coelho: I knew one named Bochecha, another one called Cara de Cavalo [Horse Face] who was thrown in the river, a bunch of children.

Tobias: Like four or five?

Coelho: More, a bunch.

Tobias: About how many in total?

Coelho: In total, per month?

Tobias: No, altogether, in the two years you've been in the street.

Coelho: Oh, shit, man, more than forty.⁵

Tobias: And who killed them?

Coelho: Mostly other street kids, but the death squads kill too.

Early one morning I went into the center of Recife where I was to meet Beto who wanted me to visit his mother. We had agreed to rendezvous at Ruas e Praças. When I arrived, one of the street educators was reading a newspaper story aloud to a small gathering of children. A boy named Cristiano had been murdered. He was found by another street kid in an abandoned house. It was not clear if the torture had been inflicted while Cristiano was alive or only on his lifeless body, but in addition to his being shot, his mouth and throat had been stuffed with rocks and his head was left face down in a toilet. The cruelty with which Cristiano had been murdered made many activists certain that it had been the work of the death squads. "Kids might murder, but not like that," one street educator told me. Yet as the article was being read aloud, the children listened impassively.

The National Movement of Street Children organized a protest near the square where Cristiano spent his days. They had rented a sound car, one of the city's ubiquitous old station wagons equipped with diesel-powered boom speakers, but the vehicle never showed up. Cristiano was murdered during the frenzy of municipal elections so the organizers were able to convince a city council candidate to lend his sound car. But the eulogies for Cristiano were interspersed with advertisements for the candidate's campaign and for the bread shop he owned, a shop that, as the would-be politician repeated time and again, "has always supported the abandoned children of Recife." Zé Luis, another homeless youth that the newspapers described as Cristiano's best friend, planted a flower in the public square, set loose a white dove in the name of "peace," and issued a stinging rebuke on violence against children. Then a few weeks later he purportedly confessed to the murder of Cristiano.

During the initial 13 months I was in Recife I begrudgingly kept a tally of the street children who died. The list included eight names: Bonérgio, Luquinha, Cristiano, Roberto, Daniela, Branca, Maguinho, and Ubiratan.

Bonérgio fell off the back of a bus, but this was only the indirect cause of his death. He was hurt badly, but he did not die of his wounds. He died because he contracted hepatitis in a public hospital.

Luquinha's best friend, Marconi, staggered after me and called out my name one afternoon just as I was leaving the bread shop near my apartment. Smelling pungently of glue, Marconi insisted I record the story of Luquinha's murder.

> *Marconi*: A little while ago, I lost my best friend, on Christmas Day. Before that we had arranged to get together and have some fun out there, we were friends, brothers. . . . We did things we shouldn't do in the street, holdups, certain things you can imagine, we just didn't kill or rape anybody. All suddenly-like [*de repentemente*] I showed up at his house, and I found out he'd robbed a woman of four million, him and Jorge. . . . But before that, we had been picked up several times and taken to the Olinda Station House where we were hit. The aggression! Jesus, they wanted us to say things that we couldn't even imagine having done and to name other people. And they always swore to kill us.
>
> *Tobias*: Why did they swear to kill you?
>
> *Marconi*: They swore to kill us, when they saw us out in the

street at night, they'd kill us . . . they were going to drag us off
to the woods. . . . I'm sure it was X, because he always swore to
kill us.

Other children told a different version of the murder, saying another
youth had been responsible. In the end Luquinha's death, like most
violent deaths of youths in Pernambuco, was, to the best of my knowledge, never investigated.

The remaining six victims, according to everyone I spoke with about
them, died at the hands of their peers.[6] Cristiano, as discussed earlier,
was said to have been murdered by a street companion; Roberto was
said to have been killed by another young man from whom he had
stolen a pistol some years previously; Daniela was said to have been
murdered by Branca; friends of Daniela were outraged and in retribution beheaded Branca; and Maguinho was murdered by his previously inseparable best friend, and Ubiratan was killed by a young rival.
Thus, except for the ambiguous case of Luquinha, I heard of no instances of children who lived in the street being killed by death squads
during the first 13 months I spent in Recife.

When I returned two years later, many of the street children I knew
had died. For instance, Marconi, who spoke about the murder of Luquinha, was found about a year later on an Olinda beach with three
bullets to the head. Yet no street educators or children could think of
any children living in the street who had been killed by death squads.
There were likewise no such allegations during the three months I
spent in Recife in 1995. The death squads are a real and pervasive but
seldom fulfilled threat; while street children feared being killed by
them, over a period of more than three years, from June 1992 until
August 1995, the closest I came to documenting even the allegation
of a homeless child being killed by death squads in Recife or Olinda
was the death of Luquinha.

If street children view the police as responsible for enforcing a rule
by terror, other Brazilians often accuse street children of instigating
what could, through a twist of the imagination, be called a culture of
terror. Given their high visibility in public spaces and their frequent
use of violence and participation in crime, street children are widely
perceived as making the street a hostile milieu. And while advocacy
organizations tend to heighten the innocence and vulnerability of mur-

dered street children by showcasing the stories of very young victims,[7] those in Brazil afraid of street kids disassociate them from childhood, recasting them as dangerous *marginais* or *malandros*, categories devoid of any explicit reference to age.

Just as street children speak of how the violence they suffer trans - forms them, adult Brazilians endow the violence perpetrated by stree: children with transformative significance. Being violent renders simple *crianças* (children) either *menores* (minors) or, worse, *malandros*. To be sure, only a certain type of child can be a *menor*. Rich kids are always simply *crianças* (Schwartzchild 1987). But barefoot, dark-skinned, poo: children are frequently referred to as *menores*. The Minors' Code, ir. effect before the Children and Adolescents Act was passed in 1990. had legislatively defined delinquent or simply "needy" youths as *me- nores*. Since that time, all Brazilians under the age of 12 are first chil- dren, then, till the age of 18, adolescents, and the term *menor* is now widely viewed as contemptuous. But even so, poor and supposedly delinquent young people are still frequently spoken of as such. A: Kosminsky (1993 [1991]: 118) remarks, "Children made out to be criminals leave behind their very status as children only to be inscribec in the social order of the *menor*."

Even more dangerous is the label *malandro* or *marginal*, for here nc distinction is made between children and adults. In effect, the con- dition of *menor* is brought to fruition. A retired soccer star living ir my neighborhood tried to help a street child. Over a long period of time he cultivated a friendship with the boy, providing him with food clothing, and advice. He liked the boy very much and eventually in- vited him to live with him and his wife. After a week, the boy rar away, taking with him his nice new clothing. Later the man saw the boy in the street, running as fast as he could while pushing a bicycle. presumably stolen. The man explained to me, with great anger, that the 12-year-old had become a simple *malandro*. "He used to earn money by watching over cars. Now you can't do anything for him."

Part of the fear many Brazilians have of street children is played out in the widespread view that street children have become imper- vious to the law. Brazilian law provides wider legal protection of chil- dren than does legislation in virtually any country in the world. The Children and Adolescents Act covers the gamut of children's rights: civil, economic, social, and educational, among others. The penal laws have been the object of great criticism by those taking a tough stance on crime. Statutory children, those aged 11 and under, cannot be charged with an offense, although they may be taken into temporary custody. The maximum sentence that can be imposed on an adolescent (anyone aged 12 to 17), even for murder or rape, is three years, and convictions are extremely cumbersome to obtain. Adolescents must be caught in the act, are entitled to a public defender, and have the right to face their accusers. In the context of a compulsively ineffective judicial system, convictions for serious crimes are exceptionally rare. Research by the Office for Legal Assistance to Popular Organizations, known as GAJOP, found that of a local sample of 555 criminal cases involving legal minors, 538 (97%) did not result in sentences (*Estado de São Paulo* 1995). In any case, those accused of the most severe crimes could simply slip over a wall at CAP before being sentenced. For girls, there is no secure facility in Pernambuco where they can be sent, even if convicted. At worst they are sentenced to the Casa de Santa Luzia, where, until 1995 – when it was reinforced slightly in the wake of the FEBEM rebellion – escaping was as easy as walking out the front door. All of this contributes to a perception of children as legal untouchables. Ironically, the perception of children as invulnerable before the law may contribute to their victimization, for the solution, as many have seen it, is to enforce punishment extrajudicially.

For the poor in Brazil accustomed to a model of childhood in which sons and daughters are expected to help their mothers, live at home, and stay on the right track (*ficar na vida boa*), the violence in which street children engage creates an ever wider rift between *maloqueiros* and their siblings and young neighbors who stay at home. For poor, working "home children," the frequently violent behavior of street children is but a confirmation of the latter's allegedly deviant nature. One night, as I was waiting around in anticipation of the beginning of the city council–sponsored census of street children in Recife, I struck up a conversation with a young boy who was working alongside his father, selling coconut water. "So you're going to count all the street children?" he asked me.

"Yes," I replied.

"That's good. Afterwards you can round them up and shoot them."

Nothing seems to drive the wedge deeper between street children and the two types of domestically based childhoods discussed in Chapter 3 than active, public violence. If one believes that childhood is a nurtured state relying, inter alia, on protection by adults, then the murder of homeless children by those expected to be their guardians is the ultimate violation of the rules of childhood. If, on the other hand, children are expected to nurture the household by bringing in hard-earned resources, then the exercise of violence by children likewise defiles notions of what childhood should be; violence acted out by children is a deviation from the right track, from what working children in the matrifocal families call *a vida boa*.

The Brazilian police and death squads have been responsible for murders of street children, but it may be worth asking whether the protests may now be aimed at what, in the greater scheme of things, are infrequent events. By the greater scheme of things, I refer to the fact that by the early 1990s, in North and Northeast Brazil murder was the third most common cause of death for all males aged 15 to 45, led only by "accidents and adverse effects" and "signs, symptoms and other ill-defined conditions" (WHO 1993). In 1992, the São Paulo police were murdering nearly five civilians per day (not counting the police massacre that year of 111 prisoners), up from less than one per day in 1983 (Brooke 1992). In late 1997, Brazil's national statistics unit reported that homicide was the leading cause of death nationwide among 15- to 17-year-olds, accounting for 25.3 percent of deaths in that age category, up from 7.8 percent in 1980 (IBGE, 1997b; *New York Times*, 1997). Brazil is being torn apart by the violence of, virtually, a low-grade civil war, though the violence is manifest in a disorganized, decentralized fashion. Meanwhile, the police are torturing street children, as well as poor detainees in general, systematically and with impunity. And the consequences are devastating.

When I Die, No One Will Cry

Many street children exhibit a haunting pessimism about their own chances of survival. Two kids in FEBEM discussed violence in the street. The one answering the questions, Picolé, spoke in a high, prepubescent staccato, and while listening to the exchange I could not help but wonder if he expected to live long enough to hear his voice change.

Valber: What are you in for?

Picolé: I was sniffing glue. I went to snatch a lady's purse. The woman grabbed me and since I was high I couldn't run.

Valber: [speaking in a patronizing tone, perhaps imitating the social workers at FEBEM] Why do you do those things?

Picolé: Because life is like that.

Valber: When you get out, are you gonna do more of the same?

Picolé: Yeah.

Valber: Won't you regret it later?

Picolé: Shit, by the time I start regretting it, my feet'll be tied together and I'll be floating face down in the river.

I ask a boy, about 14, "What do you feel when a *colega de rua* [street peer] dies?" Without a pause, he replies, "Nothing. I don't feel anything. When I die, no one will cry."

Violence against and by street children is a part of the fabric of life in which these victims and perpetrators dangerously live, so much so that they interweave their fanciful dreams of someday settling down and having a couple of children with the more frank admission that they have little expectation of growing up to be adults. Violence is an aspect of identity as tragically indelible as the scars that crisscross their bodies.

When considering violence against children, what is not said is probably as significant as what is said. In contrast to the constellation of media, advocacy, and governmental attention to the death-squad murders of street children, a stunning silence accompanies the agonizing and far more widespread death among children in Brazil that is hunger. UNICEF statistics (1995: 66) indicate that 226,000 Brazilian children under the age of five died in 1993.[8] Most of these deaths can be attributed to hunger combined with disease. This mundane violence of everyday life, to borrow a phrase from Nancy Scheper-Hughes (1992) goes largely unnoticed, ignored by all except those who must endure it and all those who must watch their children slowly starve. In the 1950s, hunger was aptly described by the Brazilian geographer Josué de Castro (1977 [1952]) as a taboo, and little seems to have changed.

Whereas 122 murders of children under the age of 17 were officially recorded in the state of Pernambuco in 1994 (Governo do Estado de Pernambuco 1995), 14,160 infants aged under one died in 1987 (IBGE 1989). In other words, 116 times more infants died, mostly of malnutrition and opportunistic diseases. Journalists, activists, and observers make a rigid distinction between the active, public suffering inflicted by bullets and knives and the quiet, private death that is hunger and disease. The murders of street children occur in the public domain, in streets or open fields, garbage dumps or forests. Rather than wasting away slowly, the bodies of street children are mutilated with bullets, knives, and cudgels, rendering them prized specimens for a global obsession with child victimhood.

The Double Ethic of Rebellion and Remorse

While street children reject the drudgery of obedience expected of "home children," their own initiative also launches them into a path of self-destruction with little chance of escape. Philippe Bourgois (1995: 9) has aptly portrayed just such a contradiction in his ethnography of crack dealers in East Harlem: "[T]he street culture of resistance is predicated on the destruction of its participants and the community harboring them." While crack dealers seek an alternative to the lot of the legally waged inner-city poor who toil at inadequately paying, demeaning, working-class jobs, they also lead lives of self-destructive violence, drug addiction, and rage. Something similar can be said of street children.

Perpetrating violence and escaping the oppression suffered by nurturing children (see Chapter 3) can be interpreted by intellectuals as an act of resistance and by children themselves as the somewhat different but allied concept of *revolta*. But in the minds of street children, the use of violence carries dire consequences; in the end the tables are likely to be turned and one is apt to become a victim. Recall Camilla's words, "No one dies for no reason."

Street life is marked by a double ethic of rebellion and remorse. On the one hand, street children tend to be haughty and defiant: they are dismissive of those who seek to instill discipline in them; they perpetrate violence; they reject schools and other aspects of home life; and they defy the rules of spatial segregation that dictate where poor

"Girl without a Name," by Fernando Araújo.

children should and should not be. But they are also torn by a moral conflict over who they are and what they do. Their violence is projected not only outward but inward.

In his narrative, presented in Chapter 1, Edivaldo speaks of how he went to rob an old lady in the street. He grabbed her bag and ran away but, upon hearing her cry, decided to return the money. A number of street children told me stories like this, and I interpret them as indications that the children often feel deeply remorseful over what they do. Margarete speaks of how she steals, exchanges sex for lodging, and runs away from institutions, but in the same breath she speaks of her rebellious behavior at a shelter and her lack of self-worth: "I would beat up the girls, yell at the director, acting like I was bigger than everyone. But I am nothing."

Despite their tendency to blame themselves for the violence they suffer, street children also often say "We are sufferers" (*A gente é muito sofredô*). And it would be misleading to suggest that they believe their suffering is simply a merited consequence of their immersion in *that life*. Although street children frequently portray the violence against them as punishment, almost an affirmation of the bad things they say they do, their lot as sufferers is also seen as testament to the injustices of the world in which they live. The Menina Sem Nome, or Girl without a Name, was a young child who was raped and murdered on a Recife beach. No one claimed her body but the poor are said to have given her a proper burial. Venerating her as a popular saint, street children and others visit the tomb to leave votive offerings and make wishes. The suffering of the Girl without a Name doubtless resonates with street children's outrage at their own condition, at the ruthlessness of the violence they endure and at the prospect of being left to die anonymously and unclaimed in streets that are both their home and their worst enemy.

6

CURING STREET CHILDREN,
RESCUING CHILDHOOD

Regardless of the true number of homeless children in Brazil, that conundrum touched on in Chapter 4, one thing is certain: the number of programs for street children has burgeoned throughout the country. In Rio, for instance, one study counted 39 institutions that catered exclusively to street children (Valladares and Impelizieri 1991: 9). This survey noted that all of these programs had been created around or after the mid-1980s and that their numbers changed rapidly: in the course of the five months it took to complete the study, four new programs were created. Likewise, a gamut of projects has emerged in Recife, with government, civil, and religious organizations all vying for a role. In contrast to the impression given in many reports about "millions" of abandoned children beyond the reach of adult intervention, the relatively small number of children living in the streets of Recife typically have contact with adults from a variety of institutions. Most of the city's street children have been to at least one live-in program (Recife had four in 1992 and six by 1995). Of 26 children who lived in the street at the time of my interviews, 19 had lived in at least one shelter. Nearly all street children have been approached by a variety of outreach workers in the street, some over a period of many years.

Table 5 contains information about the number of adult personnel in the organizations working with street children. Because the universe of programs is quite fluid, I have chosen the period from mid-1992 to mid-1993. It should be noted that the groups not working exclusively, or at least predominantly with children living in the street have been omitted, as have a number of semifunctioning groups such as the Comunidade do Povo sem Casa (Community of the Homeless,

Table 5. *Adults in Recife and Olinda in Mid-1992 to Mid-1993
Working with Street Children, by Organization*

Organization	Approximate number employed or full-time volunteers	Comments
CAMM; Centro de Apoio ao Menore à Mulher (Support Center for Minors and Women, known as Admilson and Roberta's farm)	3	Approximate count (CAMM has about 7 employees but also works with non–street children.
Casa de Passagem (House of Passage)	20	
Capim de Cheiro (Capim de Cheiro Farm)	3	Many more people are involved, but 3 people dedicate most of their time to the project.
Centro de Formação (Training Center)	5	
Prefeitura, Recife (Recife Municipal Government)	10	This number was set to at least double, in late 1993, with the hiring of street educators and personnel for group homes.
Comunidade dos Pequenos Profetas (Community of Little Prophets)	7	
Desafio Jovem (Young Challenge)	6	Many more people are involved, but the equivalent of at least 6 full-time people work with the street kids.
FUNDAC	200	This includes 150 interns. The additional 50 is a conservative count of the administrators, supervisors, educators, drivers, guards, messengers, medical personnel

Table 5 *(cont.)*

Organization	Approximate number employed or full-time volunteers	Comments
		and others who work with street girls at the Projeto Renascer and with street boys at a facility in Abreu e Lima. This figure excludes the vast number of people working at CAP and other branches of FUNDAC.
Oficina de Papel (The Paper Workshop)	7	
A Granja do Padre Ramiro (Padre Ramiro's farm)	8	
Pequenos Educadores (Little Educators)	5	
Ruas e Praças (Streets and Squares)	13	
Sobe e Desce (Going Up and Down)	10	
SOS Criança (SOS Children)	1	Takes into account only the staff member who works specifically with street children.
Total	298	

comprising 10 volunteers) and the Associação pela Restauração do Homem (Association for the Restoration of Man, which was established only as I was leaving Brazil in 1993). Those individuals whose particular tasks do not relate primarily to street children have been excluded, as have whole categories of people who work with street children on a daily basis, such as the personnel at CAP and the judges at the Children's and Adolescents' Court because their official mandate is not to work specifically with street children but rather with children in general. I have also excluded the militants at the National Movement of Street Children, since their work relates most directly to poor children in general; the same with the personnel at the human rights organization CENDHEC. Personnel at other institutions like the field offices of UNICEF and Save the Children have been omitted because, even though they fund projects for street children, the scope of their work is relatively wide and street kids are only one part of it. For the same reason, members of the municipal councils on children and adolescents in Recife and Olinda (created as a result of the 1990 Children and Adolescents Act) have been left out. In short, the count is extremely conservative. It should be pointed out that, for one reason or another, on an average day a great many of these people are not actually working. For instance, of the 150 interns at FUNDAC in 1993, I doubt more than 20 actually went out to the street on a typical day.

The number of people working with street children in Recife comes to at least 298, 64 more than the combined number of kids found sleeping in the streets of Recife and Olinda (see Chapter 4).[1] I recall more than one occasion when I went out with street educators and we had difficulty finding any street children at all. On other occasions, like the one described in the first pages of this book, street educators from various groups would be competing for the children's attention. At the Praça Maciel Pinheiro in downtown Recife, it was not unusual for the children to be accompanied by street educators from FUNDAC in the morning, Ruas e Praças in the afternoon, and Pequenos Educadores in the evening. On the other hand, children in certain other parts of the city, far from the center, rarely if ever had contact with street educators.

All of the groups and programs (with the exception of the CAP detention center) are relatively new, having been founded in the mid-1980s or even the 1990s. And there is a rapid turnover. Three institutions, the Oficina de Papel, Restauração do Homem, and the city government project, came into existence only during my first 18-month stay in Brazil. In the two years I was away from Recife, between mid-1993 and mid-1995, a number of NGOs had closed while others

Lunchtime at a live-in shelter.

had been formed, and the state and city programs had been restructured.

The conditions in which most NGOs work are difficult. The salaries for street educators are low, generally in the range of US$50 to $150 per month in 1992 and 1993. Some even work for less than a minimum wage (in the range of US$50 to $90 per month at the time, depending on the exchange rate). Conditions are precarious enough for street educators in some groups to experience hunger in the middle of the day because they cannot afford to buy lunch. "I'm starving" (*a fome é demais*), I heard mumbled at different times. One of the street educators in Olinda at Sobe e Desce suffered painful headaches because she needed glasses, but the glasses cost the equivalent of what she earned in three months. A few of the groups work at a grueling pace. At Ruas e Praças the educators speak of themselves as *militantes* (militants) rather than *empregados* (functionaries, or employees) and some worked as many as 60 hours per week in 1992 and 1993.

The NGOs are mostly funded by charities and foundations abroad, with small supplemental grants from state or municipal sources. Before 1994 when Brazil adopted its new currency, the real, dollars went a long way. But after the middle of 1994, the situation for foreign funding changed dramatically. The comparatively high price of the real meant that U.S. and European currencies no longer had ample purchasing power in Brazil and most NGOs came under great pressure. In addition, funding from abroad tends to be short-term, and the end of a single grant can spell the end of an organization. In 1995, the Training Center (Centro de Formação) was faced with the prospect of closing when its principal grant expired.

Although most government functionaries earn menial wages, the state of Pernambuco manages to spend vast sums of money in the name of street children. During 1995, a study sponsored by the state of Pernambuco counted 356 children in the streets, both working and sleeping (Cruzada de Ação Social 1995). Although I believe that for once they vastly underestimated the true number (for surely there are many more children who work and beg in the streets), all government agencies seemed to be basing their work on the premise of there being fewer than 400 homeless and working children in the street. Following the July 1995 rebellion at CAP that destroyed the detention center, a government spokesman declared that the funding for street children would be increased to 1 million reals per month (Lucena and Andrea 1995: 1). If true, this works out to about US$2,800 for each of the 400 children the city was then saying worked and lived in the streets.

Reclamation, Salvation, and Citizenship

The Cruzada de Ação Social (Crusade for Social Action) is a philanthropic government institution run by Pernambuco's first lady (the governor's wife) that supplies prescription lenses, artificial limbs, and other emergency assistance. In 1995, the Crusade had plans to distribute free bumper stickers that read "The street is no place for children" (*A rua não é lugar para crianças*). As heterogeneous as the various religious, nongovernmental, and state organizations are in their philosophies and modus operandi, they all seem to be guided by the idea distilled in the Cruzada's slogan. Although few other agencies engage in such wishful thinking as to believe that bumper stickers will deter mostly illiterate children from frequenting the public spaces of the city, all groups working with street children in Recife aim in one way or another to distance children from the streets. The belief that children are antithetical to streets seems to hark back to ideas deeply entrenched in Brazilian social history about the opposing realms of street and home.

Taken together, the home and the street have functioned as something of a prism through which to view Brazilian society.[2] The home, in its almost symbiotic form of the *casa grande* (the big house) and *senzala* (slave quarters), was the locus of Brazilian society during the colonial era. Thus in *Casa Grande e Senzala*, Gilberto Freyre, Brazil's celebrated social historian, places the home at the center of his arguments about economy, politics, race, and other aspects of Brazilian society.

The big house and the slave quarters coupled with the *engenho* (the old-fashioned sugar mill) or the *fazenda* (plantation or ranch) became formidable economic and social institutions. Historians and sociologists have often highlighted the far-reaching autonomy of this form of home in colonial Brazil (e.g., Wagley 1971 [1963]: 31). Until the twentieth century, Brazil was an overwhelmingly rural society. In this respect it was similar to the rest of Latin America, indeed to most of the world. Yet in Brazil the locus of political and economic power was entrenched in the rural house, not in the urban center (Smith 1954: 527). It is thus not surprising that Freyre found in the house certain keys to understanding the evolution of Brazilian identity. The *casa grande* and the *senzala* are constituted by two social categories, respectively, the masters and the slaves. But within the *casa grande* there existed a hierarchy not only of white over black, but of husband over wife, and of father over son. Fathers exercised near total domination over children. "In patriarchal Brazil, the authority of the father over a minor son – and even one who was of age – was carried to its logical conclusion: the right to kill" (1968 [1936]b: 59).

With the decline of slavery came the decline of the *casa grande*. The *casa grande* was replaced by urban and suburban mansions, and the *senzalas* by shanties. Thus Freyre's sequel to *Masters and Slaves* is entitled *The Mansions and the Shanties*, or *Sobrados e Mocambos*. This shift brought the then waning patriarchal family into close proximity with the street. Freyre portrays the relationship between the street and the home as an uneasy one. "Brazilian patriarchalism, when it moved from the plantation to the town house, did not at once come to terms with the street; for a long time they were almost enemies, the house and the street" (30). The paterfamilias had to struggle to keep the females and children of the household out of reach of the street. The attempt to separate the house from the street, Freyre (1968 [1936]a) argues, can be seen in the very architecture of the urban mansion.

> The Big House in Brazil may be said to have become a type of domestic architecture designed for an almost Freudian purpose: to safeguard women and valuables. The women behind grilles, lattices, screens, shutters, or, at most, allowed into the backyard or inner court or garden . . . the jewelry and money, hidden underground or in the thick walls. (109)

The streets, Freyre observes, were not public in the sense of public for all. They were a space for men and had a polluting effect on women and children. Parks, promenades, and squares, he writes,

> were for the use and enjoyment of the man of a certain social position, but only for the man. . . . The boy who went out to fly his kite or spin his top in the street was looked upon as a vagabond. A lady who went into the street to shop ran the risk of being taken for a street walker. (xxvii)

Like the children who suggest that the street exerts an addictive transformative power over their lives, as discussed in Chapter 4, adult Brazilians likewise point to the morally contaminating effects of the street. Parents will complain, "We teach our children one thing at home and they learn another in the street." Although the middle class may give scant thought to what it is like to live in a hot, cramped *favela* shack, it is taken for granted that the street is the worst place for children to be. In 1995, the Cruzada de Ação Social was even bent on clearing the streets of working children. An advisor to the governor's wife assured me that they planned to pay a minimum wage to the families of working children so that the mothers would place their children in school, this notwithstanding the fact that when actually functioning the schools are in session only four hours each weekday, or during about just 18 percent of a child's waking hours in a typical week. In any case, the prevailing minimum monthly wage of about US$115 would leave the family still mired in abject poverty and with little incentive to stop sending the children out to work and beg in the streets.

Three main components of institutional help for street children in Recife and Olinda can be identified. The first is what the groups call *abordagem*, that initial contact in the street when the *educadores* first approach the children. Typically they might offer pens and paper with which to draw, a game to play, or another activity such as sewing. In addition, the *educadores* ask how the children are faring in the street and offer advice on a wide range of subjects, such as health or family problems, and discuss possibilities for leaving the street. Simple exercises in reading and writing are also undertaken. A second type of work with street children involves vocational training undertaken away from the street in a permanent facility and typically in one of the following activities: silk-screening, carpentry, sewing, broom making, and typing. The third element of assistance takes the form of shelters where children are offered a place to live. Generally these are located in rural areas.

In all its forms, work with street children, I would argue, is shaped by moral judgments of how childhood ought to be. If childhood in Northeast Brazil can be represented by two ideal types – the nurtured child and the nurturing child, as I have suggested in Chapter 3 – it would seem that programs for street children aim to make their beneficiaries more akin to one of these two ideal types. The international NGOs seem to favor a refashioning of street children in the model of protected, rich childhood; the local organizations in Recife tend to work in different ways to shepherd the kids back into the more familiar model of poor childhood. This section examines the different motifs employed by agencies working to help street children leave the street. As will be evident, there is both contradiction and overlap among these motifs, and most agencies appeal to more than one simultaneously.

Reclamation: Making Little Workers, Remaking the Family

Padre Ramiro, a Spanish priest who has worked with poor children in and around Recife for many years, has two farms where street boys live. There were about eight on each farm when I visited in April

1993. One farm is next to a highway, just outside Jaboatão and about 30 kilometers from Recife; the other is situated, intentionally, in a remote location because some of the boys there have been *jurados*, that is, issued a death sentence, by enemies of one sort or another.

Padre Ramiro, a self-styled liberation theologian, described his philosophy of working with kids as a "therapy of sweat." The boys, indeed, are made to sweat. They work long hours under the hot sun, tilling the soil, planting, and harvesting. They tend the goats which Padre Ramiro has imported from Europe and which he argues could solve the problem of malnutrition in the Northeast if only people would overcome their prejudice against goat's milk. The children arrive through FEBEM under the orders of a judge. Padre Ramiro asks them whether they want to stay and work hard. Most of them, he explained, head straight for the road back to Recife, but some, of course, stay.

On one visit, Padre Ramiro handed me a book.[3] He said that the three engravings it contained summed up the objectives of his work with children. On the cover, a bony, barefoot boy with threadbare clothing and untamed hair saunters down the street, eating a piece of fruit and carrying a bucket of food, probably culled from rubbish bins. A dog attempts to remove scraps from the bucket. "This is the street child," Padre Ramiro said. Print number two shows two children, a dog, and a grown woman in a narrow path between shacks. "This is the neighborhood of the street child where he must return." The final print shows a young man, thin and angular but kempt, carrying a small case. Like the boy on the front cover, he is barefoot. "This is what we return to society," Padre Ramiro told me, "a working child."

Padre Ramiro speaks of his goal: *recuperar as crianças*, to recover or reclaim the children. He says his approach is based on the philosophy of sweat – that is, teaching the kids to toil under the hot sun. "The street children must *mudar de vida*" – literally, "change lives," in the sense that one might change clothing. Padre Ramiro's approach is one of remaking street children, molding them into a form closer to the ideal of working children in the urban Northeast. They are encouraged to live in houses, not in the street, and not to use drugs or engage in crime. Teaching them to work – on the farm, clearing fields, planting, harvesting, taking care of the father's imported goats – is seen as a means of providing them with the psychological and moral wherewithal to find jobs similar to those held by other poor people.

Padre Ramiro seeks to effect a transformation through work similar to what one might experience in a religious conversion. Although Padre Ramiro is a Catholic priest, I did not observe him speaking to the street children about God. Rather, he spoke about goats, hoes, and cheese. Although he runs sessions for the mothers of working children in which passages from the Bible are studied and compared to day-to-day events, his office contains no religious images and one member of his staff is even a Pentecostal Christian. Padre Ramiro sees work as both a means to *mudar de vida*, change lives, and an end in itself. In his approach to street children, work seems to take the place of religion.

Teaching street children to work is one aim of nearly every agency in Recife. All, with the exception of Demétrio's Comunidade dos Pequenos Profetas (Community of Little Prophets, discussed later), offer some vocational training. The Casa de Passagem, which works only with girls and young women, has two centers in the city, the Casa I and the Casa II. The first, which serves as the headquarters, is a drop-in center where street girls can wash their clothes and get a meal and where counseling and educational activities are undertaken, while the second house offers vocational courses. In 1992 and 1993, these courses consisted mostly of the socially defined "female" activities of sewing, typing, and cooking.

Centers as diverse as the Escola dos Jovens Trabalhadores (School of Young Workers), which prides itself on its radical view of social transformation, and the far more traditionally oriented, government-run FUNDAC offer almost identical vocational courses – silk-screening, woodworking, printing, and the like – even though their explicit philosophies are radically different. Work is the widely agreed-upon medium for reinserting street children into "society," and work inevitably means the low-prestige, low-wage toil that is the lot of Brazil's "structured" underclass – precisely the types of employment that "successful" nurturing children in the *favelas* might look forward to having.

Reclamation can take place in ways other than through work. When I first met Demétrio, the founder and leader of the Comunidade dos

Pequenos Profetas, he told me that some of the kids who lived with him had taken to calling him *Pai*, or Dad. "At first I resisted this," he told me. "Then I realized that it satisfied a need in the children and I accepted it." Demétrio calls his group a community, and the community simulates in many ways, implicitly and explicitly, a family. His farm is a family setting in the sense that everyone eats together, and the main building was originally a house, to which some additions have been built. Demétrio pays for the children to attend private school and he even chides them to clean up their rooms.

Demétrio describes his methodology as "body to body" (*corpo a corpo*). "We work the self [*o ser*] first. We're not interested, initially, in imparting vocational training. First you must work on the child, reconstruct the universe that the child lost. . . . [You can't forget] that the child has the right to be a child." Demétrio seems to imply that being a child is something unattainable in the street. I do not believe it would be reading too much into his words to suggest that "the universe that the [street] child lost" is childhood itself. The idea, in other words, is to restore to children a childhood they allegedly lacked in the street.

The notion that people who have spent their early years on the street have been deprived of childhood itself is quite common among NGOs. At the first meeting I attended at the National Movement of Street Children in Recife I found it difficult to distinguish between some of the *meninos* (boys) and the *educadores* (adult street educators), for there was little difference in terms of physical size, apparent age, and even style of dress. Because they grew up in the street, street youths are said to have never had a childhood. One of the ironies of work with street children under the Children and Adolescents Act is that only a small minority of street "children" are statutory children, that is, under the age of 12, and a large portion are actually statutory adults, 18 or older.

Integrating street children into the family situates them in a present where childhood is synonymous with domesticity and offers them a future by rescuing them from street life. It is no accident that Demétrio's farm is located well outside Recife, far from the city and far from the street. As one impressed American observer remarked to me, "You can't do anything for street kids in the street. You have to get them out of the city."

The rural setting and the "family" ambience were staple ingredients in work with what were once called "dependent children" in the United States. Ashby (1984: 3) describes the Allendale farm for boys, founded in 1895 in Illinois, as being "predicated on the belief that placing a city waif in a rural environment, and raising him in a setting that contained a sense of family and community, would make it possible to 'recreate this boy.' "

While collectively Brazil's street children are widely seen as dangerous, individually they are widely seen as needing care and attention. Charles Loring Brace, the founder of the New York Children's Aid Society, warned of the dangers of street urchins in America acting collectively and threatening the public. "Herding together," Boyer (1978: 96) quotes him as saying, they "form an unconscious society." One of Brace's solutions was to ship street urchins from the industrial cities of the East to towns in the West where they lived with local residents who took them in in exchange for their labor.

In the context of Brazil, recreating society within the family and in the rural milieu recalls the theme of the *Casa Grande*, where cities were relatively unimportant and the family-run plantation was the locus of society.

In Chapter 3, I discuss "child shifting," or what in Portuguese has been referred to as *crianças em circulação*. For Fonseca (1989), this is the phenomenon of children spending their formative years away from their progenitors. The attempt on the part of Demétrio, the leader of the Comunidade dos Pequenos Profetas, to legally adopt some 25 street children is a quite literal attempt at shifting the children to his care. But elsewhere the attempt is more symbolic.

The Brazilian state at national and local levels has seen to it that street children are included in the family, if only an imaginary one. When Recife was gearing up for its mayoral elections in August and September 1992, none of the candidates could afford not to talk about street children and the need to help them. When powerful men are elected to office, they typically give their wives the task of caring for the poor and for street children. For example, when Fernando Collor de Mello was elected president in 1990, his wife Rosane was named head of the Legião Brasileira de Assistência (The Brazilian Assistance Legion). At age 26 and with no prior experience in administration, the first lady assumed control of an institution of 9,400 employees and an annual budget of US$1 billion.[4] In Recife, the wife of the mayor traditionally runs the Lar de Assistência de Recife (Home for Assistance of Recife), technically an NGO but, to all intents and purposes, a municipal agency located in the very headquarters of the city government. The acronym of this group, LAR, means home, or hearth. Similarly, it is the governor's wife who runs the Cruzada de Ação Social (Crusade for Social Action) and it is no surprise that the first lady, Magdalena Arraes, whose husband was elected governor for the third time in 1994, took a keen interest in street children. In the city of João Pessoa in the neighboring state of Paraíba, street children were a vital part of Lúcia Braga's campaign for mayor in 1992 and of her image as matriarch. Campaign footage was shot at the República dos Meninos e Meninas de Rua de João Pessoa (The Republic of Street Children of João Pessoa), featuring the would-be mayor among her young charges.

As Roberto DaMatta has observed, in Brazil "Everything outside the home is 'the government's problem' " (1991 [1985]: 23). Accordingly, street children are frequently portrayed as a problem for the government, and seemingly dispossessed children are shifted to the personalized, "protective," patriarchal care of the state. At the same time, First World advocates for street children urge their audience to think of street children as their own, for doing so ushers them into a familiar notion of childhood and situates grownups as protectors. As Patricia Holland (1992: 148) has observed, the image of the vulnerable child has the effect of confirming adult power.

Salvation

Consider the names of some of the projects and institutions that cater to street children: Childhope, Comunidade dos Pequenos Profetas (Community of Little Prophets), Restauração do Homem (Restoration of Man), Casa de Passagem (The House of Passage), Projeto Renascer (Project Rebirth), Retome Sua Vida (Reclaim Your Life), and Semente de Amanhã (Seed of Tomorrow). The motifs of hope, restoration, passage, and rebirth are all components of a theme encapsulated in the name of the British charity – Save the Children. And where salvation is not suggested in any part of the institution's name, it is often an aspect of its public image and implicit in the institutional philosophy.

Salvation is a theme with great appeal to journalists. Take, for instance, the opening paragraph of an article about the Casa de Passagem written by the British journalist Anthony Swift (1991b) and published in *Oxfam News*:

> When Ana Vasconcelos talked with young girls living on the streets of Recife, Brazil, a group told her they were going to hell. When she asked why, they replied: "This is the passage to hell." She asked if they would like to make a place from which they might go to heaven. She said: "Let's construct our own internal feeling which allows us to go to heaven instead of hell." They wanted to try. (10)

Among agencies in Recife, there is talk of offering street children *uma vida nova*, or a new life. The Pentecostal organization Desafio Jovem (Young Challenge) speaks of offering a new life through Jesus. "Vices" such as sniffing glue, sleeping in the street, and stealing, which when grouped together constitute *essa vida* (that life), are blamed on temptation by the devil, sometimes even hundreds of devils, and labeled as sin. The discipline at Desafio Jovem, where activities such as religious study, literacy classes, and agricultural work are rigidly programmed and where leaders aim to reshape the moral character of those in their care, recalls the children's Houses of Refuge of the first half of the nineteenth century in the United States.

> In 1839 a writer described them as designed for poor, idle, and "vagabond" children, even though they "may not have been convicted of any specific crimes." In 1851 the Boston Children's Friend Society urged the confinement of any child whose family situation might "tend" to make him an eventual social problem. (Boyer 1978: 95–96)

Desafio Jovem brings together everyone from men just released from jail to eight-year-old boys literally abandoned and living in the street. While the sleeping quarters are separated into three age groups – young children, adolescents, and men – the previous lives of all those at Desafio Jovem seem to be tarred with the same brush. The group's efforts at rescuing are dependent on portraying the past lives of their charges as vice-ridden. The rebirth involves not only Bible study, prayer, and the acceptance of discipline, but also the exchange of the *vida errada*, or iniquitous life, for the *vida boa*, the righteous life. One symbol of this transformation at Desafio Jovem is a change in the very names of the children. Street children are usually known to one another by nicknames. But those who join Desafio Jovem are called only by their legal names. The nickname is seen as a tainted vestige of street life to be left behind before the child commences a "new life."

The agencies most adept at cultivating a notion of salvation attractive to foreign donors are those whose very institutional identity is enmeshed in the personal identity of the leader. Under the direction of Ana Vasconcelos, the Casa de Passagem launched a masterful public relations campaign that made the tiny NGO known widely in Brazil, the United States, and western Europe. In Britain, the NGOs Womankind International and Childhope promoted the Casa de Passagem. In 1991, when articles appeared in the press about violence against street children, these two NGOs wrote letters to editors, both thanking the publications for bringing attention to the injustice and introducing readers to the Casa de Passagem. One letter published in the *Independent* read as follows:

> Zoe Heller rightly draws attention (5 May) to the horrific murder of street children in Brazil. Violence on this scale, perpetrated against the most vulnerable members of society, is indeed shocking and your readers may well wonder what, if anything, can be done to protect these young people.
>
> A human rights lawyer in Recife, Ana Vasconcelos, has attempted to address that question by setting up a safe house for street girls. It is known as the Passage House. . . .
>
> We hope that your readers will be encouraged to know that, against all odds, someone has had the courage to take a stand against the death squads which are slaughtering Brazil's children. (Young and Fenton 1991)

The letter pits the anonymous mayhem of street life against the personal warmth and commitment of the institution's leader. With the exception of Padre Ramiro's organization and the Pentecostal Desafio Jovem, none of the groups discussed here is explicitly religious. But curiously, the strongest hints of salvation seem to come from some of the secular organizations.

The themes of salvation, work, and family mirror approaches to the poor in Britain during the Industrial Revolution. With the poor masses flocking to the cities, those with something to lose sought ways to make the destitute safe. The secular response was to encourage economic individualism. The religious response was salvation of the sinning poor. There seems to be a natural affinity between the notion of recreating the family and that of saving children. The two motifs are complementary. The reports that marked the beginning of a surge of interest in street children within UNICEF contained in their titles the invented word "MyChild." In the preface to one of these, the author writes,

> This second report, which seeks above all to be the voice of some 25 million street children in Brazil, is dedicated with great love and respect to a son named Luis Carlos whom I knew for only an hour in Porto Alegre as he searched for his father, and to all my sons and daughters on Brazilian streets called "garoto" [boy]. May all who call them their children too and who seek to give them new lives achieve together what no one of us can possibly do alone. May we learn from the anguish of the garotos, and may we bring them joy. Our world needs all of them very much. (Taçon 1981a)

Here the author seems to suggest that street children are looking for parents and that it takes only a warm heart to become one. And being a "parent" of street children gives extraordinary power. The author suggests that it enables one to give children "new lives" and to be their voice – the voice of "25 million" of them.

It is the alleged powerlessness of destitute children in the Third World that tugs at the emotional purse strings of the middle classes in the First World. As Patricia Holland writes,

> Children living in poverty, children suffering from neglect or disadvantage, children who are the victims of wars or natural disasters – they figure in imagery as the most vulnerable, the most pathetic, the most deserving of all of our sympathy and aid. They are on the receiving end of an oppression in which

they can only acquiesce. Children are seen as archetypal victims; childhood is seen as weakness itself. As the children . . . reveal their vulnerability, we long to protect them and provide for their needs. Paradoxically, while we are moved by the image of a sorrowful child, we also welcome it, for it can arouse pleasurable emotions of tenderness, which in themselves confirm adult power. (1992: 148)

Salvation is based on the notion that street children exist in a sort of hell or, at best, purgatory on earth. To be rescued from this state, street children must be reinserted into a recognizable form of childhood. Different actors among the universe of advocates for street children portray this return to childhood in different ways. Sometimes it is the chance to play, enjoy life, and be protected like "regular kids" in the industrial world. At other times, the effort is to make street children more like the ideal of the poor, working child – for example, through Padre Ramiro's program. But leaders of institutions that metaphorically save children rather than simply reclaim them are often credited with the greatest power.

Another way of saving street children is far more materialistic. It consists in offering street children an alternative to the street so cushy they would be hard pressed not to accept. Campinas is a small city about 100 kilometers from São Paulo. At first glance, one could easily imagine this to be a modern European town. It is clean and organized, and its shopping centers offer the city's mostly middle-class residents a wide array of conveniences. The roads, paved and well maintained, are busy with family cars and modern buses. It is hard to imagine that Recife and Campinas are cities in the same country. But just below the surface, Campinas shares some of the same problems as Recife. I was shown around by two street educators, university students who first worked on their own with street children as part of their studies in education and later joined a Catholic priest from the United States.

The priest ran a farm where about 20 street children lived. At the time of my visit, he accepted only boys, though he had plans to build another house for girls. The shelter occupied the picturesque grounds of a former plantation. The administration building was located in

Two boys and an anthropologist playing tic-tac-toe in Campinas. Photo by Isabel Balseiro.

what was once a stately mansion, which today could double as an upscale country inn. The kids were playing outside their house when I arrived. In fact, they seemed to play most of the day. Previously the children had had a teacher, but this arrangement did not work out. So at the time of my visit, the only interruptions to their games were two prayer sessions and three meals (the latter prepared for them by professional cooks). The kids tended some animals – rabbits and a horse, among others. Otherwise they had no responsibilities. At night they slept in their own bunk beds under freshly laundered sheets and blankets. One of the former street kids liked it so much that he invited his two little brothers back in the *favela* to move in too. After visiting the site where the house for the street girls was to be built, I asked one of the street educators how many girls were sleeping in the street. She told me that at that time there were none. As shelters go, this was a five-star hotel, ready to scoop up street girls who did not yet exist. The idea seemed to be to give street children (real and imagined) the closest institutional equivalent of a First World childhood.

Citizenship

The tactics described previously focus on transforming street children. The National Movement of Street Children, in contrast, speaks of

changing Brazilian society. It refers to children as agents involved in
the forging of their own histories.

> The MNMMR was founded on the belief that children and ad-
> olescents are agents with the potential to effect change, actors in
> the creation of their own history. In the struggle for a society
> that is more just, fraternal, and egalitarian, the Movement does
> not think for or work in place of children. Rather, the Movement
> carries out its work at all times *with* the children and adolescents,
> the latter being agents in the construction of the Movement.[5]
> (MNMMR-PE 1992: 30)

It would be difficult to overstate the extent to which the National
Movement of Street Children and so many other NGOs in Brazil have
been influenced by Paulo Freire's theories on critical consciousness as
a liberating process. A native son of Recife, though widely revered
throughout Latin America, Freire argued in *The Pedagogy of the Oppressed*
(1972 [1970]) that

> the great humanistic and historical task of the oppressed [is to]
> liberate themselves and their oppressors as well. The oppressors,
> who oppress, exploit, and rape by virtue of their power, cannot
> find in this power the strength to liberate either the oppressed
> or themselves. Only power that springs from the weakness of the
> oppressed will be sufficiently strong to free both. Any attempt
> to "soften" the power of the oppressor in deference to the weak-
> ness of the oppressed almost always manifests itself in the form
> of false generosity. (28–29)

Citizenship is seen by many groups as part of what Freire speaks of
as the liberation of the poor that emerges not from false generosity
but through the combination of critical consciousness and action.
Freire writes,

> Reality which becomes oppressive results in the contradistinction
> of men as oppressors and oppressed. The latter, whose task it is
> to struggle for their liberation together with those who show
> true solidarity, must acquire a critical awareness of oppression

through the praxis of this struggle. One of the gravest obstacles to the achievement of liberation is that oppressive reality absorbs those within it and thereby acts to submerge men's consciousness. Functionally, oppression is domesticating. To no longer be prey to its force, one must emerge from it and turn upon it. This can be done only by means of the praxis: reflection and action upon the world in order to transform it. (36)

Citizenship is the flip side of the now much maligned concept of *assistencialismo. Assistencialismo* is difficult to translate directly into English but it refers to paternalistic handouts of immediate utility, such as used clothing that, although important in themselves, do nothing to resolve long-term structural inequalities. *Assistencialismo* is, in short, the false generosity spoken of by Freire, and whereas it reinforces hierarchies rooted in dependence and condescending largesse, citizenship appeals to an ideal of equality.

The National Movement of Street Children speaks of the *organização*, or organization, of children as being one of its principal tasks. The movement is composed of *núcleos de base*, or base cells, of children who either participate in a similar profession, such as watching over cars, or, as is more common, live in or frequent the same neighborhood. Some of the núcleos have very little adult participation, such as one group called Força Jovem. In the Força Jovem meeting I attended, there were no "adults" present, except myself, but two leaders of the group were veterans of the movement, both aged 18, and most of the participants seemed to be in the age range of 16 to 19. Other núcleos meet in a more clearly adult-directed way. For instance, Ruas e Praças organizes monthly *encontros*, generally held over a weekend. In these meetings, the children participate in different events such as dance, theater, and discussion groups. Each meeting has a theme, such as *São João* (the June festivals), sexuality, or the Children and Adolescents Act. Representatives of the various base cells around Recife and Olinda meet on a weekly basis in the office of the movement to discuss what the cells have been doing and any general business.

An activist with the movement argued for the importance of impressing upon the kids both the social dimensions of their predicament and their individual rights as citizens.

> For a child in the *favela* it is a heroic act to leave home. In the *favela* there is no room to dream, there are no colors, everything is dark. In the street there are bright colors, the children can have fantasies and dreams. You need to take advantage of the potential of this act. When you ask the kids why they are in the street, they usually say it's because their family is so poor, because they are immigrants from the countryside, because their mothers hit them. But they don't see that there are no bourgeois kids in the street. They see leaving home as an individual act. They don't see that there are social factors involved.

The activist's words echo Freire's belief that so long as one internalizes the ideals of the oppressor, liberation is not possible. "Only in the encounter," Freire (1972 [1970]: 186) writes, "of the people with the revolutionary leaders – in their communion, in their praxis – can this theory be built."

Citizenship is a complicated notion in Brazil. As DaMatta (1991 [1985]) has pointed out, in most situations the idea of citizenship carries deeply negative connotations. DaMatta's argument is based on the premise that in Brazil laws are conceived of as being relational: "In Brazil, no one escapes from family ties or from certain links of friendship, in much the same way that in the United States it is impossible to escape from one's alma mater, from one's social security number, or from one's credit card" (99).

DaMatta observes that merely referring to someone by the term *cidadão*, or "citizen," nearly always borders on a slur. As a citizen, one loses the relational ties of family and friendship. One becomes anonymous. When confronted simply as citizens by the authorities in the anonymity of the street, Brazilians may ask, "Do you know who you are talking to?" In so doing, they hope that the relational laws will protect them since the universal ones almost never do: "In Brazil, the individual who is isolated and lacks relationship . . . is considered very negatively, revealing only the solitude of someone . . . who is a marginal human being in relation to others in the community" (84).

Historian Linda Lewin (1987) has argued persuasively that the extended family, *parentela*, has been pivotal in twentieth-century oligarchic politics both in the Northeast and nationally. The elaborate kinship networks of the elite, fortified through first-cousin marriages and intertwined economic enterprises, do not have a corollary among today's urban poor but, even so, street children do not want to be identified as lacking a family and a neighborhood. When on a number of occasions I took street kids to hospitals or clinics, I noticed that they always claimed to live at home, with their mothers, in a specific neighborhood, even if they had not shown their faces there for years. Similarly, many of the children who told me that they lived at home and only came to the street during the day to work or play revealed later, when I came to know them well, that they also slept in the street. The relational ties to their families remained crucial to them, if only in an emotional and, frankly, imaginary way.

The notion of rights, so fundamental to citizenship, is viewed ambiguously in Brazil. Margarete once described the street girls at a particular agency as being *cheias de direitos*. When I asked her to explain what she meant by "full of rights," she said that they were bossing one another around, trying to "be bigger" than one another. Even a street educator, referring to the movement's farm, confessed to me, ' The first time the kids go, they are cooperative. But then they adopt an attitude. They think they have a series of rights and they stop cooperating."

Notwithstanding the lack of a priori appeal inherent in the idea of citizenship, some groups such as Ruas e Praças strive to encourage the notion among street children. In contrast to other groups that seek special medical attention for street children, Ruas e Praças seeks to make impersonal and frightening public institutions – clinics and hospitals – accessible to street children just as they are, in theory, to all Brazilians.

If citizenship is a complicated notion in Brazil at the theoretical level, it is also a difficult notion at the practical level. When street kids explain why they do not work, they often say it is because they do not have documents; frequently one of their vague plans for the future is "to get my documents" (*tirar meus documentos*). By this they refer to six or seven legal papers ranging from birth certificates to military registration, from voter registration to work permits. Typically, street kids lack all of these. The children often speak of their ability to work or advance in life as being inhibited by the seemingly endless series of bureaucratic hurdles implicit in getting their documents. Thus Ruas e Praças, as well as other groups, will sometimes help children obtain one or two of the more vital documents, such as birth certificates. When I asked an *educador* at Ruas e Praças why the group helped kids to get their documents, he replied simply, "These are important for all citizens."

The most vital of the documents is the General Registration Card, usually known as the *carteira de identidade* or identity card. For kids who are under 18 but look as though they could be *de maior* (of legal age), it is desirable to have an identity card. On the other hand, for those who are over 18, the document is not usually convenient; it means they must be taken to adult police stations if arrested, and it implies a legal termination of the status of being *meninos de rua* (street children), rendering them, almost officially, adult *malandros*, or dangerous rogues.

Reclamation, Salvation, and Citizenship: Moving from Street to Home

Describing social conflicts during the early period of urbanization in Brazil, Gilberto Freyre (1968 [1936]a: 107–108) wrote: "Many a former slave, degraded by freedom and the living conditions of the town, became a street idler, ruffian, thief, prostitute, and even murderer – the terror of the bourgeoisie of the mansions." It would not be farfetched to view alarmist images of the *maloqueiros* as the contemporary equivalent of Freyre's description of the "degraded" freed slave. Unfettered from rural bondage and resituated in the city street, the manumitted slave struck fear in the world of the patriarchal home; likewise, impoverished children, moved from *favela* shack to thoroughfare, from home to street, have become the dread of contemporary urban Brazil.

Roberto DaMatta (1991 [1985]: 100) observed that "no one lives in a fully social way without a family, without the imperative and instrumental network of personal bonds." By living physically separated from families in the impersonal milieu of the street, street children are a living oxymoron. Their very existence is made in some way illicit through the manner in which protective laws are interpreted in Brazil: when poor children are photographed in the street doing almost anything, even sleeping, their eyes are covered over with black bands, a practice that, to my dismay, was necessary to follow in this book. Although the explicit rationale is to avoid harm to the children from the likes of death squads, the effect is to make the very status of being a street child appear illicit.

While street children have been used by some to exemplify the vulnerabilities of childhood, they have also been refashioned in another way – as harbingers of the danger posed to society (inevitably construed as a world that does not include street children) by the unsupervised young. The approximately two dozen police officers called in to rid the Law Faculty of street children and street educators in the episode that opens this book were clearly sent on behalf of those who perceived young people in the streets as dangerous.

A few groups have attempted to address children within the milieu of the street – that is, they have concerned themselves with rights that are part and parcel of an incipient notion of citizenship. But the house remains the dominant motif of work with street children; street kids are encouraged to be more like the poor children who work and inhabit the *favelas*, or they are elected for salvation into a home that elevates their saviors. This latter "home" may imply a notion of protected, nurtured childhood, which is said to be natural and appropriate, or else be the symbolic Brazilian home favored by politicians, where the condition of children is indicative of the well-being of the Brazilian nation.

7

STREET CHILDREN AND
THEIR "CLIENTS"

A 12-year-old who left home at age six told me that he had spent six years in the street, three in a shelter. Because the arithmetic so obviously did not work out, I asked him to explain what he meant. He repeated himself, only clarifying that during three of the six years that he had been *na rua* (in the street) he had been in a shelter. Such exchanges raise a question – do the children see institutions as a means of leaving the street or merely as one element of a larger concept of street life? If the institutions aim to reclaim children (*recuperar as crianças*), uproot them from the street (*tirar eles* [sic] *da rua*), offer them a new life (*uma vida nova*), or give them rights as citizens, what do the kids see in the institutions?

In all of the talk about street children, there is scant analysis of the institutions that seek to represent, aid, or even rescue these children. What little is said about the institutions seems aimed only at raising money for them. Whereas the previous chapter sought to examine the approaches of agencies that help street children, this final chapter turns the tables and examines how the kids see the institutions. I argue that street children in Recife tend to view the social service institutions as an integral part of street life, not as a way out. They may even envisage the institutions as *freguêses*, a concept introduced in Chapter 2 and elaborated on here that I translate as "clients." Their own visions of change, however, are remote from the adult concepts of salvation, reclamation, and citizenship.

Where gender-appropriate, I asked in my survey whether respondents had been to each of a series of institutions. Those who said they had were asked whether they had liked the place, why or why not,

Table 6. *Anthropological Interviews: Reasons for Leaving Shelters*

Questions and responses	Number
Why did you leave the place (the shelter)? (*Porque você saiu de lá?*)[a]	
I felt like it	13
I didn't like the rules	4
I had to leave	3
I had fights with other kids	3
The food was bad	2
Other	7

[a] $N = 32$ responses from children who had left a live-in shelter. Question posed in an open-ended fashion.

and why they had left. Of the sample of 50, 39 respondents had been to at least one live-in institution.

Typically children who had been to an institution said they had liked the place. In all, 19 of the 23 who had returned to the street from an institution said they had liked at least one shelter. When asked why they had left, the answers varied widely. Sometimes it was because they had turned 18 and were forced to leave, sometimes their mothers had fetched them. But of those who left of their own accord, most explained their departure by saying, "I felt like it" (*porque eu quis*), while a number cited poor food, fights with other kids, or restrictions such as not being able to smoke or having to take a bath.

For the institutions, it is more often than not a patent challenge to convince kids to stay and a bitter disappointment when they do not. The children's perceptions of the shelters typically clash with those of the *educadores*. For instance, as noted in the preceding chapter, Padre Ramiro speaks about "reclaiming" (*recuperando*) children through the "methodology of sweat"; the kids, on the other hand, speak admiringly of the father's imported goats. Discussions about sexuality are a staple service at the Casa de Passagem, but the girls spoke to me instead about such immediate benefits as a place to wash their clothing and get a meal.

While street educators at different projects may talk of the larger goals of social or spiritual change (e.g., through the discovery of God, at Desafio Jovem), the kids more typically mention material benefits. When discussing why they liked the shelters, the kids would frequently cite such perks as "You get fed at the right time" (*tem a comida na hora certa*) or "You get a place to sleep, there's television, and you can swim in the river" (*tem dormida, tem televisão, tem banho de rio*). The end result is something akin to what Snow and Anderson (1993: 93) have called a "revolving door" phenomenon when speaking of homeless people and shelters in Austin, Texas; the institutions in both settings may offer their beneficiaries a respite from the street without extricating them from it.

Included here are some exchanges and comments concerning institutions in Recife that I believe both illustrate some of the findings of the survey and serve as a point of departure for discussing how the children view the institutions.

> *Tobias*: Have you been to Desafio Jovem?
> *Tuco* [*male, aged 16*]: Yes.
> *Tobias*: Did you like it?
> *Tuco*: Yes.
> *Tobias*: Why?
> *Tuco*: There was a lot of food, a lot of work, a place to sleep. They have everything.
> *Tobias*: So why did you leave?
> *Tuco*: I liked it, but I missed the street [*fiquei com saudades da rua*].
> *Tobias*: Have you been to Padre Ramiro's farm?
> *Tuco*: Yes.
> *Tobias*: Did you like it?
> *Tuco*: No, I didn't like it because you have to get up at five o'clock in the morning, put on boots, get dressed, and clear the forest.
> *Tobias*: Why did you leave?
> *Tuco*: There was a kid threatening to kill me.

> *Female* [*aged about 16*]: The Casa de Passagem? Since the first time I went I thought it was very good, excellent [*legal*]. But

on the other hand, I think the Casa de Passagem is horrible [*ruim*] because there are girls there who are motormouths, they like to argue with the other girls. They grab a knife, a fork, to hurt you! They horse around, bug the technicians. The Casa de Passagem, right? There you get supper at the right time [*na hora certa*], breakfast at the right time, which is in the morning.

Robson [aged 12]: Yeah, I've been to Desafio Jovem. It's good there, we're the ones who make the rules in the house, there's a house for us to live in, a bunch of us *maloqueiros*.

Tobias: Did you stay there for a while?

Robson: I only spent a week, then I left.

Tobias: But if you liked it, why did you leave?

Robson: You eat every day, take a bath, have breakfast, dinner, all those things.

Tobias: Did you get tired of that, the bath, the schedule?

Robson: Yes. Whenever you want to leave you can. So I left and came back here [to the street].

Cheira [male, aged 17]: Yeah, I've been to Padre Ramiro's farm. I worked there cutting grass. It's good there, there's lots of vocations they teach you. And the priest is great with us.

Tobias: How long did you spend there?

Cheira: Four months. There's Desafio Jovem too.

Tobias: Have you been to Desafio Jovem?

Cheira: Yes.

Tobias: How long were you there?

Cheira: I didn't spend much time there. About two or three months.

Tobias: Why did you leave those places?

Cheira: I didn't like them because when you go to eat, there's no meat, you can't smoke, there's no coffee, just tea, you eat only yam and cassava, because they say that if you eat meat it makes you want to smoke. . . . I got fed up so I left. I didn't like it. I went back to the street to steal, smoke pot, take Rohypnol.

Pipoca [male, aged 17]: FEBEM [pausing, looking off into the distance and sounding philosophical], FEBEM is like a hotel, and the *monitores* are our waiters. They may catch us today, but before it's tomorrow we've blown that joint.

Opinions on the institutions are clearly mixed, the contrasting views often expressed amid an "on the one hand" this and "on the other hand" that. The children tend to express happiness about the things they receive, such as food, clothing, or a place to sleep, but dissatisfaction with restrictions such as not being able to smoke and toward the fights that break out when so many street children are brought together in a confined space. When conflicts erupt in the street, *meloqueiros* tend to move on to a new spot for a while. The ease of spatial mobility in the city serves to diffuse tension. So when such conflicts erupt at shelters, as they so often do, the most obvious form of resolution short of violence is moving on.

If the need to avoid confrontations makes shelters an unlikely place at which to stay indefinitely, conflict resolution is also a part of what makes the shelters attractive in the first place. If the police, another youth, or anyone else has made a credible threat and staying in the street is deemed imprudent, the most obvious place to go for children unwelcome or unsafe at home is a shelter. Children sometimes even show up voluntarily for detention at FEBEM. But to the extent that shelters are a place to wait for a threat to subside, their appeal is only a passing one.

In a study of male alcoholics in the skid row areas of U.S. cities, Wiseman (1970) examined how (to use her term) "social controllers" such as police officers, social workers, and missionaries saw the services (and regulations) they enforced in very different ways than did the alcoholics themselves. Generally devoid of formal training, job references, a fixed place of residence, and a predictable and steady income, skid row men would need to be ingenious and persistent in securing the resources necessary for their existence – shelter, food, drink, and medical care being the most essential. The skid row resident's existence depended in part on his ability "to locate things that can become resources to supply food and shelter if they are used in a way other than that generally intended. Even the institutions and organizations created specifically to provide necessities as a charity can be redefined and 'worked' so as to offer more than bare comfort" (18). Skid row alcoholics employed diverse strategies to secure maximum benefit from all available resources.

> For instance, some of the missions provide bed facilities, although usually only on a nightly basis unless the man decides to accept the rehabilitation program that is offered. One man conjured up a picture of Skid Row alcoholics playing a sort of gigantic musical chairs with this resource: "Actually, you could get a free bed every night if you went to all the churches and missions around here. You could get by taking a different one each night." (23)

Skid row men captured the normative objectives of charities and would sometimes even feign conversion to Christianity to please their benefactors; they would likewise redefine certain social institutions to suit their own needs. Thus, alcoholics in need of a warm place to sleep would actually on occasion ask the police to arrest them. In a more contemporary examination of homeless people in the United States, Snow and Anderson (1993) have likewise portrayed the divergent ways in which the homeless and the caretaker institutions view the services offered by the latter:

> Many of the homeless . . . view participation in rehab programs as a last-ditch effort to survive. A large number do not perceive themselves as having substance-abuse problems, and an even larger number have little faith in the agencies' promises of success. . . . Nonetheless, in order to gain access to the facilities and services, they often present at least a facade of openness to the agency's ideology. (288)

Street children in Recife also "work" the institutions, appealing to the latter's moral framework when convenient, and spurning it when not. In Portuguese there is a verb that I believe is useful in describing the way *maloqueiros* see the process of securing resources. *Descolar* is used in informal Brazilian speech to signify to "score" or "come up with." For instance, *descolar uma grana* means "to come up with some money." Literally, the word means "to unglue": *colar* meaning "to paste," and *des* being equivalent to the English prefix "un-." Although

Brazilians may no longer associate *descolar* with its etymological roots, the idea of ungluing serves as a poignant metaphor to explain how street children in Recife and Olinda conceive of the task of obtaining the daily necessities of food, clothing, and money. All of these things are there; they simply need to be unstuck.

Shoplifting is referred to as *descuido*. *Descuido* means "carelessness." When no one is watching, when the shopkeepers are being "careless," one can snatch clothing, candy, or anything tempting. The verb refers to what others are failing to do – watch over their merchandise – not to what the kids are positively doing. Likewise, all sorts of things can happen when someone *dá um vacilo*, that is, lets down his guard or screws up. One youth summed up how he gets money and things: ' I beg, panhandle, steal, whatever falls in the net is fish [*o que cair na rede é peixe*]."

To a large extent, I think, the institutions are viewed as one type of fish that falls into the nets of street children. In the same way that kids ask for money in the street, they ask for clothing, food, money, and other favors at the institutions. Generally they are not surprised when they do not get what they request, but this by no means prevents them from persisting in their mission. And if there's no meat in the stew, they will complain.

During a visit to one shelter I met a group of children who told me that they did not plan to go back to the street. I had no reason to doubt them. They seemed well adapted at the shelter and they did not need to worry about the violence and danger of sleeping in the street. There was plenty of food, though they had to prepare it them-selves, and although they had serious chores they also had extensive leisure time to play soccer or dominoes, watch television, or dance. But several weeks later I found three of them in the street sniffing glue and asking passersby for spare change. I sat down to talk with them to find out why they had left. "We're on vacation," one of them told me. "But we'll go back after New Year's."

The endless demands and complaints of street children coupled with their failure to embrace what their benefactors view as important op-portunities are a source of deep frustration in the work of street ed-ucators. I remember my own dismay when trekking into the city at dawn one day to take Camilla to the doctor. She insisted she would not go without fresh clothing so I had assembled a pair of shoes, a skirt, and a top. Rather than showing gratitude for what I saw as my largesse in making the special dawn venture into town, being willing to wait for hours at the clinic, and coming up with clothing, she instead complained that I hadn't brought her any soap. Street educators who earn paltry salaries and work in difficult conditions speak of being worn down by the constant demands of street children. One friend commiserated, "I can't even buy new shoes for my own son and I spend the whole day out working with street children. 'Lady, give me a pair of shorts, find me some sandals.' They never stop asking you for things."

In Chapter 2, I referred to a conversation between one of my neighbors and two street children. My neighbor asked one of the boys where he had gotten a nice new shirt and pair of shorts. He said from a *freguesa*. Hozana was shocked at his use of the word. She explained to me, "*Freguesa*, if you look it up in the dictionary . . . say I always go to the same market stall to buy meat. The butcher will call me a *freguesa*. But for him [one of the kids], it's the person who always gives him clothing."

Its etymology is ambiguous, but most dictionaries suggest *freguês* (the masculine form of the noun) comes from the Latin *filiu ecclesiae*, or son of the church (see, for instance, Machado 1952). Indeed, one meaning of the word in Portuguese is parishioner. But today, it tends to be used in reference to a regular client of a business. However, *freguês* has a double meaning. It can refer to a regular purchaser *or* to a regular vendor. One might conceive of the children as *freguêses* of the agencies in the sense that they are members of the "parish" and also regular clients of the services. But one could also look at the relationship the other way around, seeing the agencies that fall into the wide "nets" cast by the children as members of the street children's parish. Some *maloqueiros* even suspect the latter depend on them.

Speaking of one leader of an institution in Recife who made a film about street children, a youth said,

> I presented something of what I know how to do, others presented what they know how to do, which is shooting up. . . .
> And what did he give us? Nothing. Nothing more than a simple

basket of food, two kilos of beans, two kilos of rice, and he wanted us to live on that for a year! Now he profited. He took the film abroad. Abroad a film about us, about the street children of Pernambuco, is worth more than a porno flick!

Referring to the leader of the same institution, a 19-year-old who had grown up in the street said, "He grew at our expense" (*subiu à custa da gente*). The kids, especially the older ones, tend to be suspicious of visits by foreigners to local institutions. More than once I heard the complaint, "They're showing us off so they can get money from the *gringos*." It is in order to draw attention to the ways the children render a service for the agencies and to how they conceive of the agencies as an integral part of street life that I speak of the latter as "clients."

Children will often spurn what those at the institutions and else-where view as monumental opportunities. Toward the end of my stay in Recife, a boy I knew, Adriano, had met a man who sold jewelry in the street. The man liked him and offered to teach Adriano how to make jewelry that he might eventually sell on his own. The man invited Adriano to stay at his house, an offer the boy accepted gladly. But Adriano stayed only long enough to eat everything in the refrig-erator and grab some jewelry before he made his way out through a window. He had acted in a similar fashion at SOS Criança. SOS Criança is an advocacy organization that in principle offers no direct services, but the director often helps out individual street kids in different ways. She had once allowed Adriano to sleep inside the office. He stayed for a period of about two months. Then one night he ate all the cheese in the refrigerator and slipped away.

Every institution around the city seems to be able to tell of countless similar cases. The leader of one group offered extraordinary assistance to one young woman. He bought her a small house in a *favela*, gave her a job with the vital *carteira assinada* (social benefits), and took care of one of her babies. But in time, she quit the job, abandoned the house, went back to the street, and demanded the return of her daughter, who was later seized by the police and placed in the Casa de Carolina.

My neighbor and friend Hozana invited the boy briefly adopted by the soccer star (see Chapter 5) to live with her. "You'll be part of the family, you'll have your own room, you won't sleep outside – only dogs sleep outside," she told him. "You'll have to work – not be a servant, but help out just like my children help out – and obey me. Would you like that?" The boy nodded shyly and Hozana shed a few tears, thinking she was going to truly transform the boy's life. I too was overcome with emotion, because it seemed to me that for once I was going to see a happy future for a street child. But when he declined to make a firm commitment, Hozana said the boy could think about it overnight and come back and tell her the next day. Yet he did not stop by her house for quite some time, and only then to ask for food.

Although the material trappings of shelters or offers to live with middle-class families are attractive to street children, many aspects of these situations are in direct conflict with a street ethos based on spontaneity, insubordination to authority, and solidarity with other deeply rejected young people. What are in short supply are stories of children who have lived in the street for a prolonged period of time and made what can be assumed to be a definitive departure. One of the very few such youths I met is the one I refer to as David in Chapter 4. He had spent two years in the street without going back home. He recalled how he made the decision to leave the street.

> I've known about Ruas e Praças for a long time. They taught me so many things that clicked with me. They said that we had to change our lives [*mudar de vida*] and so on, that if I didn't make a move I wouldn't become anything. So the thing to do was go forward and I went forward [*o jeito era caminhar e caminhei*].

But David was exceptional in that once he decided to leave the street, he never slept there again in subsequent years. During my fieldwork I met many kids who had left the street for institutions or who even returned to their mothers, but it was by no means certain that their departure from the street was definitive. One boy named Dogival who left the street and went to live with the Pentecostal Christians at Desafio Jovem asked to take my tape recorder to a quiet spot to record a message for what he called "vice-ridden" children (*viciados*) in the street. On the tape, he said that when he had been in the street he had known only "false witnesses," that he had lived "stealing and sinning." He urged other kids to do what he had done, telling them to leave the street, cease to sin, and come to Jesus. But when I returned

to Desafio Jovem a couple of weeks later I was told that he had run
away.

When children leave institutions they tend to use the word *fugir* –
literally "to flee" or "to escape." The *educadores* find this term offensive
and prefer the term *sair*, "to leave." "After all, no one is tied up here "
said a volunteer at Desafio Jovem. The one place about which it is
acceptable to use the word *fugir* is the state institution CAP, where
children do need to flee to get away. But even when they escape from
CAP or a shelter, their flight is by no means definitive. In a six-month
period in 1992, CAP records show 17 children actually returned vo.-
untarily.

It is readily apparent to the kids that the institutions aim to "uproot" them from the street. One young transvestite even described
CAP as a potential route for leaving the street: "[CAP] is a way of
changing a child's life – if the child toes the line [*se ela seguir a reta*]."
But the kids themselves seem to hold views of how one leaves the
street that are generally very different from those held by the inst -
tutions discussed in the previous chapter.

When children live in the street, home remains a constant point of
reference. As explored in Chapter 4, street children speak of the street
and their lives in it in opposition to the homes where they once lived
and which they possibly still visit. Home is typically seen by the
children and their would-be benefactors alike as the only escape from
the street aside from death. Perhaps because of the great stigma, not
to mention the hardship, of living in the street, *maloqueiros* tend to
cling to the belief that they should – and, moreover, will – leave the
street. They often ridicule the adults who are homeless, radically separating themselves from them. As they physically mature, they struggle to retain their links to childhood in different ways: through the
use of glue (which is considered a kid's drug), through hanging out
with children younger than themselves, through lying about their age,
and through referring to themselves and others of their own age as
maloqueiros or even *meninos*. There are even a few *maloqueiros*, like those
mentioned in the Introduction, who are in their early 30s. *Maloqueiros*
distinguish themselves from the homeless adults, I believe, by holding
on to a sort of bourgeois dream of eventually marrying, working, being
a homeowner, and having a couple of children. Below are examples of

what two kids, both about 17, thought it took to leave the street. The two exchanges took place in CAP.

Tobias: Have you spent some time in the street?

José: I spent a year and two months in the street, then I spent two more months. I went back to my house. I ran away again. . . . I spent two years sniffing glue. I saw it wasn't getting me anywhere [*vi que não dava resultado*] and I found myself a girl that was, oh so good – you know what I mean? I liked her, she tripped me out, I tripped her out [*ela fez minha cabeça, eu fiz a dela*].

Tobias: So you quit using glue, Rohypnol, pot and went home?

José: I quit everything and now I need some strength [*tô precisando de uma força*]. I'm going to see what I can get out of that judge,[1] see if he'll find me a job or do something for me. By the look of things he might just be the goody-goody type [*tem assim uma cara de bonzinho*], but he rattles on at the mouth too much. No, it looks like he's punishing us, we're all full of fury [*raiva*], I think we're going to start a rebellion. . . . What we want is some strength [*uma força*]. All that judge does is talk and pocket what's his. He has to help us get on the right track [*andar certo, na linha*].

Cheira: We [street children] rob one another, because it's the only way we have to survive. We don't have a profession. Some of us know how to read, some don't, and we have to take life like it comes, we have to steal. But one day, I hope to quit this life and work, have a kid, a wife, live in a quiet house, walk in front of the police without anyone thinking I'm a thief. You know, be like an honest person, earn my money without being called a thief, without being called names. When the police hit you and everyone stares, you feel embarrassed. . . . To quit this life [*pra pessoa deixar essa vida*] you have to have a lot of willpower.

The two exchanges, I believe, exemplify views commonly held by street children about leaving the street. Consider the second passage first. Cheira inserts his dream of leaving the street between descriptions of how he experiences life in the street; it is but a brief respite between "we have to take life like it comes, we have to steal" and "When the police hit you and everyone stares. . . ." The thought seems to cross his mind between the moment he is caught and the next moment when the blows from the policeman's club come raining down on his head. Like most street kids, he speaks of the street as a form of life – *essa vida*. In order to quit that life, what is needed is *força de vontade*, or willpower, something that presumably comes from inside. Leaving the street, in other words, requires quitting one "life" for another, giving up the lived reality for a distant dream. The vehicle for making the transition is personal effort. That street children would believe that what they need in order to leave the street is mostly their own willpower is congruent with their portrayal of the street as a deviant form of life. Because they tend to blame themselves in explaining why they are in the street, they tend to view those who aim to help them in various ways: with gratitude, since their "clients" are offering something immediately useful; with dislike, because the "clients" are "stingy" and do not offer enough; and with disdain, for they suspect their benefactors are gaining something at their expense.

José speaks of the humiliation he suffers at having his mother appear at his hearings, and of the *raiva* that grows in him while locked up in FEBEM. He says it was he who decided to "quit everything," the drugs and the street alike, and how a girlfriend was a part of his decision to quit. But while he hints at the need for *força de vontade*, willpower, he also speaks of another sort of *força*, the *força* that comes from an external source, in this case the judge. *Força* means force, strength, vigor, compulsion, or, perhaps more figuratively, a helping hand. In his use of the word, José asks for something concrete, a job or "something for me," but at once expresses his need for something of an almost spiritual nature, something to make him walk *na linha*, literally straight along the line or, figuratively, on the right track. So even though it is something coming from the outside, a change in himself is implied.

If street children see *essa vida*, that life they lead in the street, as a betrayal of motherdom (see Chapter 4), it is not surprising that they tend not only to blame themselves for their predicament but also to place the onus of responsibility for leaving the street on their own shoulders. The implications of this for institutions are far-reaching. It means that adult motifs of "salvation" from an outside benefactor are irrelevant, that street children believe themselves unlikely to become working children, and that discussions of citizenship and rights fail to resonate. What is left for street children when they view institutions is an opportunity within the street. Although the institutions may say they are offering a new life, the kids may merely seek a pair of rubber sandals. Acts of *assistencialismo*, the short-term paternalistic handouts shunned by most activist organizations, are cherished by the kids.

Although street children speak of living in the street as a vice, for most the fantasy of leaving street life, *essa vida de malandragem*, remains just that, a flicker of a dream within an everyday life of drugs, crime, and violence. Rejected in their own homes and in the *favelas*, street children find a solidarity among their peers that otherwise eludes them. In a world where they are the ultimate outcasts, it is this shared sense of difference and of glaring ostracism that offers street children a sense of belonging. While many agencies wish to *uproot* children from the street, the kids are busy *ungluing* what is immediately useful to them within street life; while benefactors speak of giving the children a new life, the latter plead for a pair of shorts, money, and a snack. Street kids view the resources of the institutions as there for the taking, though one must be cunning and persistent to extract them. And when one has no need for them, why hang around?

CONCLUSION:
THE EPHEMERAL LIVES OF
STREET CHILDREN

In the Introduction, I outlined why this book does not have the re-
strictive aim of proposing policy recommendations. I argued, among
other points, that if one's goal in writing about street children is to
offer ideas on how to eradicate a problem, one can hardly view those
people seen to embody the problem as autonomous beings in a social
world. Reduced to something to be cured, street children become objects in a distant debate among adults. This book has aimed to treat
street children as socially significant protagonists while also bringing
into focus the adult debates in which they are enmeshed. Yet, while
I believe it base, even harmful, to reduce street children to a problem,
the lives of children growing up in the streets of Recife and other
Brazilian cities are fraught with problems. A danger is therefore implicit in refusing to think in terms of change. Feigning the role of
the detached observer in the face of an intolerable status quo is to
accept tacitly that same status quo or, worse, to hide behind the cyr-
ical vogue of treating the brutality of social life as so much text.[1] Th s
final chapter employs the main themes of the ethnography – identity,
violence, the relationship of street children to institutions, and the
idea of childhood itself – to reassess the problem-ridden worlds of
street children and considers the question of the future, that is, of
what may lie ahead for street children.

Violent Representations

In *Threatened Children: Rhetoric and Concern about Child-Victims*, Joel Best
(1990: 177) argues that the success of the missing children's movement in the United States in the early to mid-1980s lay in "the

organization and culture of the contemporary social problems market-place and in the appeal of the crusaders' message." The message was appealing because no one was in favor of children going missing; be-cause the well-organized advocates were riding a tide of activism rooted strongly in the civil rights movement of the 1960s; and because new alternative television news and quasi-news programs such as *To-day, Sixty Minutes*, and *Donahue* – all with time slots to fill and in search of emotionally captivating topics – were conducive to spreading the message of the advocates for missing children.

Appropriated into an adult-driven marketplace for social problems, street children have become somewhat like the photographs of missing children whose faces briefly populated milk cartons in the United States, symbols of larger debates. In the case of street children, these debates relate to, among other things, the vulnerabilities of unpro-tected children and the danger posed by unsupervised children. While advocates for missing children focused attention on cruel, deviant adults who abducted, raped, and killed children, campaigns in behalf of street children have privileged a concern for undeniably vulnerable children over a serious engagement with the oppressive socioeconomic conditions under which both domiciled and homeless Third World children live.

The first piece I regrettably wrote on street children is a fine ex-ample of how street children have been recruited into an issue-hungry adult world. As mentioned in the Introduction, I was asked by an NGO to write a booklet about street children as a background doc-ument for a meeting of parliamentarians. The conference in fact was about family planning, but the "street children problem" was brought in to widen the appeal of the event. In a planning session it was decided that street children were, literally, "a sexy topic." The idea was clever, if cynical: whereas family planning is controversial in many countries, street children, on a certain level, are not. No one is in favor of children growing up homeless.

What is controversial in Brazil about street children is not only the violence against them, but the crimes they commit. During a visit to the Aníbal Bruno men's prison, I met a smartly dressed man who at first I took to be a lawyer visiting his client. He turned out to be a prisoner sentenced on several charges of bank robbery to more than 100 years. Despite facing what sounded like a dim future, Jefferson wasn't worried. "Money talks!" (*o dinheiro fala mais alto*), he would exclaim at regular intervals during our long conversation, explaining with bravado how he had already escaped from jail on two occasions. the last time from a maximum security facility. We began discussing one of the street youths I was visiting, and he let me know how, in an almost fatherly way, he had been trying to convince the boy to give up petty theft.

> Look, I told him: you have two choices: either get a job, or move on to something more ambitious, like bank robbery. If you go and hold up some poor man in the street who's wielding a pickax, he'd rather kill you than hand over his month's salary. But if you go into a bank where the people are dressed in suits, they won't shoot you. And there's a lot more money there.[2]

Jefferson had a point. A friend of mine who used to work in a bank reminisced one day about how his colleagues looked forward to hold-ups because in the confusion that ensued they could always stuff their own pockets with money. In Brazil, while condemnation tinged with quiet resignation is expressed in the face of white-collar crime and corruption, a more violent reaction is often reserved for those who practice small-time, street-level crime. Petty crime renders street children feared and hated and vulnerable to retribution. Sometimes mugging several people a day, Recife's self-described *maloqueiros* live with exceptional risk.

Concerned adults outside Brazil generally focus on the victimhood of children who grow up in the street and attribute the violence against such youths to an alliance of state (police) and business (merchants who lose customers frightened off by the presence of unruly youths).[3] Elements of both groups, particularly the police, live up to the accusations against them, but at some point it is also necessary to consider the violence and crime in which street children engage, if for no other reason than because the principal victims are other children. I refer not merely to the violence that street children self-destructively inflict on one another, but to the small number of street children, sometimes wielding knives, razors, or broken glass, who hold up dozens of people each month. As the bank robber Jefferson suggests, petty thievery renders street children easy targets for adult rage.

Conclusion

High-profile campaigns to protest death-squad murders of street children in Brazil have undeniably had a few positive effects. They helped create the environment that has allowed the National Movement of Street Children, which has fought in behalf of the rights of all poor children, to become a leading social movement in Brazil; they may have helped move forward efforts to implement the Children and Adolescents Act, for they focused attention on the conditions of young Brazilians; and they put the police under scrutiny.

But as argued in Chapter 5, relatively few children living in the street are murdered by death squads today. Attention could usefully be refocused on police torture, ranging from vigorous slaps to the hand to electric shock, from pistol whippings to leaving prisoners hanging upside down, practices that affect poor detainees of all ages, regardless of whether they live in the street or in homes. Although I found that street children in Recife were more likely to die at the hands of their peers than at the hands of the police or death squads, violence carried out by the authorities no doubt encourages the children to act out the violence they themselves experience. In the case of the *preso de ordem* system, in which prisoners are made to torture other prisoners, the police are clearly setting up their "helping hands" to be murdered. Street children and poor children in general would be aided more if attention were focused not on the rare, tabloid-friendly executions of sleeping children but on the pervasive, everyday abuse on the part of the police and other officials.

One of the worst forms of abuse must be that experienced by some young children confined to the juvenile detention center and molested by their older peers or locked up in the illegal solitary confinement chamber. It used to be the case that some children literally grew up in FEBEM; now, with the Children and Adolescents Act, detentions cannot legally exceed 45 days. As set out in the act, the function of facilities such as CAP (as the old FEBEM in Recife is now called) is that of a sort of triage center where children caught for an infraction or, in some cases, lost or in danger are held temporarily until appearing before a judge. The judge has a variety of options, including releasing the children to their families, sending them to another institution such as a shelter for street children, or sentencing them (if aged 12 or older) to a secure facility. Yet 45 days for a young child never exposed to an institution like CAP can be devastating, as the testimony of Edson (in

Chapter 5) illustrates. Beyond bureaucratic inefficiency or the desire to use CAP as a jail, there is probably no reason to force children to stay more than 24 hours. Although the law on this waiting time is unlikely to be altered, organizations such as the National Movement of Street Children should be supported in their efforts to make the period as brief and humane as possible.

This book makes the case that the concern over violence affecting children needs to go beyond the street to take into account the violence children suffer at home. In their homes and neighborhoods, children are exposed to beatings and sexual assault, but above all, they are exposed to the violence of hunger and poverty that renders the street a materially attractive alternative. Focusing exclusively on the crimes committed against a small but highly visible population of street children does little for the vast, hidden population of "home children"; rather it gives the probably misguided impression that there is nothing worse than growing up in the street.

Street Children, Childhood, and the Street as a Right for "Home Children"

In his history of U.S. children of newly urbanized, working-class families in the first two decades of the twentieth century, David Nasaw (1985: 41–42) writes that "There was nothing new or extraordinary about asking children to go to work. Only recently has childhood become – almost by definition – an age of irresponsibility." Viviana Zelizer (1985) has argued that by the 1930s changes in the social value of children in the United States had consolidated to the extent that children came to be viewed as economically worthless while emotionally priceless. Today, children in the United States, as in most advanced industrialized countries, are nearly always a financial liability to their families. An article in the magazine *Working Mothers* (O'Connell 1997) cited data from the Department of Agriculture indicating that U.S. families with incomes in excess of $55,000 spend on average $10,510 annually on their children from birth to the age of two years. Although children in the First World have come to represent an economic burden for their parents, their noneconomic value has come to be deemed incalculable.

Among the poor of Northeast Brazil a contrasting – and once far more widespread – logic prevails: children are valued, in part, according to their success at contributing to the household economy. This is not to suggest that *favela* parents do not place a high noneconomic value on their children; rather, families whose survival requires continuous resourcefulness expect children to nurture the household, and children take pride in doing so. Successfully helping their families is likely to enhance their status in the household. Thus, discouraging poor urban children in Brazil from working in the street, far from protecting them, will likely weaken their ties to the home.

To an extent, urban children can contribute to the household while physically at home, especially by minding younger siblings. But the household's survival, of course, ultimately depends on the ability of its members to secure money or goods from outside. Poor urban children in Northeast Brazil have an important role in bringing in resources, but their options are limited. Some of the principal means of earning are:

- hawking items that require little capital, such as popsicles or chewing gum
- apprenticing with a mechanic, furniture maker, or another working-class adult
- working as a guide for visitors (an especially common practice in Olinda)
- doing odd jobs such as washing store windows or carrying around goods at the market
- helping their parents in their work
- begging
- scavenging for items that can be sold, such as glass bottles, cans, and cardboard
- petty theft.

A cursory look at these options reveals how problematic they are: even the cost of the styrofoam box needed to carry around popsicles is prohibitive for many families and, while the profit margin is small, the competition is great; there is little demand for apprentices; Olinda, the principal tourist destination in Pernambuco, already has more than 100 young guides and on a typical day only a small fraction as many visitors willing to pay for a tour; in many situations, children are not allowed to work alongside their parents (this is often the case, e.g., when the mother is a maid) and do not necessarily augment household

A young guide showing a visitor the view from the Alto da Sé in Olinda.

income when they do; begging is a competitive arena with a dearth of prospective donors; scavenging for cardboard, bottles, and cans requires capital, in the form of a cart, is competitive, and offers little financial return; petty crime is dangerous for the children and generally shunned by mothers. In short, the informal sector opportunities open to children are competitive, sometimes dangerous, and offer only meager financial rewards. Nonetheless, at different times most poor children in urban Northeast Brazil engage in some of these or similar activities.

As if the difficulties inherent in these working strategies were not enough, children's strivings to nurture the household are stymied in another way. Their aspirations are in conflict with global moves toward discouraging child labor and with the notion, particularly strong in Brazil, that the street – the principal venue for urban children's remunerated work – is a contaminating realm, perforce out of bounds to children. For poor families in Northeast Brazil living almost hand to mouth, the economic contribution of young children can literally make the difference between survival and starvation. Children in Northeast Brazil rarely fulfill their dreams of giving their mothers as much as they would like to – many of the children I knew told me their greatest dream was to give their mothers a new house – but most give a lot, especially if their contribution is measured in terms of effort.

Poor children speak not only of the obstacles they face in their attempts to nurture the household, but of the consequences of failing to succeed. It is worth revisiting the words of the boy quoted in Chapter 4 who explained his view of the origins of street children.

> Perhaps because there is so much popcorn being sold in the street, a kid won't be able to bring money to his mother. So his mother gets worried, frustrated because there's nothing to eat, and hits the kid. The kid, afraid to go back home without money and get hit, just sleeps in the street. He picks up the vice [*pega o vício*] of sleeping in the street. He gets hooked [*fica viciado*], afraid to go home. Then he picks up other vices like sniffing glue, smoking pot, and so on.

Street life is an alternative to home life, but it is a violently unappealing one for most children precisely because it is a confirmation of their failure to nurture the household.

Street children live within larger political and moral economies that both shape their existence and are shaped in subtle ways by their existence. On a number of occasions I was recruited by mothers in the *favelas* to photograph their babies. The mothers would always scurry to collect as many artifacts of impersonal capitalism as they could find and place them around their babies – laundry soap in a brightly colored box, a tin of infant formula, a transistor radio, the odd plastic toy. While the urban poor (including street children) of Northeast Brazil pay homage to the trappings of a consumer society from which they are largely excluded, they are also well aware of their position in relation to what we might call a larger political economy.

The political economy, a term I use loosely to denote the macrolevel political and economic systems under which power relations are played out and resources distributed, is a part of the backdrop against which street children assess the benefits of leaving the street and returning to the fold of working, nurturing childhood, and it is the political economy that makes it clear to street children that, materially, home life has little to offer them. Asked to tell me about all the things in

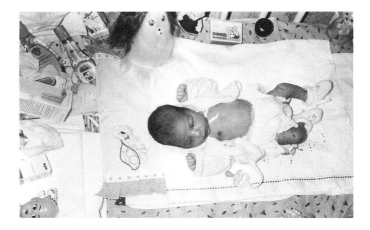

Baby amid a halo of consumer goods.

her house, a five-year-old called Negona could only think to mention "mosquitoes" and then, after a moment of reflection, "mud."

Why then do so many children stay at home? Why was the rigorous census of street children sponsored by the city council of Recife (described in Chapter 4) able to identify only 212 children and adolescents sleeping rough, rather than the tens of thousands that the city would have if it conformed to UNICEF's suggestion that Brazil has at least 7 million street children?

This book could surely be criticized for not treating extensively the question of political economy. It is, after all, only the oppressive structural conditions of urban poverty in Brazil that make living in the street a materially rational alternative for some children – an unthinkable choice on those grounds for most children in the First World. But in aiming to place children at the center of this narrative, I have attempted to privilege what I view as their ways of interpreting their predicament. Faced with a political economy that offers them little of a material nature beyond mosquitoes and mud and scant hope for the future, poor children in Northeast Brazil appeal to a moral economy that highlights the importance of their nurturing position within the matrifocal family.

The term "moral economy" I borrow, in a reshaped form, from James Scott, who, in turn, borrows the notion from Marxist historians

In his study of agrarian societies in Southeast Asia, Scott (1976: vii) argues that "The problem of exploitation and rebellion is . . . not just a problem of calories and income but is a question of peasant conceptions of social justice, of rights and obligations, of reciprocity." In a similar fashion, if children's decisions to leave home or stay home hinged merely on where they could find more food or where they could acquire more money, few poor urban children would bother staying in shacks where there is little to do and less to eat. It is the children's sense of a moral economy that makes them stay at home.

Whereas Scott writes about a moral economy that is upset by commercialization in agriculture, by the advent of the bureaucratic state, and by new systems of taxation and tenancy – that is, by outside forces impinging on the subsistence ethic of peasants – I employ the term in a similar but inverted sense, referring to the moral economy of the home that poor children in Northeast Brazil see themselves as responsible for maintaining. The incentives to live at home, work, and stick to what the children call the righteous life (*a vida boa*) are great, precisely because street life implies a breach of their obligation. Street life undermines the role of children within matrifocality, recasting the nurturing child as social pariah.

Beginning with Raymond Smith (1956), matrifocality has been studied from the adult perspective. This book has aimed to turn the tables, delving into the relationship between matrifocality and the child's sense of self. Whereas Aptekar (1988) maintains that in Colombia early independence in the form of living in the street is encouraged by matrifocal families, I argue that children in Northeast Brazil see the situation in diametrically opposed terms. Street life – what the children call *essa vida* – is a betrayal of their role in the matrifocal household. In the street, the children are physically estranged from their mothers and thus from their guidance and protection (whether real or merely yearned for); and they use resources for themselves, not primarily for the household. Although *maloqueiros* may speak of bringing home money to their mothers – and indeed many do – most of their resources are kept for themselves and quickly spent in the street. Thus, rather than the child going from the home to the street and back to the home with the purpose of harnessing the income-generating possibilities of the street for the nurture of the home, the economic life of street children begins and ends in the street.

Rather than bringing home life-sustaining necessities such as food and clothing, *maloqueiros* spend much of their money on street diversions – drugs, video games, and candy; rather than earning "good money" through work, they earn what they call "bad money" through crime.

Efforts at preventing children from working in the street threaten the position of poor urban children within the home. The more difficult it is for children to bring in resources to households that not only desperately need the fruits of child labor but morally expect them, the more vulnerable the child's status becomes. Where schools occupy at most only four hours a day of a child's time and home does not offer the physical space for children to play, the street is an invaluable resource. Poor children play mostly in the mud lanes that run near their shacks, but inevitably they also play and work on the city streets. Denying them that possibility, given the dearth of alternatives, is to enforce a social and economic apartheid likely to sink destitute households into even deeper poverty. Thus, any "solution" to the plight of street children must consider first how to make the lives of "home children" more rewarding. Declaring the street out of bounds will only make the home less viable.

The Future

Observers seem to wonder whether street children inhabit a sort of Rousseauian state of nature and innocence or whether their lives are – as in the Hobbesian embodiment of primitive society – nasty, brutish, and short. On the one hand, Aptekar (1988) argued that street children in Cali, quite unlike their image as psychologically battered drug users, were growing up in a generally healthy, adaptive way. While in no way glorifying the conditions of street children in Kathmandu, Panter-Brick et al. (1996: 441) suggest that given the comparatively worse nutritional status of children in rural areas and squatter settlements, "urban homelessness may represent an appropriate response to circumstances of poverty." On the other hand, Dimenstein (1990) described a "war" on children in the streets of Brazil, and the image of street children being hunted down by killers is common in the media.

In assessing the conditions of street children, this book treads something of a middle line. By placing street children within the context of what they have left behind – childhood in the *favelas* – it is possible

At home with my dog. Photo by Daniel Aamot.

to see that street life has certain redeeming features. Children may eat better in the street than they would at home. This is not to say that street children do not experience considerable hunger – both their incomes and their resources in kind are secured with great irregularity. But those children adept at stealing have considerable purchasing power compared with the poor in the *favelas*. Ironically, some of the street children bring in – and quickly spend – a good deal more every month than the street educators who try to help them. In addition, many street children fashion elaborate networks of support from people who give them food, clothing, and other resources. Street children often have ample time on their hands for diversion. In the neighborhood where I lived, the street children could regularly be seen playing checkers, competing at video games, drawing, flying kites, riding on the backs of buses, even paddling rented canoes. They slept when they wanted to, sought food when they were hungry, and there was no one to tell them what to do. Despite their professed adoration of their

mothers, their adage "chiefs are for Indians" (*quem tem chefe é índi*)
could probably also describe their feelings about supervision at home.

But my research in Recife did not lead me to share the sanguine
view of others that street children live amid a supportive network of
friends and are likely to simply grow up and become much like other
poor adults. Jill Swart (1990) writes hopefully of street children, or
malunde, in South Africa,

> Given the opportunity, children are likely to enter stable em-
> ployment situations. The *malunde* want to become taxi drivers,
> photographers, clerks, electricians, builders, doctors, lawyers,
> bishops, and sign writers. One wants to be a policeman. They
> plan to be people of worth in the community and to raise chil-
> dren who will not have to live on the streets. (126)

Aptekar suggests that living in the street might be "the beginning
of a heroic adventure, often in a community of peers and friends – an
adventure that has been portrayed in the literature of many cultures
as a requisite to finding one's own identity, which is, after all, the
function of adolescence" (1988: 195). Implicit in the statement is the
idea that for poor Colombian children, spending some of their early
years in the street may merely be a natural part of the life cycle, a
character-forming experience that is part of growing up.[4] Elsewhere,
Aptekar (1989: 435) has gone so far as to suggest that stints of living
in the street may have a salutary effect on children.

> For most of the children [in a sample of 56 street kids in Cali],
> being on the streets was not a permanent lifestyle, nor necessarily
> a pernicious one. Only a small group of older children were on
> the streets for long periods of time without getting assistance
> from some family member or benefactor. If these children were
> using an excessive amount of drugs, were suffering from addi-
> tional nutritional problems, or if their general emotional health
> was deteriorating with time on the streets, then the test results
> would have shown that these children had more pathology than
> the younger children. Indeed, according to our results and con-
> trary to expectation, age and time on the streets seemed to me-
> diate their problems. (435)

Aptekar explains that this is due in part to the fact that "most of the children were not actively abandoned, but were growing up in an orderly fashion that allowed them to take their place in the existing subculture of urban poverty" (435). The situation of children in Cali and in Recife may not be easily or even usefully comparable because most of the Colombian children, according to Aptekar, were returning home. But I emphasize the argument that living in the street did not hinder the prospects of success for the Colombian children who live in a milieu of urban poverty because I found precisely the opposite to be true in Recife.

In an article about children growing up in the street, Judith Ennew (1994b) recounts a conversation she had with a street child at a conference in Brazil:

> Some while ago, I shared a cigarette with 13-year-old Marcus in Rio. We were both feeling depressed by the non-productive events of the Second International Meeting of Street Children in Brazil. It was not easy to communicate – he in Portuguese, I in Spanish. But we managed somehow.
>
> After a while, I asked him about his family. He had two brothers, he said, but he never saw them. And as for parents? No, they were not a significant part of his life. He had some contact with a state institution. "But really," he said, "my friends are bringing me up." (409)

Ennew employs the anecdote as a point of departure for reassessing ideas about the peer-based affective relationships of street children. She argues that "such children develop supportive networks, coping strategies and meaningful relationships outside adult supervision and control" (410). She also draws attention to the problem of policies based on the idea that children outside adult control are perforce worse off than those at home and dangerous to themselves and to all those around them. Elsewhere, Ennew (1994a) makes the point that there are scant data on what happens with street children in the long run. Notwithstanding this important caveat, she writes,

> What [information we do have] hints . . . that they do not remain on the street. They taste its freedom as children – when

they are able to make a living there. But once they become youth it is not possible to beg, they need more money than can be gained in casual street trades, they settle for mainstream society, albeit in casual work and poverty. They marry or cohabit, have children, find a dwelling of some sort. (9)

Street children in Recife spoke to me about friendship in varied ways. Many said that they had no friends at all. "We don't have friends, just *colegas* [peers]" was how Margarete described it.[5] Others spoke warmly of their relationships, explaining that, notwithstanding the strife, "We're all friends." But none suggested anything approaching the idea that their mothers ("parents" are hardly a packageable concept for Brazil's urban poor) were "not a significant" part of their lives or that their friends were "bringing me up." On the contrary, their anxieties about the future were resolved only through wishful thinking about a reapproximation to their mothers and to homelife.

As Ennew (1994b: 413) herself has lamented, street children have been studied mostly through "anecdote or statistics collected . . . without comparison with control groups." I believe it important to add that they have been studied anachronically. Research on street children has been mostly like a snapshot, a portrait at a particular moment in time, with no effort to discover what happens over the long run. I do not pretend to redress the lack of longitudinal data here, but the devastation of human life I saw in following street children closely over a mere three years and then through the occasional news that reached me over an additional two years has led me to draw conclusions very different from those of Swart, Aptekar, and Ennew. Here is what has happened to some of the street children discussed in this book.

Margarete, of Chapter 1, was expelled from the shelter where I first interviewed her because she hit another girl over the head with a brick. After a short stay with an aunt, she returned to the street. She gave birth to a baby girl in a public hospital, then returned briefly to her aunt's house. A job was found for her in a municipal crèche. Later, she was committed to a mental hospital and her infant daughter was placed in a state institution. Margarete was then released – to the street – where she soon became pregnant once more. Shortly after her second child was taken from her she was said to have suffered a mental breakdown and then disappeared from the streets. When I returned in 1995, no one had heard from her in months. Most assumed she was dead. There was no trace even of her babies, for when I tried to track them down at the Casa de Carolina, I was told they had been given up for adoption. In 1997, to everyone's surprise, Margarete resurfaced, in the mental hospital.

Carlos, interviewed in my first radio workshop (Introduction), was in the men's prison, Aníbal Bruno, the last time I saw him. He and three companions had been accused in mid-1993 of using a brick to smash the skull of a schoolboy who refused to surrender his watch. *Alejado*, whose mother speaks of her attempts to coax him off the street (Chapter 2), was accused in the same case and so was *Manoel*, the youth who threatened to smash a large rock over the head of *Marcela* (Introduction). In mid-1995, all three were still in prison. In 1997, I learned that Carlos and Alejado had been murdered.

Beto, who interviewed Carlos, remained in the street. An NGO tried to help him set up a market stall so that he could work his way out of the street. They built a stall for him, reserved a place in a neighborhood market and gave him enough money to make his first purchase of produce. He took the money and ran. He subsequently threatened a street educator with a gun and was thereafter refused any help from the group. His brother *Zezinho* (Chapter 3) was murdered by someone he was attempting to mug.

Zé Luis, accused of murdering *Cristiano* (Chapter 5), remained in jail, the last I heard.

Mônica, the girl in Chapter 4 who said she would be a *maloca* [sic] all her life, was pregnant for the third time, the last I knew. Her first baby died, the second was taken to the Casa de Carolina. I do not know what has become of the third, but am reluctant to inquire. In 1997, I learned that Mônica had taken a job as a street vendor.

Bia (Chapters 2 and 5) participated actively for about a year in an educational program for street children. Then she suddenly abandoned the school. When I saw her in 1995, she was nearly always very high. Her body was more scarred than ever and she had few teeth left. She lived with her newborn in an abandoned, roofless house. A street educator friend wrote to me in 1996 to say that she found the baby with cigarette burns across her body. She wrote, "I became extremely anguished. My first impulse was to take her to my house, but I know that is not the best solution. Every day they [the street kids at the abandoned house] have a more depressing quality about them and less hope of improving their lives."

Sócrates, the boy who describes his beating by the police in Chapter 5 ("if a person gets kicked a lot in the belly he might what? Die! Yeah, he might die"), was arrested, accused of stealing a wallet. He spent nearly two years in Anibal Bruno, the men's prison. Upon his release, he returned to the street.

João Defunto, discussed further on in the Conclusion, was released from prison, to the street. In 1997 I learned he had been murdered.

Cheira, of Chapters 5 and 7 ("one day I hope to quit this life and work, have a kid, a wife, live in a quiet house, walk in front of the police without anyone thinking I'm a thief"), was also murdered.

I heard about *Marconi*, the youth who insisted I record his testimony of how the police had murdered his best friend *Luquinha* (Chapter 5), from the mother of my godson. In a letter she dictated for me in 1994, she recounted how Marconi was "found dead on the Olinda beach with three bullets in his head."

A 15-year-old whose words do not appear in this book stabbed to death his inseparable chum *Maguinho* (Chapter 5). That was 1993. By the time I returned in 1995, he was said to have committed two more murders.

One young boy who participated in a radio workshop at the Law Faculty (Chapter 2) fell off the back of a bus and was killed instantly when run over by another bus.

Adriano (Chapter 7), the boy who raided refrigerators whenever he got the chance, was murdered and no one was saying by whom.

Walter, spoken of as something of a bully by his chum *Eufrásio* (Chapter 2), went into hiding after committing a murder. Eufrásio, the last time I saw him, was leading much the same existence, adept as always at breaking into houses during the night. He had scarcely grown.

Iracy, who helped me with some of the interviews, wrote me a desperate letter in 1994, at that time aged about 17, to say that she was pregnant and jobless.

When I returned to Brazil in 1995, having been away for two years, I found many of the surviving children on the same corners where I had left them. Only the situation always seemed worse. *Eliane* (Chapter

2), the 15-year-old who looked no more than 12 in 1993 and who hoped to fill her mother's refrigerator with yogurt before she died, was pregnant for the third time.

Camilla, the pregnant 17-year-old mentioned in the Introduction and elsewhere (e.g., Chapters 5 and 7), was raising her baby, in the street. The gaunt toddler, aged two when I met her in 1995, was suffering from a chronic respiratory disease. She was so malnourished her hair had not grown in fully and she had never slept in a bed. Camilla, who once shunned drugs, had become a habitual user of glue and a variety of pills and, though still under the grip of her abusive boyfriend *Tadeu* (Chapter 2), she exchanged sex for money and drugs with a much older man. Although she was not using contraception, she desperately wanted to avoid another pregnancy. In 1997 Tadeu was murdered.

Marcela (Chapter 2), the transvestite, seemed to be giving up any hope of ever realizing her dream of being a designer or opening a beauty salon and she seemed to be losing her looks, of which she had been so proud.

Germano (Chapter 2) moved on from stealing bicycles to stealing cars and from statutory adolescence to adulthood, which landed him in jail. Somehow he was released, and he returned to the street.

Upon my return to Brazil, I heard no reports of children "returning home" and no reports of street children finding jobs and leaving the street except to live (for a time?) in a shelter. *Latinamerica Press* (1996) reported on a photojournalist who in 1990 took a picture of 17 young people, from the ages of 8 to 21, living in the streets of São Paulo. Almost six years later, the daily *Folha de São Paulo* looked for the children. They found that "Of the 17, eight are in prison, two are in FEBEM . . . four still live in the street, and two are dead. Only one, now 18, has changed her lifestyle and works as a domestic earning US$80 a month." The street children in Recife fare similarly, though I have never heard of any becoming domestic workers and the mortality rate is surely higher.

Agencies working with street children discuss engaging their charges in a "process," but the objective of this process is nearly always loosely defined in terms of a variety of unlikely transformations. But three institutions with very distinct approaches have had success in keeping some children (doubtless a minority of those in their care) off the street for long periods of time. These are the Comunidade dos Pequenos Profetas, where Demétrio maintains a farm with a "family" atmosphere; CAMM, where street children live without full-time adult supervision and with remarkable autonomy; and Desafio Jovem, the rigid, Pentecostal farm for drug addicts and street children. All of these institutions are dependent on the whims of foreign donors and local government agencies, and it is uncertain what will happen with these children in the long term. Demétrio plans to have them stay "forever." The directors at CAMM say they hope to reintegrate the children into their original homes (normally they only accept children with some family links). When I returned in 1995, some of the same kids were at the CAMM farm while others had simply left and returned to the street. It is uncertain what happens at Desafio Jovem, but many of the children were taken in at a very young age, some when as little as eight or nine, and are simply growing up in this Pentecostal community. Others stay for a time, and then run away. But to my surprise, some youths who had been in and out of many institutions decided to stay at Desafio Jovem. As one "recovered" lay worker at Desafio Jovem explained to me, "We substitute one drug for another, God for the street." Nowhere is the attempted transformation of street children more radical than at Desafio Jovem, where street life is equated with sin. But since street children are accustomed to speaking of street life as a vice, this philosophy seems to click with some of them.

Those who aim to turn *maloqueiros* into working children and future working adults or who wish to engage street children in political activism have remarkably few success stories. Around 1992 and 1993, NGOs in Recife seemed to point to the same two children when citing such cases. One became a militant with the National Movement of Street Children. But his return home, to a crowded hovel in a *favela*, did not solve all his problems. He remained illiterate, unemployed, even hungry, and reaching adulthood jeopardized his role in the movement. The other, David, of Chapter 4, found a steady job as a silk-screener. As the main breadwinner of the household and the only member with formal employment, he doubtless saved some of his youngest siblings from starvation. But when I visited, the family of 11 and counting lived in a two-room shack without running water.

Some street children, as discussed in Chapter 7, are offered opportunities, such as to live with middle-class families, or a relatively well paying job, but desist. Whereas Aptekar (1988) argued that the worst enemy of street children was their increasing age, I think the *maloqueiros* of Recife would say their worst enemy is what they describe as the addictive power of street life itself. Support for institutions working to remove street children from the street must start with painful recognition that many street children, when presented with seemingly attractive alternatives, still opt to live in the street. Likewise, despite large-scale efforts to effect street education in Recife, that is, to teach children in the street, I never encountered a child who had learned to read or write in the street.

But I also take something of a middle ground when it comes to discussing the importance of organizations that work with street children. Although it would be easy to cynically disregard as ineffectual much of the work being done, the value of this activism cannot be quantified simplistically in terms of how many street children have been "saved." Despite all of the frustrations that agencies in Recife have experienced in trying to awaken in street children a yearning for a new life and a new society, their persistence is not gratuitous for it forms part of a struggle for life and human dignity. Activist and service-providing organizations are gripped by the certainty that if they give up on the *maloqueiros*, they are handing them over to be killed by the police, by thugs, or by other angry children. Indeed, when observing *maloqueiros* in Recife, one has the distinct sense that childhood in the street is a fleeting condition, not because it inevitably leads to adulthood, but because it leads to early death or something equally intolerable. Efforts to change this reality cannot be dismissed.

In speaking of their own futures, I found street children walked a tightrope between two extremes. Often, they spoke of an almost formulaic dream.

Vamp [*male, aged about 16*]: [I'd like to] get a job, a woman, get married, have my children and leave street life [*essa vida*].

Whoever lives that life has nothing to lose. It's just be killed or die.

Renata [female, aged 15]: [What I want is] to have a house to live in, to not need anything from my mother, for me to have enough to give to her.

Patrício [male, aged about 17]: [What I want is] to work, have my child, my house, my wife.

They speak, on the one hand, of what I earlier referred to as a bourgeois dream (a spouse, a house, an "honest" job, and a couple of kids). On the other hand, Vamp hints at a different future he and so many other street children envisage, namely premature death – which turned out to be only too true in his case.

When asked what happiness meant for them, the children's answers varied. But there were also commonalities: houses, mothers, families, school, and work figured prominently in their answers, the same elements they spoke of when thinking hopefully of the future. In the questionnaire, I asked each respondent whether she or he would like to have children. A typical answer went as follows:

Jacilene [aged 15]: Yes, yes, I'd like to have just two, a *casal* (a girl and a boy).

In fact, of the 35 children who said how many children they wanted to have, only 5 (14%) gave an answer other than one or two. Whenever optimistic talk about the future arose, the children almost universally expressed the desire to have either one child or a *casal*. Nothing troubled me more than seeing infants in the street, and with a certain righteous determination I initially argued at length with children about the dangers of early pregnancy and encouraged them to use contraception. Speaking with boys about using condoms proved fruitless, and the closest I ever came to introducing any of the girls to the world of contraception was convincing an already pregnant Camilla to attend a sex education session at a family planning clinic, a requirement for the prenatal exam for which she never showed up. Although no girls told me they wanted to be pregnant immediately, parenthood was consistently part of what I believe is a way street children – both male and female – have of imagining their way out of the street. Thus while street children hardly cling to a belief in salvation from outside, they seem to treat their own reproduction as a type of salvation they themselves can effect.

For girls, the thought of having children may be a painful resignation to the realities of an inevitable adulthood, but it is also part of an imagined way of creating the opposite of street life, of producing the most essential component of home life – the emotional link between mothers and children. In a region where children almost universally say the person they love most is their mother, it is no surprise that motherhood and the concomitant possibility of being adored constitute a powerfully attractive hope for girls.

Street children have an ambivalent attitude toward adulthood. Being an adult means being treated as one before the law – that is, being sent to adult prisons rather than to juvenile detention centers from which escaping is easy. Living in the street, they also prefer to think of themselves as children, for being a street adult is a painful confirmation that their dreams of leaving "that life" have not been realized. For adolescent boys, parenthood, preferably with multiple women, is a means of confirming an important facet of their ideal of manhood. Riding the bus to the Aníbal Bruno jail to visit João Defunto, a *maloqueiro* who had recently turned 18, I met his girlfriend, Luanda, then pregnant by him. After being refused entry to the jail because she lacked identification, she gave me a package to deliver to her boyfriend. Upon my telling João Defunto about the package, he asked if it was "from Katia?" Katia, as I later learned, was also pregnant by him at the time.

"No," I said, a bit confused, "it's from Luanda." His mother, who was visiting at the time, giggled with evident pride and explained, "He's got women coming out of the woodwork" (*ele tá cheio de mulheres*). For young people, male and female, who literally possess nothing but their bodies, reproduction endows them with the possibility of creation. But their dreams of family life in the comfort of a home, they know, are unlikely to be realized. As I left Brazil in 1995, Camilla asked me when I would be back. When I told her it would probably be a couple of years before I returned, she said she would be dead by that time. I protested weakly, but she insisted, "Street children only have three futures: prison, insanity, or death."

Street Children, Reproduction, and Apartheid

Childhood has emerged as a specialized domain: pediatrics, compulsory schooling, child psychology, and Disneyland, to name just a few now taken-for-granted institutions, are all recent inventions. In the United States, new parents are greeted with a barrage of mail-order catalogs peddling every imaginable accoutrement for child care – each product, from breast pumps to diaper disposal machines, billed as indispensable. As Ellen Seiter (1993: 2) describes it, "The message is no less than this: mothering is the most satisfying and fulfilling experience life has to offer – so long as one has the right equipment." Another type of equipment, that used for children's play, is at present contributing significantly to the U.S. trade deficit with China, because China is the leading manufacturer of toys for American children.

Legislators in the First World debate the minutiae that color the character of childhood: school prayer, viewer ratings on movies and video games, regulations for child car seats. But what is beyond contention is that, as the habitat of humankind is inexorably transformed from rural to urban and economies from subsistence-based to market-driven, the practice of raising children has become pivotal in debates on where nations and the community of nations are headed. Sharon Stephens (1997: 10) has drawn attention to the relationship between constructions of childhood and constructions of the nation: "It is precisely because childhood so often still tends to be seen as natural and innocent, ahistorical and apolitical, that it is eminently fitted for use within nationalist visions and projects, with a wide range of consequences for the lives of actual children." At the same time that children are the subject of nationalist rhetoric everywhere from Singapore (Wee 1995) to Croatia (Povrzanović 1997), Indonesia (Shiraishi 1995) to Britain (Holland 1992), they are also appropriated as symbolic representatives of an emerging global community based in no small way around the consumption preferences and popular culture of children and youths.

Chris Jenks (1996: 67) has observed that the child has become "an index of a civilization – witness the outrage and general disapproval at the revelations concerning Romanian orphanages, an obvious signifier of the corruption of Communist structures!" Images of childhood are vital to everyday Brazilian conceptions about the United

States, and the reverse is also true. For so many Brazilians who know only a few things about the United States, one of those things is almost invariably "Disney," that is, Orlando's amusement park world of eternally happy childhood.[6] In contrast, Americans familiar with just a few things about Brazil tend to know that death squads kill homeless children there. If the state of childhood is to any degree "an index of civilization," as Jenks suggests, the lore of popular culture places street children and Disneyland as markers at opposing ends of the spectrum. First World claims to a privileged state of civilization are buttressed through condemnation of the plight of the Third World's street children. Street children, who undeniably suffer, are for the First World the obverse of its own still diverse notions of childhood, fomenting through their shock value a consensual position on the vital elements of childhood. In their negation of what is familiar and dear in childhood, street children reassure a world still ill at ease with its own patterns of reproduction, of bringing children into adulthood.

While it is problematic to essentialize the paradigm of the "world's children," I do believe there are a few essential elements in the emerging global paradigm of childhood. An increasingly urban, market-based world coupled with state-regulated education as the principal means of preparing the work force and international pressure to reduce or eliminate child labor have meant that the appropriate, "natural" – not to mention only feasible – habitats for children are school, home, and commercially ambitious play places, from amusement parks to shopping malls. Whereas in certain contexts it was thought of as natural for children to play and work in the street, for instance in New York City at the beginning of this century (see Nasaw 1985), today's street children find themselves in a prohibited realm. And it is easier and cheaper for a world troubled with its own patterns of reproduction to focus on the plight of children in a highly anomalous situation (preferably in a distant country) than to rethink the turbulent process of child rearing at home.

Brazil's street children challenge the hierarchical worlds of home and school and threaten the commercialized "public" space such as stores and shopping centers. They subvert their country's unmentioned but very real social apartheid that keeps the poor cooped up and out of view in the *favelas*. The final stages of writing this book were undertaken in Cape Town. As the two-year-old ANC government in South Africa was struggling to contend with the havoc wreaked by apartheid, I could not help but think that Brazil is moving in the other direction. Brazil may not have a Group Areas Act but in some places one would hardly know it. São Paulo now has vast neighborhoods known as *condomínios fechados*, gated communities where no one can enter without a pass and where only wealthy people can afford to live. The larger communities have their own schools, stores, and movie theaters, and some children scarcely leave these modern-day bantustans of the frightened elites. In Recife, some neighborhood streets have been blocked off by residents and declared private. And everywhere, the rich build ever-taller apartment towers fortified by high walls and armed guards, hoping to live just a little further above and more protected from the world of the street.

At a global level, inequality is enforced through separation and control of movement. South Africa's apartheid was merely an explicit, some would say generic, version of this phenomenon (Mamdani 1996), but the pattern is reproduced on many scales in many contexts, perhaps most strikingly in efforts to hermetically seal the borders of wealthy countries, as if the global movements of labor were divorced from global movements of goods, services, and capital.

The intersection of violence and children strikes emotional chords. But the chords are heterogeneous. In an examination of public debate in the wake of two gruesome cases of murder – one in the United Kingdom, the other in Norway – in which children were both the perpetrators and the victims, Stewart Asquith (1996: 102) points out that whereas the British widely called for more severe punishment of children, the Norwegians moved to ban the *Power Rangers* and *Ninja Turtles* from television: "What this surely illustrates is the way in which social, cultural and even historical differences in the explanations of childhood behaviour have to be taken into consideration." Asquith argues further that what the cases "alert us to is the malleability of childhood as a social construct, both from a historical and comparative cultural perspective, in which theories of childhood, the process of socialization and the relationship between the generations cannot be divorced from the structural makeup of society in general" (103).

A similar point can be made about violence and Brazilian street children. Part of the reason that the murders of children in Brazil's streets are widely perceived as more shocking than, say, severe malnutrition in the Brazilian *favelas* relates to the poignancy with which notions of children and adults as, respectively, in need of protection and responsible for protecting are subverted through these two tragedies. It is easier to ignore the children who, together with adults but in the privacy of their own homes, are victims of macrostructural social and economic systems than it is lone children in the public arena. Within Brazil, the murders of street children are seen as shocking and worthy of profound condemnation, but there is also a simultaneous and opposing tendency to focus on the role of children in perpetrating violence. When children and adults are seen more as beings on a continuum than opposing elements of a dyad, it follows that children must be held responsible for their action. Street children are not only held responsible, they are held up almost as the public face of violence and urban disorder, as the undoing of the nation.

The existence of impoverished, unsupervised, enraged children in the commercial centers and middle-class neighborhoods of Brazilian cities is a threat to the geographical segregation of rich and poor; and the violence in which the children sometimes engage is a threat to hierarchical class relations and to the division of power between adults and children. Violence at once endows street children with power and renders them vulnerable to retribution. Efforts to transform street children – either by turning them into working children, "restoring" to them a lost childhood, or saving them from the terrestrial hell of street life – can be seen as attempts to redress the threatening divergence of street children from familiar notions of childhood, to return them from street to home, from the libertine world of *essa vida* to the watchful eye of motherdom.

Janice Perlman (1976) was correct in arguing that at the center of the debate over marginality in Brazil is the issue of control. Whereas most of the *favelas* she studied were located near middle-class sections of the city, the government wanted to raze those *favelas* and relocate residents to remote working-class neighborhoods: "It is easier to exert police control over a distant ghetto, and easier to treat the needs of the poor in a perfunctory manner when they are no longer a visible part of the urban scene" (249–250). The problem with street children is precisely that they are so visible and yet so difficult to control. It may be easy for the elite to ignore hungry children tucked away in the *favelas*, but they cannot do this with the children who might hold them up at gunpoint as they ferry their own progeny to private schools. And the street children know this only too well. As a young adolescent explained to me with a certain tone of pleasure, "We ask people for money and they say 'I don't have anything.' You point a thirty-eight at them and then you see how fast they come up with some."

The perception of street children as a threat is rooted in the contradiction between the desire to keep children socially marginal, docile, and out of view, and the existence – precisely at the center of urban social life – of street children who often exercise violence, something normally deemed the province of adults. Street children are a reminder, literally on the doorsteps of rich Brazilians and just outside the five-star hotels where the development consultants stay, of the contradictions of contemporary social life: the opulence of the few amid the poverty of the majority, the plethora of resources amid the squandering of opportunities. They embody the failure of an unacknowledged social apartheid to keep the poor out of view. At home in the street, they are painful reminders of the dangerous and endangered world in which we live.

APPENDIX:
THE SETTING: RECIFE, OLINDA, AND NORTHEAST BRAZIL

Ten other South American countries lie contiguous to Brazil, but in Recife and Olinda, where the nearest border is thousands of kilometers away and few foreign tourists venture, the rest of the world feels small. Poor people would ask me what it was like *lá*, or there, for many had not heard of the United States.

The topography and climate of Brazil range from the dense and humid rainforests of the Amazon to the harsh, arid backlands of the Northeast known as the *sertão*, from the temperate rolling hills and fertile plateaus in parts of the South and Southeast to the vast flood-plain in Mato Grosso do Sul known as the Pantanal. The socioeconomic conditions are no less varied. Brazil is sometimes described as Bel-India, since it combines in one country the wealth of Belgium and oppressive poverty of subcontinental proportions.

Recife is the capital of Pernambuco, the state lying at the heart of the poorest region of Brazil. Pernambuco in combination with all or parts of eight other states constitutes Brazil's *Nordeste*, or Northeast. Much of the state of Pernambuco consists of the semiarid *sertão*, which also extends over vast stretches of the states of Maranhão, Piauí, Ceará, Rio Grande do Norte, Paraíba, Alagoas, and Bahia. Droughts have struck the *sertão* at least 10 times over the past century, and each time disease and starvation have ravaged the *sertanejos*, its inhabitants. Even in good times, with its cattle grazing and subsistence agriculture, the *sertão* has remained an impoverished backwater in Brazil.

The economic engine of Northeast Brazil has always been located near the coast and its fuel, historically, was sugar. Some of the first sugar mills in the New World were established in Pernambuco in the mid-sixteenth century, and to this day sugar remains the principal crop of the state. Sugar is grown in the *zona da mata*, or woodland zone, so called for the forests that once covered this fertile area embracing the coast where the rains are more plentiful and predictable. The production was initially organized around *engenhos*, the mills that processed the cane immediately after it was cut. The *engenhos* called for a combination of land, machinery, oxen, and labor. Slaves were imported from West Africa and from Angola, about 4,000 to 5,000 annually during the seventeenth century, over a million in the course of the eighteenth century. The constant replenishing of slaves from Africa resulted in an enduring African influence on Brazilian culture. The economic organization of the *engenho* was paralleled by a social and political organization that concentrated power in the hands of a white plantation aristocracy.

From approximately the mid-sixteenth century until the mid-seventeenth century, the *zona da mata* from Pernambuco to as far south as central Bahia held a virtual global monopoly on cane sugar production. Recife (under the shadow of Olinda) and Salvador da Bahia were the principal ports for the export of sugar and the import of slaves from Africa and manufactured goods from Europe. The economist Celso Furtado described Pernambuco as having once been perhaps the world's most profitable colonial agricultural territory (cited in Levine 1978: 21). But since the 1800s, the economic history of Northeast Brazil has been one of decline. Economist Nathaniel Leff (1997: 35) offers a "rough estimate" that "real per capita income in the Northeast *fell*, by approximately 30 percent between 1822 and 1913."

The destruction of many sugar plantations during a rebellion against Dutch occupation, coupled with competition from the newly sugar-producing territories of the Dutch, French, and British Caribbean and from Louisiana, pushed Brazilian cane production into a gradual backward slide. By 1900, Brazil supplied only 5 percent of the world's sugar (Skidmore and Smith 1984: 154). Sugar seemed to get a new lease on life in the late 1970s and in the 1980s from the government's policy of promoting the use of alcohol made from sugarcane as fuel for automobiles, but consumer preference for gasoline engines did not sustain the rejuvenation. In any case, sugar production

Map 3. Northeast Brazil.

in the Northeast has been chronically inefficient, and Brazil's main site of production has shifted to the Southeast. Today, the cultivation of marijuana yields as much income in some parts of Pernambuco as does sugar.[1]

Appendix

Olinda and Recife

Founded by Duarte Coelho in 1535, Olinda was one of the first permanent settlements of Brazil. The Cidade Alta (High City), as the historic center is called, is located on a knoll overlooking the Atlantic, well above the level of the marshy flatlands below. The Dutch invaded Pernambuco in 1630 and maintained a toehold in northeastern Brazil until 1654. During this time, Recife, previously a mere fishing village, became the seat of Dutch power. Shortly after their arrival, the Dutch razed Olinda, using the city's stones to build Recife. Under Johan Maurits of Nassau, governor general of Dutch Brazil from 1637 to 1644, Recife was transformed into a planned city, complete with palaces, military forts, shipping facilities, even an observatory and zoo.[2] Recife grew to become the second largest city in Brazil (after Salvador), a status it maintained until the middle of the eighteenth century (Levine 1978: 2).

Following its destruction by the Dutch, Olinda was rebuilt by the Portuguese over the next century, until 1755 when the reconstruction officially ended. The city has managed to preserve a distinctly colonial air, making it no wonder that Unesco declared it a world historical monument. The cobblestone streets are graced by views of the sea, of Recife, and of other portions of the Cidade Alta itself.

Olinda has traditionally been one of Brazil's important religious centers. In 1687, King Dom Pedro II established the Bishopric of Pernambuco, with Olinda at its center. Some 20 colonial-era churches dot the hills of the city. The Franciscans, Benedictines, and Carmelites established convents or asylums there. The Jesuit priest Father Luis de Grã gave the first classes in 1568 in what was to become the Seminary of Olinda. The Seminary slipped out of Jesuit control in 1760, when the Jesuits were expelled, but continued to operate under other auspices until recently. The Monastery of São Bento, established in 1599, still holds public masses and runs an expensive and lucrative private school.

The houses of Olinda are whitewashed or painted in soft pastels. On a typical afternoon, one will find most of the shuttered windows open, revealing the high-ceilinged interiors. Olinda maintains a certain appeal for middle-class artists, intellectuals, and other refugees from the high-rise security blocks of Recife so, unlike other parts of the

An Olinda church.

metropolitan area, rich and poor live in close proximity in Olinda. The city has two main museums and a number of private art galleries as well as craft shops. But although most visitors to the region stop here, Olinda is far from a tourist town. The half-dozen hostels and small hotels in the old city have vacancies all year except during *carnaval*, and there are few proper restaurants. Unlike Salvador da Bahia, which is frequented by tourists year round, Olinda is a place for *olindenses*.

During *carnaval* the city is visibly transformed. Every street and square of the Cidade Alta teems with *passistas*, or dancers of *frevo*, the trademark music of *carnaval* in Pernambuco. After months of practice, *Blocos*, organized groups that play music and dance in the open air, parade along different streets, sometimes along a preordained route, sometimes wherever their fancy takes them. Rural *maracatu* dancers in splendidly colorful costumes perform during special parades. Enormous *bonecos*, papier-mâché dolls representing folk heroes or public figures, sway amid the *passistas*. One guidebook (Cleary et al. 1990) assures the reader that at least 50 percent of the Brazilian population can dance better than the Supremes. In Pernambuco, where many children take their first steps to the rhythm of *frevo, forró*, or *capoeira*, the rate could well be higher.

Olinda during *carnaval*.

Only a couple of decades ago, Olinda consisted of nothing more than the Cidade Alta and several contiguous neighborhoods, such as Bomfim and Gaudalupe, and a few *favelas* such as the Ilha de Maruim. But today, with a population of about 350,000,[3] Olinda has sprawled the entire 10 kilometers north along the coast to the next municipality, Paulista, as well as inland into the areas of Peixinhos and Ouro Preto (see Map 4). Olinda contains several upper-middle-class pockets such as parts of Casa Caiada, but most residents of Olinda live in *favelas* or in working-class *vilas*.

The beaches of Olinda are not considered choice by the wealthy but they are crowded, particularly on weekends, with the poor and middle classes. The most popular stretch is in Casa Caiada, only a bus ride away from even the most distant *favelas* of Olinda and within walking distance for many residents of the city. Notwithstanding the small streams of raw sewage that flow into the ocean here and there, bathers are plentiful. Vendors ply the beach, hawking coconut water, beer, hot dogs, and ice cream. Men play volleyball and soccer; women sunbathe, typically in "dental-flcss" or very scant bikinis. Music from nearby bars, portable radios, or parked cars is played almost incessantly. *Música baiana*, or Bahian music, loosely based on reggae and various Afro-Brazilian rhythms and performed by such stars as Daniela Mercury, was the rage in 1992 and 1993. During my second period of fieldwork, in 1995, Brazilian funk and a new music called *mangue* (literally, mangrove swamp) that combines a number of forms of regional music had gained in popularity.

Most of the businesses of Olirda — shops, banks, restaurants, medical offices, and the like — are located along the main avenue that runs from Carmo, at the foot of the Cidade Alta, north along the shore through the neighborhoods of Bairro Novo and Casa Caiada. (It is precisely along this stretch that the street children of Olinda can be found.) In the other direction, along Avenida Kennedy and on nearby side streets, are located countless auto parts stores and wrecking yards, a few small industries, and vast slums such as Peixinhos.

The old center of Recife includes the neighborhoods of Santo Antonio, São José, the Island of Recife, and the area of Boa Vista (see Map 1). This is still a bustling business center, full of shops, market stalls, and offices, and parts of the Island of Recife are being refurbished. But other centers are cropping up, and the rich use the traditional downtown less and less. Boa Viagem, Recife's answer to Copacabana, contains a vast modern shopping mall, seemingly airlifted in from Miami, and countless boutiques and stores. Further south, Piedade has a shopping center of its own, complete with a most unlikely import, an ice skating rink. The neighborhood of Casa Forte has many conveniences as well. Notwithstanding the competition from the new commercial poles of Boa Viagem, Piedade, and Casa Forte, the old center remains the seat of city and state governments (enormous employers and bases of power) and an important center of transportation (the hub of most bus lines in the city).

Recife has traditionally been known by its inhabitants as the Venice of Brazil for the Afogados, Beberibe, and Capiberibe rivers that weave

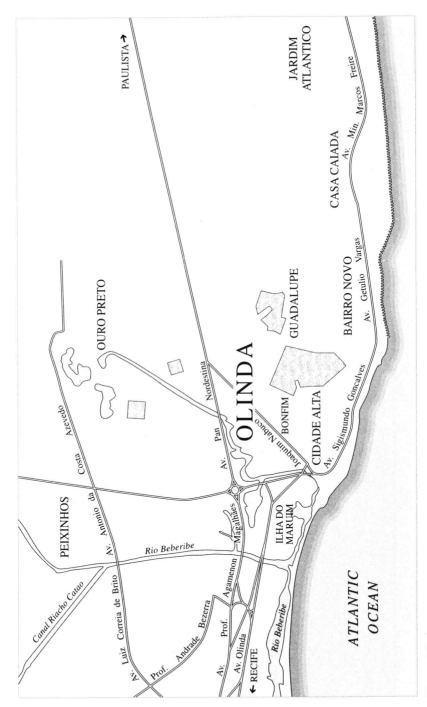

Map 1 Olinda

their way through the city. But the rivers and canals have long served as open sewers and the *catinga*, or rank smell, can be overpowering. Notwithstanding the foul state of the waterways, poor children can often be seen swimming in them. The wealthy traditionally have lived in stately mansions, though today most live in tall apartment buildings.

Neighborhoods such as Boa Viagem, Piedade, Casa Forte, and other privileged pockets here and there contain apartment towers, nearly all of which were constructed since the early 1970s. Comfortable single-family dwellings can be found in many other sections of the city. But more than half of Recife's population, as in Olinda, lives in *favelas* or in working-class *vilas*. The *favelas* are typically in areas that were recently "invaded" and contain houses fashioned from tin, cardboard, plastic, and wood, or sometimes mud and wattle. Virtually any scrap material that can be found is used. The land on which the *favelas* are built is nearly always either reclaimed swamp or a hillside. The swamplands flood and the hills are susceptible to mud slides. Most of the working-class neighborhoods such as Casa Amarela, Brasilia Teimosa, and Tres Carneiros began as "invasions" but became permanent, legal settlements where over time brick houses replaced the makeshift shacks. Because so much of the city is constructed at sea level, countless *favelas* around the city are deluged when the rains are heavy or the tides high. The sewage, which typically runs in open streams, merges with the flood waters, turning the dry earth into thick, malodorous mud.[4]

In his self-styled "sentimental" guide to Recife, Gilberto Freyre (1961: 3) was forced to confess that "no sea port in Brazil offers less to the tourist." My own first impressions were of mild shock, as the fieldnotes from my first day in the city attest: "The motorists are like bulls in Pamplona, they accelerate when they see people crossing the street. The streets are littered with rubbish and the sidewalks are mostly the territory of those who fish through the garbage for cardboard, bottles, or a meal for their animals or (perhaps?) themselves."

One's mode of transportation around the city shapes one's view of the metropolis. The poor, frequently barefoot, travel by bus or on foot. The buses are plentiful, but the routes tend to be circuitous, and in the mornings or evenings one will almost invariably have to stand. With inflation from 25 to 30 percent per month during 1992 and

1993, salaries were adjusted only four times per year, but bus fares rose every month. The fares, about US$.25 or $.50, depending on the route, become prohibitive in relation to salaries before wage adjustments.[5] One feels the heat when traveling by bus, for there is often no shade where one waits, and once on the bus the sheer mass of human bodies can be stifling. On foot one dodges open utility holes, parked cars, kiosks, and reckless drivers. Sewerage holes emit foul odors. By automobile, the experience is different. The poverty is more remote. The favelas, from a vantage point more distant and more rapidly shifting than when one walks, look almost picturesque.

The streets may all be named after the rich and powerful – senators, governors, landowners, among others – but the wealthy have, at best, a tenuous sense of ownership. They use the streets only to get from one place to another, usually as fast as possible. When they drive, they are reluctant to stop at intersections for fear of being mugged. But for about an hour each day, two large stretches of street are transformed. Between 5:30, when the sun rises, and 6:30, when the sun is more intense and people need to get ready for work, the paved path along the beach in Boa Viagem in Recife and the quiet streets closed to traffic in Casa Caiada in Olinda are inundated with walkers. Throngs of middle-class and rich people in shorts and sneakers walk along the sea. On a typical morning they encounter many acquaintances. Sometimes high-stakes business deals are struck. By 7:00 A.M., however, these streets are empty of strollers. In the evening, after dark, venturing out in these same areas is considered dangerous. But lovers park along the sea – with the windows rolled up and the doors locked – to *namorar*, or do what lovers do.

As Freyre remarks in his guidebook, Recife "is not unveiled immediately; its greatest charm lies in its ability to win one over little by little" (1961: 4). Recife probably has more difficulty winning one over today than when Freyre last revised his guidebook more than three decades ago, yet somehow maintains the ability to do just that. Hidden among lifeless concrete high-rises one finds colonial churches; around the corner from the porno kiosks lie the elegantly landscaped gardens of the Teatro Santa Isabel; lost among vendors peddling cheese, bottle openers, and plastic Xangô relics in the snaking alleys around the Mercado São José, one suddenly emerges into the Patio de São Pedro, the finely restored colonial-era square. But most of all it is the hospitality, wry humor, joy, contemplative melancholy, and myriad other charms of *recifenses* that win one over. Northeasterners have a cunning ability to turn the most unlikely situation into a celebration, to find moments of happiness despite hardship, and to personalize the most routine of social interactions.

The climate in Recife and Olinda is remarkably stable throughout the year. Temperatures typically range from lows of about 23°C (73°F) to highs of no more than 30°C (86°F). Winter refers to the rainy season, between April and August, and summer to the rest of the year. Regular rainfall in winter and occasional rain the rest of the year keep the vegetation green and lush. Trade winds blow off the ocean, with seldom a pause, so that even if one feels quite hot in the sun, any shady spot with a breeze is comfortable. At night one never needs a blanket but rarely feels so hot as to wish to throw off the sheets. Many people sleep in hammocks hung between any two hooks on the terrace or in the house.

Demographics

As of 1993, Brazil's population was about 157 million, with 3,590,000 births annually. The average annual growth rate of the population between 1990 and 1994 was 1.5 percent (UN 1996: 128). The population of the state of Pernambuco (7.1 million in 1991) is now heavily concentrated in the metropolitan area of Recife and in adjacent coastal towns. The metropolitan area is home to 40 percent of the state's population (IBGE 1992). Whereas in 1940 only one-third of the state's residents lived in cities, now over two-thirds live in urban areas.

The population of the state is very young. In 1980, 42 percent of Pernambucans were aged 14 or younger and a full 53 percent were 19 or under (IBGE-PE 1980). The population of Pernambuco rose by 19 percent between 1970 and 1980, and by 16 percent between 1980 and 1991.

Recife, the state's capital, experienced what has been termed "slow growth" until 1820, then a century of accelerated growth, followed by a period of veritably explosive growth, particularly from the 1940s onward (Assies 1991: 43). As of 1991, Recife officially had a population of 1.3 million, but if one takes into account the larger met-

Appendix

Table 7. *Population of Pernambuco*

Year	% in rural areas	% in urban areas
1940	66	34
1950	56	44
1970	46	54
1980	34	66
1991	29	71

Sources: Andrade 1979:18 and IBGE 1992.

ropolitan region, the figure rises to 2.9 million (CMPDDCACR 1994: 2).

In 1991, 41 percent of northeastern mothers of children five years of age and younger were not using any method of contraception. Of those who were, 65 percent relied on tubal ligation (BEMFAM 1991: 15). Thus, most women delay using contraception until they opt for sterilization. Although reliable data on the prevalence of abortion are rare, it is difficult not to get the anecdotal impression that unsafe, illegal abortions constitute the primary means of reproductive control for women who have not had tubal ligations. When I asked poor mothers, from time to time, whether they wanted more children, the reply, literally without exception, was "God help me!" (*Deus me livre!*).

Kinship, Race, and Religion

Favela families are often described in terms similar to the matrifocal kinship structures outlined by Raymond Smith in *The Negro Family in British Guyana* (1956). In highlighting the matrifocal elements in Recife, Parry Scott (1990) writes,

> The term "matrifocality" identifies a complex web of domestic group relations in which, even when the man is present in the household, the female side of the group is favored. In other words, mother–child relations are characterized by greater solidarity than father–child relations; choice of residence, identification of known relatives, exchanges of favors and goods, visits, etc. are all stronger on the female side, and there are likely to

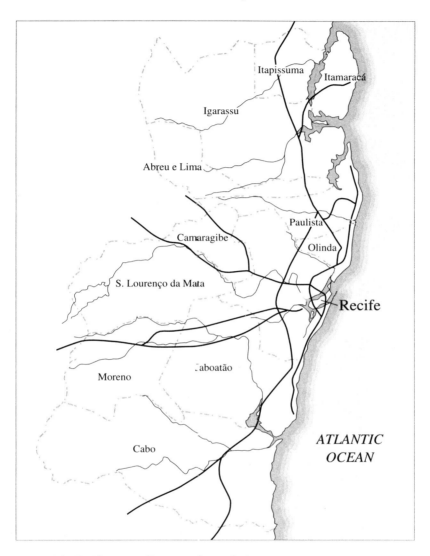

Map 5. The Recife metropolitan area. *Source:* Assies 1991: 97.

be religious and cultural manifestations highlighting the female side. (39)

Seen from the perspective of the children, the mother is typically far more important than the father.

One anthropologist has referred to families in the *favelas* as something like small-scale "survival units" (Banck 1980). Although the "economistic" view of *favela* families has been overemphasized, as Cardoso (1984: 196) rightly asserts, the family-support networks in *favelas* tend to be less elaborate and formal than among the middle classes. The middle classes are likely to maintain intricate relations with a large network of consanguineous and affinal relatives, sometimes referred to collectively as *parentela*, or kindred (Brown 1979). But at the core of middle-class families residing in apartment buildings and well-secured homes is a nuclear family with a man firmly at the helm. Moreover, the middle-class woman is expected to have her children with only one man, and the man is expected to live permanently under the same roof with his (one) wife and his children.

Recife has relatively few people that Europeans would call white or that Africans would call black. Most fall somewhere in between and have a mixture of European, African, and Amerindian ancestry. Because many poor women have children from several men, the range of color within one family can be striking. In *Masters and Slaves*, Gilberto Freyre (1963 [1933]), who studied under Franz Boas and supported Boas's thesis on the separation of genetics from culture, treats among other themes the permeation of Indian and African cultures into the life of the plantation aristocracy. Freyre argues, rather eccentrically, that under the slave regime Brazil achieved a sort of racial democracy through miscegenation and the cultural merging of the Indian, African, and Iberian elements of Brazilian society. Freyre's thesis has been widely challenged (e.g., da Costa 1966). Although class and race are not themes examined extensively in this book, the perspective of Floristan Fernandes and Roger Bastide (1978 [1951]) guides my thinking on this subject. They argue that Brazil has a rigid class structure that relegates blacks and people of mixed race to the lower class. In Recife it is true that light-skinned people can be found living in the *favelas* and fairly dark-skinned people in expensive apartment buildings, but skin color correlates approximately to wealth, such that the rich are

The Setting

Olinda artist and poet Fernando Araújo. His T-shirt reads: "WE NEED A DREAM: National Committee on Dissatisfaction."

more likely to be light-skinned and the poor more likely to be dark-skinned. Street children in Recife, not surprisingly, are mostly black, in the North American color scheme, or ranging from what Brazilians call *morenos* (dark) to *negros* or *pretos* (very phenotypically black).

People in the Recife area, like others in most parts of Brazil, are heterogeneous in their religious beliefs. Although 92 percent of Pernambucans identified themselves as Catholic in a 1980 survey (IBGE-PE 1980), Afro-Brazilian spirit-possession religions are widely practiced, especially in the *favelas*. And consulting a *mãe-* or *pai-de-santo* (a leader in one of various Afro-Brazilian traditions) or making an offering to Iemanjá (the goddess of the Sea) by no means precludes the possibility of characterizing oneself as Catholic. Catholicism, in any case, is practiced in diverse ways. Some Recife communities are sharply divided, as Robin Nagle illustrates in *Claiming the Virgin* (1997), between adherents of liberation theology who believe the church should seek to effect social transformation, especially for the poor, and those who follow the more traditional, Vatican-inspired edict that Cathol - cism and politics do not mix. *Kardecismo*, a form of spiritualism based on the teachings of the nineteenth-century Frenchman Alain Kardec, is also widespread in Recife and, along with *umbanda*, another form of spiritualism, has considerable appeal among the middle classes. Many professed Catholics will come to an *espírita* center for such purposes as spiritual surgery, while others simply leave the church to practice the *espírita* faith, which draws on Christianity, the social philosophy of Comte, the Law of Karma, and other sources (Brown 1979: 284). Depleting the proportion of Brazilians who are nominal Catholics are the Pentecostal Protestants, often referred to in Brazil simply as *pro- testantes* or *crentes* (believers). The Pentecostal churches – the Assemblies of God, the Universal Church of the Kingdom of God, the Four-Square Church, and others – have been gaining rapidly in number and strength around the country, and Recife is no exception. According to 1991 census data, 328,000 Pernambucans (4.6%) declared themselves Pentecostals and an additional 158,000 (2.2%) "Traditional Evangel- icals," which in Brazil means Methodists, Episcopalians, Presbyterians, and other practitioners of noncharismatic Protestantism (IBGE 1997a).

Economic Conditions, Education, and Other Indicators

There has been no lack of initiatives to staunch the poverty of North- east Brazil. In 1959, the Federal bureaucracy known as SUDENE (Su- perintendency for the Development of the Northeast) was established in Recife. The original objectives of SUDENE were to develop irri- gation systems in the *sertão*, relocate *sertanejos* to more fertile land in the state of Maranhão, and attract industry to the Northeast. More than three decades later, SUDENE is known as the headquarters of the *industria da seca* – the drought industry – where generous salaries and consulting fees have underwritten a First World lifestyle for those least likely to suffer the poverty of Northeast Brazil.

The public sector in Brazil as a whole and in Northeast Brazil in particular is often treated as a source of private booty for its functio- aries. An acquaintance of mine who sold hydraulic equipment in Re- cife told me that at least 10 percent of his asking price was always destined for the pockets of the government purchaser. A veteran public servant in Olinda, whose uphill battle to feed and clothe her family, notwithstanding her rank and years of service, attested to her honesty, told me that she had recently been offered, in exchange for a purchasing contract, enough money to buy a new house. Brazilians of all social classes will tell you that they would normally expect public servants to accept such offers.

They say there are only two ways to get rich in Northeast Brazil: inherit wealth, or steal it. Indeed, successful, law-abiding entrepreneurs are rare. The economy in Recife remains linked to the larger economy of sugar and to the port that historically concentrated most of the region's exports, but this is less the case all the time. In the outskirts of Recife one finds large industries such as food processing plants, cleaning product factories, and distilleries. Some people have enriched themselves through these sectors. Construction and real estate are important facets of the economy. Real estate has been a particularly vital sector since the country for decades suffered hyperinflation, and keeping money in local currency, despite sometimes attractive interest rates, was risky at best, senseless at worst.

The state employs a vast army of teachers, nurses, and civil servants, most of whom in 1992 and 1993 were earning no more than US$100 per month. When the new currency, the real, was introduced in mid-1994, salaries about doubled when translated into dollars, though most prices also rose at least to match. For families with one or two members earning a minimum monthly salary, survival is a struggle. Families without any formally employed members typically live in extreme deprivation. They rely on *biscates*, or odd jobs, such as taking in washing, catching crabs along the rivers, and street vending. Crime makes an important contribution to the income of countless households. Children are a vital resource, as they can hawk various goods, beg, steal, do odd jobs, and work in the home.

One of the most disturbing indicators about life in Recife is the homicide rate. The murder rate tripled between 1980 and 1989, from 17.4 per 100,000 inhabitants to 47.6. In comparison, the mid-1980s rate was 4.9 in Costa Rica, 3.3 in Chile, and 0.7 in England and Wales (WHO 1988). The rate for Brazil as a whole was 14.8 in 1986 (UN 1991). As discussed in Chapter 5, by 1997 homicide had become the leading cause of death nationwide for 15- to 17-year olds.

Middle-aged people in Pernambuco speak of a time when the public schools were viable, and it was even possible for children to study only in state or municipal schools and gain access to universities. But education has never been a political priority in Pernambuco. In the early 1890s, Governor Barbosa Lima complained that Pernambuco invested more in prisons and barracks than in schools (Levine 1978: 162). Today the public schools are in a state of perpetual crisis. The official statistics reveal part of the picture.

- In 1988, 31 percent of children "failed" first grade. An additional 22 percent simply dropped out during the year, leaving only 47 percent who passed directly on to second grade.
- Only 28 percent of children aged 10 to 17 have completed four or more years of school. (UNICEF 1992; CMPDDCACR 1994)

Teachers were paid only about US$160 per month in 1995, supplies are forever missing, and strikes are routine. But even when the schools are in session, many children are too hungry to concentrate or too bored to sit still. Families with any resources at all send their children to private schools. A full 63 percent of schools in Recife are private (CMPDDCACR 1994). Today it is virtually unheard of for a child educated in state schools to be admitted to a university.

In 1990 the Population Crisis Committee (cited in Assies 1991: 5) rated 100 large cities around the world in terms of quality of life. They took into account such indicators as health, education, and sanitary conditions. Recife ranked 96th. Statistics on the city are consistently bleak. According to UNICEF (1992), in 1989:

- infant mortality stood at 74 per 1,000 live births
- 19 percent of children had height/age ratios indicative of malnutrition
- 23 percent of children under age five had suffered diarrhea in the two weeks prior to a national health survey.

The plight of poor, urban children is one aspect of the downside of Brazilian economic growth between the end of World War II and 1980. The drive to industrialize also spawned a vast urban underclass. Despite high rates of economic growth – GNP per capita rose by an average annual rate of 6.3 percent between 1965 and 1980 (UNICEF

1995: 76) – the living conditions of the majority of Brazilians failed to improve. Wealth was being amassed by a small middle class and a much smaller elite. Recession ravaged Brazil in the 1980s. The growth between 1980 and 1992 was negligible, at an average of 0.4% (UNICEF 1995: 76) with some of those years actually showing negative growth. Between 1980 and 1988, the minimum wage fell by about a third in real terms (Rizzini et al. 1994: 57).

Perhaps nowhere in Brazil are the contrasts between rich and poor more evident than in Pernambuco. The assets of one family I knew, whose businesses flourished under tax breaks facilitated by SUDENE, were estimated at US$500 million; but according to UNICEF (1992), 69 percent of families in Pernambuco have incomes of less than half the monthly minimum wage, that is, less than what then amounted to about US$45 per month.

It would be easy to think of Northeast Brazil as a cauldron of misery. Indeed, the official statistics do little to capture the dimensions of the suffering. Yet it must also be said that, despite the harrowing oppression of being poor in Brazil, *nordestinos* have a knack for making life a worthwhile experience. As one friend advised me, when I was telling him of a family whose house had been flooded by the winter rains, "If you think about those things too much, you'll go mad." Hunger, violence, and ostracism, likewise, may be the context in which street children exist, but their lives can hardly be reduced to those elements.

GLOSSARY

Aníbal Bruno   Recife's men's prison. When a street youth turns 18, he may be incarcerated at Aníbal Bruno, where typically he is placed with 10 other inmates in a cell that lacks even beds. Prisoners, even when arrested on minor charges, are sometimes forced to wait years before seeing a judge.

Artane   a "prescription only" drug (Trihexyphenidyl) with a euphoric effect used widely by street children and poor youths in general. A synthetic antispasmodic, Artane has an inhibiting effect on the nervous system and is often prescribed for people with Parkinson's disease.

assistencialismo   A derogatory term employed to describe patronizing handouts, such as of used clothing. It implies doing things *for* one's beneficiaries, rather than *with* them.

bad money   see *dinheiro errado*.

barracos   a crude hut fashioned from scrap material, normally wood but also sheet metal, cardboard, and plastic.

bigu   street children use the term to refer to a ride on the back bumper of a bus, as in to *pegar bigu*, or to catch a ride.

bocada (sometimes called *boca*, as in *boca de fumo*)   a place where illegal drugs are sold.

CAP (Centro de Acolhimento Provisório)   The Center for Provisional Reception (frequently referred to as FEBEM). When children are detained for an infraction or when lost, they are held at CAP as they await a hearing with a judge at the Children's and Adolescents' Court next door. Under the Children and Adolescents Act, children can be held up to 45 days. In fact they are often held longer. Before the act was passed into law, many children who were lost or abandoned literally grew up in the facility. Recife's CAP was destroyed in a violent riot in 1995.

carnaval the pre-Lenten festival celebrated in the streets of many Brazilian cities.

Casa de Carolina the state-run facility in Recife where abandoned or abused young children (up to age six) are interned.

Casa de Passagem House of Passage, a Recife NGO for street girls.

casa grande literally, the big house. The *casa grande* was the slave master's home and the locus of power in Brazil before abolition.

cheira-cola a glue sniffer.

Cidade Alta literally, the high city, the term is used to refer to the colonial center of Olinda.

colegas peers.

descolar literally, to unglue; figuratively, to come up with, "to score."

dinheiro errado bad money. Children use this term to refer to money earned in the street by means of stealing or prostitution. They say *dinheiro errado* gets spent faster than other money and that their mothers often reject it.

dinheiro suado good money. Children use this term to refer to money earned by the "sweat of one's brow," as opposed to *dinheiro errado*. They say *dinheiro suado* lasts longer.

documentos documents, specifically, the legal papers such as birth certificates, working permits, and voter registration cards that are obligatory to hold but, especially for illiterate people, a bureaucratic nightmare to obtain.

educador/a (m./f.) literally, educator; used frequently to refer to an *educador de rua*, or street educator, that is, to a person who works in the street with street children.

engenho sugar mill; plantation complex.

essa vida literally, that life; used by street children to describe the things they do in the street, such as stealing, using drugs, and other things they deem no good.

Estatuto da Criança e do Adolescente the Children and Adolescents Act, voted into law in 1990 to replace the repressive Código do Menor, or Minor's Code. The act, 267 sections long, defines the rights of children and the obligations of the state and families toward them.

favela   a shantytown, or informal settlement, usually built on "invaded" land. The homes are mostly *barracos*. In Recife the *favelas* tend to be built on low marshy land that floods frequently or on hillsides that are susceptible to mudslides.

FEBEM (Fundação Estadual do Bem-Estar do Menor)   State Foundation for the Well-Being of Minors, established in 1954 under the military government; although FEBEM was a larger bureaucracy of services and penal institutions for children, the term was and continues to be used to refer to the government-run holding tanks for juvenile delinquents, now known (in Recife) as CAP. Technically, FEBEM has become FUNDAC, but the name has great staying power.

freguês/freguesa (m./f.)   literally parishioner; a client received or vendor visited habitually; used by street children to refer to a person who helps them on a consistent basis by giving them food or clothing.

FUNDAC (Fundação do Criança e do Adolescente)   Foundation for Children and Adolescents. State-run network of detention centers and social services.

galera   a gang of young people.

homem   literally, a man; a man who does not practice receptive anal sex; a policeman.

madruga   a mispronunciation of the word *madrugada* (meaning dawn); the act of stealing from houses in the middle of the night.

malandragem   debauchery, living by one's wits, trickery.

malandro   a rogue; one who practices *malandragem*.

maloca   shack; sometimes a shortened form for *maloqueiro*.

maloqueiro   in general usage, a rascal, or a naughty or dirty child; a slum dweller; among street children in Recife the term is used to refer to themselves, especially to the older ones who have been in the street for some time.

maloquero   alternative pronunciation of *maloqueiro*.

marginal   literally, marginal; street criminal.

Menina sem Nome   the Girl without a Name; a young girl who was raped and left dead on a beach. The poor gave her a proper

burial and she has become a popular saint. Street children sometimes visit her tomb in Rec.fe's Santo Amaro Cemetery.

menino   male child; homosexual; in certain contexts, a child paramour.

menino/a de rua   boy/girl of the street.

monitores   the adult supervisors at FEBEM who are responsible for
keeping order.

motherdom   a term used here to refer to the moral and economic
logic of the matrifocal home, according to which children are
expected to live at home, bring in resources to the household,
and heed the advice of their mothers.

Movimento Nacional de Meninos e Meninas de Rua   *see* **National
Movement of Street Children.**

National Movement of Street Children   a nongovernmental organization founded in 1985 that brings together children and street
educators into a large and vibrant Brazilian social movement that
aims to defend the rights of children.

NGO   acronym for nongovernmental organization.

nordestinos   the residents of Northeast Brazil.

nurtured children   a term used here to refer to middle-class and
rich children who have few responsibilities at home, who are not
expected to work or bring in resources to the household, and who
are nurtured by their parents over a long period of time.

nurturing children   a term I employ to refer to poor children in
matrifocal households who from a young age are expected to assume many responsibilities within the home, such as minding
younger siblings, and who bring in resources from outside.
Rather than representing endless expenditures for their parents,
they nurture the household.

olindenses   residents of Olinda.

pontos   hangouts, turf; places where street children congregate.

preso de ordem   a prisoner in a police station who, after several detentions, is given special duties such as cleaning the station
house, running errands, and torturing other prisoners. Being
made to torture other prisoners places one on the victim's "hit
list" so that after being released a *preso de ordem* may be murdered.

Projeto Renascer   literally, "Project Rebirth." This **FUNDAC** project (subsequently renamed Center for Reception and Referral) operated on weekdays, offering girls lunch, medical attention, and a variety of educational activities.

raiva   rage; rabies.

recuperar   to recover; used to refer to the "reclamation" of street children converted into little workers.

revolta   rebelliousness. Children say that the violence they suffer makes them *revoltar*, or strike back.

Rohypnol   a "prescription only" drug (flunitrazepam, a sleeping pill) favored by street kids and poor youths.

senzala   the slave quarters.

sertão   the rugged, dry hinterland of the Northeast.

viciados   people with vices; street children often say they have become viciados or *aviciados* [sic] as a result of street life.

vida boa   the righteous life; in the parlance of poor children, the life they lead at home when they help their mothers and do "good" things such as working.

vida errada   the bad or iniquitous life; for poor children, the life they say they lead when in the street, stealing, using drugs, and generally doing "bad things."

vida nova   a new life; institutions often say they are offering street kids a *vida nova*.

vila   a working-class neighborhood.

Xangô   Afro-Brazilian spirit possession religion; the Afro-Brazilian God of thunder and fire equated with Saint John.

zona da mata   literally, the forest zone, for the trees that once covered the fertile strip along the coast of Northeast Brazil from Pernambuco to Bahia.

NOTES

Introduction

1. FEBEM, or Fundação Estadual de Bem-Estar do Menor (State Foundation for the Well-Being of Minors), was created shortly after the 1964 Revolution that ushered in Brazil's military dictatorship. Despite the philanthropic-sounding name, the most notable feature of the nationwide structure was the network of juvenile delinquent detention centers operating at the state level that doubled as holding tanks for orphaned, unwanted, or lost children. In the past, many children literally grew up in FEBEM institutions. The proper name for the facility in Pernambuco since 1990 has been the Centro de Acolhimento Provisório (CAP), or Center for Provisional Reception. In this book the acronyms FEBEM and CAP are used interchangeably since street children and the wider public use both terms.
2. One of the main differences between CAP and the Aníbal Bruno prison for men is that whereas escaping from CAP is merely a question of scaling a wall or even slipping out the front door, breaking out of Aníbal Bruno is nearly impossible.
3. The first question was generally answered with something to the effect of "I would kill them all one by one." To the second, most replied that the government ought to build houses for the street children.
4. Only 13 percent of the youths counted in the city government's survey of street children were female (CIELA 1993).
5. When referring to the street children "of Recife" in this book I am referring to those in the larger metropolitan area, including in Olinda.

1. Speaking of the Street

1. The reader is reminded that the acronyms FEBEM and CAP are used interchangeably. See Glossary or the Introduction's note 1 for an elaboration.

2. See discussion of the relationship between glue and hunger in Chapter 2.

3. Margarete expressed the desire that I use her real name when writing about her. At the time of her request, she was 19, of legal age.

2. *Being in the Street*

1. One group that did manage to work in the Gramado had mixed results. While generally unable to influence the kids' behavior, they found that the youths welcomed their presence, especially that of one foreigner volunteering for the group, because it offered a cover for stealing. Between forays to grab wallets, especially of old people, the kids would come over and play games with the street educators. Being around the foreign woman was especially helpful because the police seemed to assume she would not be in the company of thieving children.

2. For a discussion of the semistructured questionnaire and the sample to which it was applied, see Introduction.

3. As will be discussed in an elaboration on this theme in Chapter 7, *freguês* can also have the inverse meaning, that is, of a regular vendor. Thus, a client might also refer to the man who habitually sells her meat as her *freguês*.

4. With limited mathematical skills, many poor and street children in Northeast Brazil are unable to distinguish between the question "How many years ago?" from "How old were you at the time?"

5. The reader is reminded that the sample size varies because it was not always possible or logical to ask all questions of all informants. In addition, sampling error (for instance, skipping questions by accident) and ambiguous answers reduced the number of valid responses in some instances.

6. For a more clinical view on the possible detrimental effects of glue sniffing to health, see O'Connor 1983.

3. *"Home Children": Nurtured Childhood and Nurturing Childhood*

1. Alison Lurie, in *The Language of Clothes* (1981), argues that by the nineteenth century children's dress in North America and Europe was distinct from that of adults, with the emergence of such styles as unisex sailor outfits and the Fauntleroy suit for boys. Nonetheless, it is also true that even at the beginning of the twentieth century, it was common for children, particularly working-class ones, to be dressed like miniature adults. Only later did a distinct and widespread children's attire, exemplified by playclothes, become the norm. Curiously, now, under the globalizing in-

fluence of The Gap and other enterprises, adults are dressing much like children.

4. *Betraying Motherdom*: Maloqueiros *and "That Life" in the Street*

1. According to the United Nations data (UN 1996) 111 million Brazilians lived in urban areas in 1991. The UN defines "urban areas," in the case of Brazil, as "urban and suburban zones of administrative centres of *municipios* and districts" (175). Increasing this figure by 1.5 percent per year, the average annual population growth for the country as a whole during that period, the 1993 population would have been upward of 114,350,000.
2. This figure includes 17 infants and children under the age of 4, nearly all accompanied by a homeless adult, usually their mother.
3. Of a sample of 46 children who either currently lived in the street or had lived there in the past, only 7, or 15 percent, could correctly identify the movement. Most children said they had never heard of it or else confused it with such things as a type of music or, more frequently, a street gang.
4. Today, *maloca* is normally used to mean shack. It derives from the Tupi words *mâr-oca*, or house of war (Machado 1952). The *Novo Dicionário Aurélio da Língua Portuguesa* (1986) defines *maloqueiro* as follows: "Common denomination for rascals who wander through the street barefoot and dirty, normally in a group, asking for money and who practice petty theft. Some of them spend the nights on the beaches in hideouts in the sand, called *malocas.*"

5. *When Life Is Nasty, Brutish, and Short: Violence and Street Children*

1. Much as I tried, I was unable to find statistics on the proportion of youth murders actually resulting in trial. But if Pernambuco serves as an example for other states, the rate is quite low indeed. While the special adolescent and children's police division in Pernambuco keeps records on the autopsy reports of murdered children, it does not keep track of what happens with the cases after the bodies have been buried. Unfortunately, it is not possible to cross-check police records on murder statistics with court records of murder trials, as the latter are not available to the public. Here, the quantitatively minded reader will have to excuse my imprecise assertion that the "vast majority" of murder cases are not brought to trial. Nonetheless, after prying as far as I could with a police statistician and interviewing lawyers and social workers at the Children's and Adolescents' Court, this seemed a safe, if inexact, assessment.

2. The confusion between "four months" and "a year and four months" suggests that both estimates should probably be read as "a long time."

3. He was murdered subsequently and I have chosen to use his real name.

4. FUNDAC, the network of social service and detention centers, is the new
name for the entire bureaucracy that used to be known as FEBEM.

5. The number 40 should probably be considered not an actual numerical
estimate but a way of saying "a whole lot."

6. Here, for reasons of confidentiality, it is not possible to reveal the specific
sources of my information. Notwithstanding a presumption of innocence
until guilt has been proved, the universal perception among those who
knew the details of the incidents was that the perpetrators were indeed
other street youths. This perception was even shared by those street educators who tended to blame most of the violence on the police.

7. Most young Brazilians who are murdered are not small children but adolescents. In Pernambuco, for instance, 59 percent of all those under the
age of 18 who were murdered in 1994 were 16 or 17 years of age (Governo
do Estado de Pernambuco 1994).

8. The official statistics on child mortality in Brazil are appallingly deficient.
In contrast to this UNICEF figure for 1993, the *United Nations Demographic
Yearbook* (UN 1996: 420) estimates the number of deaths of children under
five in 1990 at 113,000, half the UNICEF figure.

6. Curing Street Children, Rescuing Childhood

1. It should be pointed out that the censuses of street children did not take
into account those sleeping in institutions, about 150. In mid-1993, there
were about 30 children with Demétrio, 30 at CAP, 16 at CAMM, 16 with
Padre Ramiro, 40 at Desafio Jovem, 6 at the Casa de Santa Luzia, and 15
at the Olga Guerros Reeducation Center (essentially a jail for adolescents).
Yet, had the census taken into account those sleeping in institutions, it
would then have been necessary also to take into account the number of
adults working at CAP, the Casa de Santa Luzia, and other institutions
whose employees have been excluded from the count.

2. See, for instance, Freyre 1968 [1936]a, DaMatta 1991 [1985], and Graham
1988.

3. Vainsencher 1987.

4. Her reign was short-lived, however. The first lady was accused, inter alia,
of awarding contracts valued at nearly half a million dollars to her immediate relatives. One contract, awarded to her brother, without competitive bids, involved the distribution of water by truck to 25,000 people in
the state of Alagoas. The brother later admitted he owned no water trucks.

He did manage, however, to build himself a swimming pool twice the size of the local reservoir (Brooke 1991).

5. For a discussion of the idea of participation of children in social movements, see Hart 1992.

7. *Street Children and Their "Clients"*

1. The children at CAP are all supposed to appear before a judge from the Children's and Adolescents' Court.

Conclusion: The Ephemeral Lives of Street Children

1. The author of a recent book on street adolescents in Hollywood (Ruddick 1996:3) writes that "My fascination with the topic was largely theoretical. Homeless youth pose a challenge to a series of theoretical premises that have become fashionable within critical theory." Street youths, for this author, seem to obligingly illustrate various academic points, such as about the "material power of symbolism" (4) and "new forms of marginality" (5).

2. Unlike other excerpts of conversations in this book, this particular passage was not tape-recorded and is therefore based on my recollection of the exchange.

3. Huggins and de Castro (1996:80) write, "Most commonly, the perpetrators were on- and off-duty police, lone citizen 'justice makers' (*justiceiros*), death-squad extermination groups, and private police. . . . Prospective victims get auctioned off to the lowest bidder; some shop owner and commercial associations keep assassination teams on a retainer".

4. Also implicit here is the suggestion that adolescence has a broad, cross-cultural meaning, a problematic suggestion when considering that Latin Americans often affirm that adolescence (as a social – as opposed to a biological – stage) is a recent import from the United States and Europe that, in any case, has relevance only to the middle and upper classes, not to the bulk of the region's population.

5. Some children said there was no difference between friends (*amigos*) and *colegas* while others made a distinction. While I initially had translated the word *colega* as "chum," I settled on "peer" instead, to emphasize that the association was based more on a shared condition than the result of purposeful selection.

6. For an excellent examination of Disneyland in relation to global notions of Childhood, see Hunt and Frankenburg 1990.

Appendix: The Setting: Recife, Olinda, and Northeast Brazil

1. I am indebted to a personal communication from Robert Levine for this information.
2. For a general history of the Dutch period, see de Mello 1987; for an analysis of architecture, art, and science during this period, see Whitehead and Boeseman 1989.
3. The United Nations estimated the population of Olinda at 341,000 in 1991 (UN 1996).
4. According to municipal statistics, only 38 percent of homes in the city are connected to sewerage systems or septic tanks (CMPDDCACR 1994: 15).
5. Monthly minimum salaries were typically about US$90 at the time of adjustment but, after being held at the same number of cruzeiros for four months, fell to less than US$40 as a result of the relentless devaluation of the cruzeiro; the currency fell at almost exactly the same rate that inflation rose.

REFERENCES

Adler, Patricia A. 1993. *Wheeling and Dealing: An Ethnography of an Upper-Level Drug Dealing and Smuggling Community.* New York: Columbia University Press.

Allsebrook, Annie, and Anthony Swift. 1989. *Broken Promise: The World of Endangered Children.* London: Headway.

Alvim, Maria Rosilene Barbosa, and Lícia do Prado Valladares. 1988. "Infância e sociedade no Brasil: Uma análise da literatura." *Boletim Informativo e Bibliográfico de Ciências Sociais (BIB)* 26 (2): 3–37.

Amado, Jorge. 1989 [1937]. *Capitães da areia.* Rio de Janeiro: Record.

Amnesty International. 1990a. *Brazil: Torture and Extrajudicial Execution in Urban Brazil.* London: Amnesty International.

Amnesty International. 1990b. "Child Victims of Killing and Cruelty." *Focus* (September): 3–6.

Andrade, Gilberto Osório de. 1979. *Migrações internas e o Recife.* Recife: Instituto Joaquim Nabuco.

Aptekar, Lewis. 1988. *Street Children of Cali.* Durham, N.C.: Duke University Press.

Aptekar, Lewis. 1989. "Characteristics of the Street Children of Colombia." *Child Abuse and Neglect* 13 (3): 423–437.

Ariès, Philippe. 1973 [1960]. *Centuries of Childhood.* Harmondsworth: Penguin.

Ashby, Leroy. 1984. *Saving the Waifs: Reformers and Dependent Children (1890–1984).* Philadelphia: Temple University Press.

Asquith, Stewart. 1996. "When Children Kill Children." *Childhood* 3 (1): 99–116.

Assies, Willem. 1991. *To Get Out of the Mud: Neighbourhood Associativism in Recife, 1964–1988.* Amsterdam: Centrum voor Studie en Documentatie van Latijns Amerika (CEDLA).

Avancini, Walter, and Sandra Werneck. 1994. *Boca.* Feature film. Republic Entertainment.

References

Babenco, Hector. 1980. *Pixote: A lei do mais fraco*. Feature film. Unifilm/Embrafilme.

Banck, Geert A. 1980. "Survival Strategies of Low-Income Urban Households in Brazil." *Urban Anthropology* 9 (2): 227–242.

Barker, Gary, and Felica Knaul. 1991. *Exploited Entrepreneurs: Street and Working Children in Developing Countries*. New York: Childhope.

BEMFAM. 1991. *Pesquisa sobre saúde familiar no nordeste do Brasil*. Demographic and Health Surveys. Rio de Janeiro: Sociedade Civil Bem-Estar Familiar no Brasil.

Benthall, Jonathan. 1992. "Child-Focused Research." *Anthropology Today* 8 (2): 23–25.

Best, Joel. 1990. *Threatened Children: Rhetoric and Concern about Child-Victims*. Chicago: University of Chicago Press.

Bitar de Fernandez, Victoria. 1989. *Proyecto regional: Niños de la calle y drogas*. Washington, D.C.: Organización de los Estados Americanos.

Bourgois, Philippe. 1995. *In Search of Respect: Selling Crack in El Barrio*. Cambridge: Cambridge University Press.

Boyden, Jo. 1990. "Childhood and the Policy Makers: A Comparative Perspective on the Globalization of Childhood." In *Constructing and Reconstructing Childhood: Contemporary Issues in the Sociological Study of Childhood*, edited by Allison James and Alan Prout, 184–215. London: Falmer Press.

Boyer, Paul. 1978. *Urban Masses and Moral Order in America, 1820–1920*. Cambridge, Mass.: Harvard University Press.

Brooke, James. 1991 (6 September). "There's Cooking in the Palace, Clucking in the Press." *New York Times*, A4.

Brooke, James. 1992 (4 November). "Brazil's Police Enforce a Law: Death." *New York Times*, A3.

Brown, Diana. 1979. "Umbanda and Class Relations in Brazil." In *Brazil: Anthropological Perspectives*, edited by Maxine L. Margolis and William E. Carter, 270–304. New York: Columbia University Press.

Burns, E. Bradford. 1993. *A History of Brazil*. New York: Columbia University Press.

Campos, Maria Machado Malta. 1993 [1991]. "Infância abandonada: O piedoso disfarce do trabalho precoce." In *O massacre dos inocentes: As crianças sem infância no Brasil*, edited by José de Souza Martins, 117–153. São Paulo: Hucitec.

Campos, Regina, Marcela Rafaelli, Walter Ude, Marilia Greco, et al. 1994. "Social Networks and Daily Activities of Street Youth in Belo Horizonte." *Child Development* 65 (2): 319–330.

Cardoso, Ruth C. L. 1984. "Creating Kinship: The Fostering of Children in

References

Favela Families in Brazil." In *Kinship, Ideology and Practice in Latin America*, edited by Raymond T. Smith, 196–203. Chapel Hill, N.C.: University of North Carolina Press.

Castro, Josué de. 1977 [1952]. *The Geopolitics of Hunger*. New York: Monthly Review Press.

Childhope. 1992 (10 June). "What Is the Going Rate for Killing a Street Child?" *Guardian* (London), 19.

Childhope. n.d. *Fact Sheet on Street Children*. New York: Childhope.

CIELA. 1993. *Primeiro relatório da segunda pesquisa realizada pelo CIELA sobre meninos e meninas de rua do Recife: Os que vivem e dormem na rua*. Olinda: Centro Interuniversitário de Estudos da América Latina, África e Ásia.

Cleary, David, Dilwyn Jenkins, Oliver Marschel, and Jim Hine. 1990. *Rough Guide to Brazil*. London: Harrap Columbus.

Clifford, James. 1988. *The Predicament of Culture*. Cambridge, Mass.: Harvard University Press.

CMPDDCACR. 1994. *Formulação de política municipal de defesa e promoção dos direitos da criança e do adolescente: Situação das crianças e adolescentes*. Recife: Conselho Municipal de Promoção e Defesa dos Direitos da Criança e do Adolescente da Cidade do Recife.

Connolly, Mark. 1990. "Adrift in the City: A Comparative Study of Street Children in Bogotá, Colombia, and Guatemala City." *Child and Youth Services* 14 (1): 129–149.

Connolly, Mark, and Judith Ennew. 1996. "Introduction: Children Out of Place." *Childhood* 3 (2): 131–145.

Costa, Viotta da. 1966. *Da senzala à colonia*. São Paulo: Difusão Européia do Livro.

Cruzada de Ação Social. 1995. *Pesquisa sobre meninos de rua*. Recife: Cruzada de Ação Social.

DaMatta, Roberto. 1991 [1985]. *A casa e a rua*. Rio de Janeiro: Guanabara Koogan.

deMause, Lloyd. 1974. *The History of Childhood*. New York: Psychohistory Press.

Dimenstein, Gilberto. 1990. *A guerra dos meninos*. São Paulo: Brasiliense.

Dimenstein, Gilberto. 1991. *Brazil: War on Children*. Translated by Chris Whitehouse. London: Latin America Bureau.

Diógenes, Glória Maria Santos. 1994. *Historias de vidas de meninos e meninas de rua de Fortaleza*. Fortaleza: Governo de Estado do Ceará.

Ennew, Judith. 1994a. "Less Bitter than Expected: Street Youth in Latin America." *Anthropology in Action* 1 (1): 7–10.

Ennew, Judith. 1994b. "Parentless Friends: A Cross-Cultural Examination of

References

Networks among Street Children and Street Youth." In *Social Networks and Social Support in Childhood and Adolescence*, edited by Frank Nestmann and Klaus Hurrelmann, 409–426. Berlin: Walter de Gruyter.

Estado de São Paulo. 1995 (19 July). "Menores infratores são impunes, diz pesquisa." São Paulo.

Felsman, J. Kirk. 1982. "Street Urchins of Cali: On Risk, Resiliency and Adaptation in Childhood." Ph.D. dissertation, Harvard University.

Fernandes, Florestan, and Roger Bastide. 1978 [1951]. *A integração do negro na sociedade de classes*. São Paulo: Ática.

Filgueiras, Ana. 1992. "Among the Street Children." *World Health* (May–June): 6–8.

Fine, Gary Alan, and Kent L. Sandstrom. 1988. *Knowing Children: Participant Observation with Minors*. Sage University Paper Series on Qualitative Research Methods. Newbury Park, Calif.: Sage.

Fonseca, Claudia. 1989. "Pais e filhos na família popular (início do século XX)." In *Amor e família no Brasil*, edited by Maria Angela d'Incao, 95–128. São Paulo: Editora Contexto.

Fortes, Meyer. 1970 [1938]. *Time and Social Structure and Other Essays*. London: Athlone Press.

Freire, Paulo. 1972 [1970]. *The Pedagogy of the Oppressed*. Translated by Myra Bergman Ramos. New York: Herder and Herder.

Freyre, Gilberto. 1961. *Guia prático, historico e sentimental da cidade do Recife*. Rio de Janeiro: José Olympio.

Freyre, Gilberto. 1963 [1933]. *The Masters and the Slaves: A Study in the Formation of Brazilian Society*. Translated by Samuel Putnam. London: Weidenfeld & Nicolson.

Freyre, Gilberto. 1968 [1936]a. *The Mansions and the Shanties: The Making of Modern Brazil*. Translated by Harriet de Onís. London: Weidenfeld & Nicolson.

Freyre, Gilberto. 1968 [1936]b. *Sobrados e mocambos: Decadência do patriarcado rural e desenvolvimento urbano*. Rio de Janeiro: José Olympio.

Gama, Mara. 1991 (18 December). "Maquiagem inútil: Collor tenta convencer os italianos de que a questão do menor por aqui não é tão feia como pensam." *Istoé O Senhor*, 29.

Glauser, Benno. 1990. "Street Children: Deconstructing a Construct." In *Constructing and Reconstructing Childhood: Contemporary Issues in the Sociological Study of Childhood*, edited by Allison James and Allan Prout, 138–155. London: Falmer Press.

Governo do Estado de Pernambuco. 1994. *Estatísticas básicas*. Recife: Secretaria da Segurança Pública, Diretoria de Polícia da Criança e do Adolescente.

References

Governo do Estado de Pernambuco. 1995. *Estatísticas básicas*. Recife: Secretaria da Segurança Pública, Diretoria de Polícia da Criança e do Adolescente.

Graham, Sandra Lauderdale. 1988. *House and Street: The Domestic World of Servants and Masters in Nineteenth-Century Rio de Janeiro*. Cambridge: Cambridge University Press.

Hardman, Charlotte. 1973. "Can There Be an Anthropology of Children?" *Journal of the Anthropological Society of Oxford* 4 (11): 85–99.

Hart, Roger A. 1992. *Children's Participation: From Tokenship to Citizenship*. Innocenti Essays, no. 4. Florence: UNICEF, International Child Development Centre.

Hernández Cava, Felipe. 1994. "Rio, en presente de indicativo." *Ronda Iberia*: 22–32.

Holland, Patricia. 1992. *What Is a Child? Popular Images of Childhood*. London: Virago Press.

Huggins, Martha K., and Myriam Mesquita P. de Castro. 1996. "Exclusion, Civic Invisibility and Impunity as Explanations for Youth Murders in Brazil." *Childhood* 3 (1): 77–98.

Human Rights Watch. 1994. *Final Justice: Police and Death Squad Homicides of Adolescents in Brazil*. New York: Human Rights Watch/Americas.

Hunt, Pauline, and Ronald Frankenberg. 1990. "It's a Small World: Disneyland, the Family and the Multiple Re-representations of American Childhood." In *Constructing and Deconstructing Childhood: Contemporary Issues in the Sociological Study of Childhood*, edited by Allison James and Alan Prout, 99–117. London: Falmer Press.

IAPG. 1990. *High Infant Mortality and the Plight of Street Children: Special Problems in Latin America and the Caribbean*. New York: Inter-American Parliamentary Group on Population and Development.

IBGE. 1989. *Anuário estatístico do Brasil*. Rio de Janeiro: Instituto Brasileiro de Geografia e Estatística.

IBGE. 1992. *Anuário estatístico do Brasil*. Rio de Janeiro: Instituto Brasileiro de Geografia e Estatística.

IBGE. 1997a. Web page: http://200.20.101.8/.

IBGE. 1997b. Web page: http://www.ibge.org

IBGE-PE. 1980. *Anuário estatístico de Pernambuco*. Rio de Janeiro: Instituto Brasileiro de Geografia e Estatística.

Impelizieri, Flávia. 1995. *Street Children and NGOs in Rio: A Follow-up Study on Non-Governmental Projects*. Rio de Janeiro: Amais.

International Child Resource Institute. 1995 (26 February). "Stop the Killings of Street Kids in Brazil." Public e-mail communication.

James, Allison. 1993. *Childhood Identities: Self and Social Relationships in the Experience of the Child*. Edinburgh: Edinburgh University Press.

References

James, Allison, and Alan Prout, eds. 1990. *Constructing and Reconstructing Childhood: Contemporary Issues in the Sociological Study of Childhood*. London: Falmer Press.

Jenks, Chris. 1996. *Childhood*. New York: Routledge.

Kael, Pauline. 1981 (9 November). "Childhood of the Dead." *New Yorker*, 170+.

Kendall, Sarita. 1975 (29 May). "Street Kids of Bogotá." *New Society*, 117–118.

Kitzinger, Jenny. 1990. "Children, Power and the Struggle against Sexual Abuse." In *Constructing and Deconstructing Childhood: Contemporary Issues in the Sociological Study of Childhood*, edited by Allison James and Alan Prout, 157–183. London: Falmer Press.

Kosminsky, Ethel Volfzon. 1993 [1991]. "Internados – Os filhos do estado padrasto." In *O massacre dos inocentes: As crianças sem infância no Brasil*, edited by José de Souza Martins, 117–153. São Paulo: Hucitec.

Kvale, Steinar. 1996. *InterViews: An Introduction to Qualitative Research Interviewing*. Thousand Oaks, Calif.: Sage.

La Fontaine, Jean. 1986. "An Anthropological Perspective on Children in Social Worlds." In *Children of Social Worlds*, edited by Martin Richards and Paul Light, 10–30. Cambridge: Polity Press.

Lamb, Christina. 1991 (June). "Why Rio Is Murdering Its Children." *Marie Claire*, 48–52.

Latinamerica Press. 1996 (16 May). "Time Stands Still for Street Kids." 5.

Leff, Nathaniel. 1997. "Economic Development in Brazil: 1822–1913." In *How Latin America Fell Behind: Essays on the Economic Histories of Brazil and Mexico, 1800–1914*, edited by Stephen Haber, 34–64. Stanford, Calif.: Stanford University Press.

Levine, Robert. 1997. "Fiction and Reality in Brazilian Life: *Pixote*." In *Based on a True Story: Latin American History at the Movies*, edited by Donald F. Stevens, 203–216. Wilmington, Del.: SR Books.

Levine, Robert M. 1978. *Pernambuco, in the Brazilian Federation, 1889–1937*. Stanford, Calif.: Stanford University Press.

Lewin, Linda. 1987. *Politics and Parentela in Paraíba: A Case Study of Family-Based Oligarchy in Brazil*. Princeton: Princeton University Press.

Linhares, E. D. R., J. M. Round, and D. A. Jones. 1986. "Growth, Bone Maturations, and Biochemical Changes in Brazilian Children from Two Different Socioeconomic Groups." *American Journal of Clinical Nutrition* 44: 552–558.

Louzeiro, José de. 1977. *Infância dos mortos*. Rio de Janeiro: Record.

Lucchini, Riccardo. 1996. "Theory, Method and Triangulation in the Study of Street Children." *Childhood* 3 (2): 167–170.

References

Lucena, Claudia, and Margarette Andrea. 1995 (23 July). "Projeto Mão Amiga lançado pelo governo após rebeliões no CAP." *Jornal do Commercio* (Recife), 1–2.

Lurie, Alison. 1981. *The Language of Clothes.* New York: Random House.

Machado, José Pedro, ed. 1952. *Diccionario Etimólogico da Língua Portuguesa.* N.p.: Confluência.

Malinowski, Bronislaw. 1944. *A Scientific Theory of Culture, and Other Essays.* Chapel Hill: University of North Carolina Press.

Mamdani, Mahmood. 1996. *Citizen and Subject: Contemporary Africa and the Legacy of Late Colonialism.* Princeton: Princeton University Press.

Martins, José de Souza, ed. 1993 [1991]. *O massacre dos inocentes: As crianças sem infância no Brasil.* São Paulo: Hucitec.

Mead, Margaret. 1977 [1928]. *Coming of Age in Samoa: A Study of Adolescence and Sex in Primitive Societies.* London: Penguin.

Mello, José Antonio Gonsalves de. 1987. *Tempo dos flamengos: Influência da ocupação holandesa na vida e na cultura do norte do Brasil.* Recife: Fundação Joaquim Nabuco.

Milito, Cláudia, and Hélio R. S. Silva. 1995. *Vozes do meio-fio: etnografia.* Rio de Janeiro: Relume-Dumará.

MNMMR. 1992. *Teses e Propostas.* Brasilia: Movimento Nacional de Meninos e Meninas de Rua.

MNMMR-PE. 1992. *Relatório Anual.* Recife: Movimento Nacional de Meninos e Meninas de Rua-Pernambuco.

Morch, Jesper. 1984. "Abandoned and Street Children." *Ideas Forum* (UNICEF journal), 1.

Muñoz, Cecilia, and Martha Palacios. 1980. *El niño trabajador.* Bogotá: Carlos Valencia.

Nagle, Robin. 1997. *Claiming the Virgin: The Broken Promise of Liberation Theology in Brazil.* New York: Routledge.

Nandy, Ashis. 1992. *Tradition, Tyranny, and Utopias: Essays in the Politics of Awareness.* Delhi: Oxford University Press.

Nasaw, David. 1985. *Children of the City: At Work and at Play.* Garden City, N.Y.: Anchor/Doubleday.

Needham, George C. 1884. *Street Arabs and Gutter Snipes: The Pathetic and Humorous Side of Young Vagabond Life in the Great Cities, with Records of Work for Their Reclamation.* Boston: D. L. Guernsey.

New York Times. 1997 (18 November). "Brazil Youth Killings Soar." A4

Novo Dicionário Aurélio da Língua Portuguesa. 1986. Rio de Janeiro: Nova Fronteira.

O'Connell, Vanessa. 1997 (April). "Budgeting for Baby: Five Smart Steps to Take Before Your Little One Arrives." *Working Mother*, 14–16.

References

O'Connor, Denis. 1983. *Glue Sniffing and Volatile Substance Abuse*. Aldershor, UK: Gower.

Opie, Iona, and Peter Opie. 1959. *The Lore and Language of School Childrer*. Oxford: Oxford University Press.

Ortiz de Carrizosa, Susana. 1992. "Latin American Street Children: Problerr, Programmes and Critique." *International Social Work* 35 (4): 405–413.

Panter-Brick, Catherine, Alison Todd, and Rachel Baker. 1996. "Growt1 Status of Homeless Nepali Boys: Do They Differ from Rural and Urba1 Controls?" *Social Science and Medicine* 43 (4): 441–451.

Parker, Richard G. 1991. *Bodies, Pleasures, and Passions: Sexual Culture in Con‑ temporary Brazil*. Boston: Beacon.

Patel, Sheela. 1990. "Street Children, Hotel Boys and Children of Pavemenr Dwellers and Construction Workers in Bombay – How They Meet Their Daily Needs." *Environment and Urbanization* 2 (2): 9–26.

Pereira, Raimundo Rodrigues. 1994 (16 March). "Em busca da infância per‑ dida." *Veja*, 66–75.

Perlman, Janice E. 1976. *The Myth of Marginality: Urban Poverty and Politics in Rio de Janeiro*. Berkeley: University of California Press.

Piaget, Jean. 1982. "The Necessity and Significance of Comparative Research in Developmental Psychology." In *The Sociology of Childhood: Essential Readings*, edited by Chris Jenks, 207–218. London: Batsford Academic.

Povrzanović, Maja. 1997. "Children, War and Nation: Croatia." *Childhood* 4 (1): 81–102.

Prout, Alan, and Allison James. 1990. "A New Paradigm for the Sociolog‑ of Childhood?" In *Constructing and Deconstructing Childhood: Contemporar‑ Issues in the Sociological Study of Childhood*, edited by Allison James and Alan Prout, 7–34. London: Falmer Press.

Qvortrup, Jens. 1987. "Introduction" [to special edition on the Sociology of Childhood]. *International Journal of Sociology* 17 (3): 3–37.

Radcliffe-Brown, A. R. 1970 [1940]. Preface. In *African Political Systems*, ed‑ ited by Meyer Fortes and E. E. Evans-Pritchard, xi–xxiii. Oxford: Oxford University Press.

Reynolds, Pamela. 1995. "Youth and the Politics of Culture in South Africa." In *Children and the Politics of Culture*, edited by Sharon Stephens, 218– 240. Princeton: Princeton University Press.

Rialp, Victoria. 1991. "Street Children." *World Health* (March–April): 8–10

Rizzini, Irene. 1995. "Crianças e menores – do pátrio poder ao pátrio dever um histórico da legislação para a infância no Brasil." In *A arte de governa‑ crianças: a história das políticas sociais, da legislação e da assistência à infâncie no Brasil*, edited by Francisco Pilotti and Irene Rizzini, 99–168. Rio de Janeiro: Amais.

Rizzini, Irene, Irma Rizzini, Monica Muñoz-Vargas, and Lidia Galeano. 1994. "Brazil: A New Concept of Childhood." In *Urban Children in Distress: Global Predicaments and Innovative Strategies*, edited by Cristina Szanton Blanc, 55–99. Florence: UNICEF/International Child Development Centre.

Rocha, Jan. 1992 (3 June). "Major Pressed to Raise Brazil's Child Killings." *Guardian* (London), 6.

Rubin, Herber J., and Irene S. Rubin. 1995. *Qualitative Interviewing: The Art of Hearing Data*. Thousand Oaks, Calif.: Sage.

Ruddick, Susan M. 1996. *Young and Homeless in Hollywood*. New York: Routledge.

Save the Children. 1993. *Criança notícia: Crianças e adolescentes na imprensa brasileira*. Recife: Save the Children Foundation.

Scheper-Hughes, Nancy. 1992. *Death without Weeping: The Violence of Everyday Life in Brazil*. Berkeley: University of California Press.

Schildkrout, E. 1978. "Roles of Children in Urban Kano." In *Sex and Age as Principles of Social Differentiation*, edited by Jean La Fontaine, 109–137. London: Academic Press.

Schwartzchild, Michael Rainer. 1987. "A criança, o adolescente e o 'de menor.'" *São Paulo em Perspectiva* 1 (1): 26–29.

Scott, James C. 1976. *The Moral Economy of the Peasant*. New Haven: Yale University Press.

Scott, R. Parry. 1990. "O homen na matrifocalidade: gênero, percepção e experiências do domínio doméstico." *Cadernos de Pesquisa* 73: 38–47.

Seiter, Ellen. 1993. *Sold Separately: Children and Parents in Consumer Culture*. New Brunswick, N.J.: Rutgers University Press.

Shiraishi, Saya S. 1995. "Children's Stories and the State in New Order Indonesia." In *Children and the Politics of Culture*, edited by Sharon Stephens, 169–183. Princeton: Princeton University Press.

Skidmore, Thomas E., and Peter H. Smith. 1984. *Modern Latin America*. New York: Oxford University Press.

Smith, Raymond T. 1956. *The Negro Family in British Guyana: Family Structure and Social Status in the Village*. London: Routledge & Kegan Paul.

Smith, T. Lynn. 1954. *Brazil: People and Institutions*. Baton Rouge: Louisiana State University Press.

Snow, David A., and Leon Anderson. 1993. *Down on Their Luck: A Study of Homeless Street People*. Berkeley: University of California Press.

Stephens, Sharon, ed. 1995. *Children and the Politics of Culture*. Princeton: Princeton University Press.

Stephens, Sharon. 1997. "Editorial Introduction: Children and Nationalism." *Childhood* 4 (1): 5–17.

References

Stone, L. Joseph, and Joseph Church. 1973. *Childhood and Adolescence: A Psy-chology of the Growing Person*. New York: Random House.

Swart, Jill. 1990. *Malunde: The Street Children of Hillbrow*. Johannesburg: Wi-watersrand University Press.

Swart, Jeane Margaret [Jill]. 1988. "An Anthropological Study of Street Chi-dren in Hillbrow, Johannesburg, with Special Reference to Their Moral Values." M.A. thesis, University of South Africa.

Swift, Anthony. 1991a. *Brazil: The Fight for Childhood in the City*. Innocen-i Studies. Florence: UNICEF/International Child Development Centre.

Swift, Anthony. 1991b. "Passage Out of Hell." *Oxfam News*, 10–11.

Taçon, Peter. 1981a. *MyChild Minus One*. Unpublished UNICEF report.

Taçon, Peter. 1981b. *MyChild Minus Two*. Unpublished UNICEF report.

Taçon, Peter. 1981c. *MyChild Now*. Unpublished UNICEF report.

Taussig, Michael. 1987. *Shamanism, Colonialism, and the Wild Man: Study in Terror and Healing*. Chicago: University of Chicago Press.

Taylor, M., K. Veale, A. Hussein Ali, and M. Elamin El Bushra. 1992. "Victimisation amongst Street Children in Sudan and Ethiopia: A Pre-liminary Report." Paper presented at Conference on Understanding Crime and Crime Control, Rome.

Thorne, Barrie. 1993. *Gender Play: Girls and Boys in School*. Buckingham: Open University Press.

Time. 1978 (11 September). "Brazil's Wasted Generation." 32+.

UN. 1991. *1989 Demographic Yearbook*. New York: United Nations.

UN. 1996. *1994 Demographic Yearbook*. New York: United Nations.

UNICEF. 1992. *Crianças e adolescentes em Pernambuco: Saúde, educação e trabalho*. Recife: United Nations Children's Fund.

UNICEF. 1995. *State of the World's Children*. Oxford: Oxford University Press

Vainsencher, Semira Adler. 1987. *Centro Educational Dom Bosco: Uma experiência com menores de rua*. Recife: Secretaria de Educação do Estado de Pernam-buco.

Valladares, Lícia, and Flávia Impelizieri. 1991. *Ação invisível: O atendimento à crianças carentes e a meninos de rua no Rio de Janeiro*. Rio de Janeiro: Instituto Universitário de Pesquisas de Rio de Janeiro.

Veale, Angela. 1992. "Towards a Conceptualisation of Street-Children: The Case from Sudan and Ireland." *Trócaire Development Review*: 107–121.

Wagley, Charles. 1971 [1963]. *An Introduction to Brazil*. New York: Columbia University Press.

Walton, Christopher R. 1991. "Surviving the Ultimate Crisis: What Hap-pened behind the Scenes at Covenant House that Led to Its Rapid Growth and How It Survived the Wrenching Departure of Its Founder." *Fund Raising Management* 22 (4): 24–28.

References

Wee, Vivienne. 1995. "Children, Population Policy, and the State in Singapore." In *Children and the Politics of Culture*, edited by Sharon Stephens, 184–217. Princeton: Princeton University Press.

Whitehead, P. J. P., and M. Boesman. 1989. *A Portrait of Dutch 17th Century Brazil*. Amsterdam: North Holland.

WHO. 1988. *World Health Statistics*. Geneva: World Health Organization.

WHO. 1993. *1992 World Health Statistics Annual*. Geneva: World Health Organization.

Williams, Christopher. 1993. "Who Are 'Street Children'? A Hierarchy of Street Use and Appropriate Responses." *Child Abuse and Neglect* 17: 831–841.

Wiseman, Jacqueline P. 1970. *Stations of the Lost: The Treatment of Skid Row Alcoholics*. Englewood Cliffs, N.J.: Prentice-Hall.

Wright, James D., Martha Wittig, and Donald Kaminsky. 1993. "Street Children in North and Latin America: Preliminary Data from Proyecto Alternativos in Tegucigalpa and Some Comparisons with the U.S. Case." *Studies in Comparative International Development* 28 (2): 81–92.

Young, Kate, and Nicolas Fenton. 1991 (12 May). "Hope for Brazil's Children." *Independent* (London), 22.

Zelizer, Viviana A. 1985. *Pricing the Priceless Child: The Changing Social Value of Children*. New York: Basic Books.

INDEX

Index

Index

Index

Index

Index